THE PRESS, PRESIDENTS, AND CRISES

THE PRESS, PRESIDENTS, AND CRISES

Brigitte Lebens Nacos

Columbia University Press
New York

COLUMBIA UNIVERSITY PRESS
NEW YORK   OXFORD

Copyright © 1990 Columbia University Press

Library of Congress Cataloging-in-Publication Data

Nacos, Brigitte Lebens.
  The press, presidents, and crises / Brigitte Lebens Nacos.
    p. cm.
  Includes bibliographical references.
  ISBN 0-231-07064-0
  1. United States—Politics and government—1945–   2. United
States—Foreign relations—1945–   3. Press and politics—United
States—History—20th century.   4. Government and the press—United
States—History—20th century.   5. Presidents—United States—
History—20th century.   I. Title.
E839.5.N33   1990
973.92—dc20   89-37161
                                                                                      CIP

Casebound editions of Columbia University Press books are Smyth-sewn
and printed on permanent and durable acid-free paper

Printed in the United States of America
c 10 9 8 7 6 5 4 3 2 1

CONTENTS

ACKNOWLEDGMENTS

Reading and coding thousands of articles from microfilm in even the friendliest of library settings, is—as I experienced in the many months of research for this book—a lonely enterprise. Otherwise, however, I was fortunate enough to benefit from lots of advice, constructive criticism, and encouragement by many people.

Most of all, I am indebted to Robert Shapiro at Columbia University who was instrumental in helping me shape my research design and who offered very detailed and always valuable advice during each phase of this project. I do not know, Bob, how many times I asked you to read and critique yet another draft or how often we met to talk about one or the other aspect of my work, but I do know that you were more than generous with your expertise and time. Thank you!

Charles Hamilton's work on the role of crises in the American governmental process inspired me to look into press coverage during crisis periods. His crisis theory and his thoughtful suggestions were especially helpful in my search for patterns in the news coverage of crises.

I am grateful to Ralph Levering, one of the referees for Columbia University Press, whose thoughtful report and detailed suggestions helped me to clarify several concepts and especially the characterisics of the examined crises. I also drew from the constructive criticism of several scholars who read an early draft of the manuscript, namely Richard Pious, Joshua Freeman, Benjamin Page, and an anonymous reader. John Young helped me a great deal with the computer analysis of my data.

It was a privilege to work with Kate Wittenberg and Leslie Bialler at Columbia University Press and to benefit from their professionalism.

Joan Gozaloff assisted generously in the preparation of several manuscript versions.

Last but not least, I thank the three Js—my husband Jimmy and my sons John and James—for their support and encouragement.

Brigitte Lebens Nacos
Manhasset, New York
January 1990

THE PRESS, PRESIDENTS, AND CRISES

INTRODUCTION

"REPORTERS ARE ALWAYS AGAINST US"

Defending the Reagan administration's decision to bar the American media from covering the U.S. invasion of Grenada in the fall of 1983, Secretary of State George Shultz complained bitterly that "these days . . . it seems as though the reporters are always against us." Shultz observed that the attitude of the press had been different in earlier times and that during World War II journalists often had reported on combat operations "and on the whole, they were on our side."[1] If there was any doubt about what exactly was meant when Shultz spoke of the press as being against "us," President Reagan explained that meaning during a press conference in December 1983, when he said that his Secretary of State had meant "all of America."[2] In late 1986 Reagan blamed the press for the embarrassing Iran–contra scandal that followed the revelation of a secret arms-for-hostage deal between the White House and the government of Iran. "This whole thing," the President charged angrily, "boils down to a great irresponsibility on the part of the press."[3]

President Reagan, officials in his administration and their supporters were not the first to complain about a hostile press. Most, if not all American presidents have had their quarrels with journalists. However, during the 1970s and 1980s there was a growing perception that the events and experiences during the last year of the Johnson and the nearly six years of the Nixon administration had fundamentally altered the way the news media reported about public officials and especially about presidents.[4] Even some members of the fourth estate have expressed the belief that the press–president relationship has changed. Pierre Salinger, White House press secretary during the Kennedy administration, has pointed out that there was always an adversarial relationship between press and president, but that this relationship has changed into a "hostile" one. *Time* columnist Hugh Sidey agreed with Salinger, when he observed, "It seems that we [press and presidents] are enemies."[5] Are the media institutions in America indeed acting like enemies of presidents and their administrations? Is the press unpatriotic, oppositional, and, as Daniel Patrick Moynihan once suggested, "more and more influenced by attitudes genuinely hostile to American society"?[6]

Other observers are convinced that the media's confrontational stance that began in the late 1960s was merely a temporary phenomenon during what Samuel Huntington calls a "creedal passion period," when "the media have no recourse but to challenge and expose the inequities of power."[7] James Schlesinger, for example, who served in the cabinets of both Richard Nixon and Jimmy Carter, has observed that in the changing relationship between the press and the government "the pendulum has started to swing back toward the skeptical from the cynical mode."[8] Huntington and Schlesinger recognize that the interaction between the press and government officials is affected by the "mood of society."[9] In the late 1970s and early 1980s, the antigovernment sentiment seemed to subside and with it the mostly confrontational press–government and press–president interaction.

Who, then, perceives the relationship between press and recent presidents correctly? Those who argue that the Vietnam–Watergate era has resulted in fundamental changes and in a deep-rooted and lasting hostility of the media toward the White House? Or other observers who believe that after an episode of increased hostility the relationship has moved toward the traditional mixture of adversarial and cooperative stance?

To answer these questions, this book examines press coverage of six crises the United States faced during the last three decades—three before and the other three after the period between 1968 and 1974. The Vietnam–Watergate era is often identified as the turning point in press–president relations. It seems more acurate to pinpoint the year 1968 as a watershed in this respect. Daniel C. Hallin has convincingly demonstrated that media coverage of the Vietnam War was overwhelmingly pro-administration, especially up to the Tet offensive in early 1968.[10] Other events in 1968, namely the assassinations of Dr. Martin Luther King and Senator Robert F. Kennedy and the clashes between police protesters during the Democratic National Convention in Chicago, as well as the publication of the Pentagon Papers, revelations about My Lai, the secret bombing of Cambodia, and the Watergate scandal during the following years polarized the nation. Because the news coverage during those years was often critical of Presidents Johnson and Nixon, this period is commonly characterized as having altered the press–president relationship. Therefore, it is more precise to speak of the 1968–1974 turning point in press–president relations rather than of the Vietnam–Watergate watershed.

There are good reasons to choose crises periods to look at the way the press has covered presidential policies and actions. Crises represent the most fateful and crucial times for the nation and its presidents. In times of emergencies the American people look to the chief executive to deal with the problems at hand, because, as Herbert Gans has pointed out, "[h]e is the final backstop for domestic tranquility and the principal guardian of national security."[11] Also, the performance of presidents in office is ultimately judged according to their successes or failures in managing and solving those crisis situations with which they are faced. Richard Pious has pointed out that "[w]e identify the presidency with the resolution of great crises."[12] And Thomas Cronin has recognized a "tendency to examine the presidency in the context of crisis."[13] Given that the well-being of the nation and a president's place in history depend at least in part on his crisis management skills and on the way those skills are perceived by political elites and by the general public, it is not surprising that presidents, administration officials, and their supporters seem especially sensitive to news coverage during crises. It is precisely for these reasons that the press–president relationship deserves special attention in the context of crises.

Closely related to the debate surrounding the manner in which the press covers presidents and their policies are media critics' charges that the press reports the news in a biased or distorted fashion. Therefore, the question of bias in the news is also examined in the case studies of six crises.

POWER AND INFLUENCE OF THE PRESS

Why is there so much interest in the manner in which the news media cover all aspects of the governmental process? The reason is obvious: Elected and appointed officials and the general public are convinced that the news media (the terms press, media, and news media are used interchangeably in this book) have political power and influence, can make or break politicians—presidents included—and can obstruct a president's ability to lead the nation and its governmental decision making.[14] President Johnson's decision not to seek reelection in 1968 and President Nixon's resignation in 1974 are among the more dramatic events which have been directly attributed to the role of the press.

Richard Neustadt has pointed out that not the formal constitutional and statutory prerogatives but public prestige and professional reputation are the most important sources of a president's influence and power and thus of his effectiveness to govern.[15] Interviews have revealed a strong belief among White House staffers that a president's reputation in the Washington community of political elites and his prestige among the general public are crucial determinants of his influence and effectiveness. Moreover, White House staffers are convinced that the press is the most important factor in influencing both a president's professional reputation and public prestige.[16]

Given this conviction that the news media occupy a central place in a president's ability or inability to persuade political elites and the public at large, it is not surprising that modern presidents and their administrations are extremely interested and often preoccupied with any aspect of press coverage that concerns them.

However, while it is widely believed that the press is influential in the political realm, it has proven very difficult to demonstrate and to pinpoint media influence precisely. This recognition led columnist Rowland Evans to describe the influence of the press to be "so intangible, so difficult to define, that it is like catching grains of dust in a sunbeam."[17]

Research has indicated that citizens' policy preferences have some effect on policy making in the United States.[18] It is also known that modern presidents follow the ups and downs of presidential popularity polls closely and adapt their policies accordingly.[19] But there is no conclusive empirical evidence of media influence on public opinion—especially on attitude change. Those who deny that the press has such a capacity can point to a series of social scientific studies that found the mass media to have at best "minimal effects" on the attitudes of individuals.[20] More recently, however, experts in the field have questioned the minimal-effect conclusions and researchers have offered empirical evidence of an "agenda setting" effect of the media.[21] These research results have confirmed Bernhard Cohen's often quoted thesis: "It [the press] may not be successful much of the time in telling people what to think, but it is stunningly successful in telling its readers what to think about."[22] Finally, some researchers have reported a substantial relationship between media content and the public's policy preferences.[23] It has also been suggested that public officials consider the news media to be "stand-ins" for public opinion—at least until the result of the next opinion polls are available.[24]

While much of past and more recent research has concentrated on the effect of the media on public opinion, there is reason to believe that the impact of press reports is greater on political elites because the media's relevant content tends to be more closely related to elite concerns and interests than to that of the public at large.[25] One comprehensive study found that government officials are especially open to be influenced by the media and that "press considerations are so much a part of policy-making [in Washington] as to be indistinguishable from it."[26]

But regardless of the evidence or lack of it, there is no doubt that decision makers, and especially presidents, presume that the media have great influence and behave accordingly. Otherwise, presidents would hardly make the great efforts they do undertake to manage the news and to prevent reports that portray them, their policies, and their ability to lead in an unfavorable light.

QUESTIONS ABOUT OBJECTIVITY AND BIAS

Given the conviction that the media are very influential, it is not surprising that those who object to the way the news is reported often and quickly accuse the press of presenting the news in a biased fashion. Conservatives have attacked the press as left-slanted, opposed to conservative politicians and policies, and supportive of liberal politicians and policies. Looking at the news media from the viewpoint of the "New Right," Richard Viguerie has stated, "Most political observers agree that liberals have effective control of the mass media—a virtual monopoly on TV, radio, newspapers, and magazines."[27] During a Washington conference in 1984, one conservative participant wondered aloud, "[W]hy is [sic] the American media pro-Soviet?" He also suggested that there were probably "active Soviet agents" within the American press corps.[28]

Critics on the left charge that the press is conservative, that it upholds the existing political, economic, and social arrangements, and thus supports the status quo. Summing up this media view, Robert Cirino has argued, "Whether it's your local newspaper, your television news, *Life, Time, Reader's Digest* or the *New York Times,* you will see that bias is there, and it is consistently a one-sided bias that favors the status quo and the establishment that it sustains." Cirino leaves no doubt that in his opinion the overall media bias is placed "to the right on the political spectrum."[29]

Many journalists and many of their critics believe that objectivity must be the standard of serious journalism. The idea here is that he press is or at least should be like a mirror that reflects what is going on in the world. One leading media representative explained the dissatisfaction with the press with factors beyond the control of the news media, claiming, "The task of journalists is to hold a magnifying mirror before our society to show warts and all. . . . As the problems have multiplied so have the means of communicating news. Newspapers, television, radio, and magazines jam these problems into an already irritated public conscience and the bearer of uncomfortable news is never loved."[30]

The notion of the press resembling a messenger, what Edward Jay Epstein calls "the mirror metaphor," has weaknesses.[31] TV-journalist Bill Moyers once said that "[o]f all the myths of journalism, objectivity is the greatest."[32] The mere fact that reporters, editors, and producers decide day-in and day-out what topics to report about, what sources to select, how many column inches or air time to dedicate to various views, and whether to place a news item on the front page or at the top of a broadcast indicates that value judgments are made all the time. As Ben Bagdikian correctly pointed out, "None of these [judgments] is a truly objective decision."[33]

Referring to the print media, Gladys Engel Lang and Kurt Lang have argued, "The political character of a newspaper affects its coverage."[34]

Michael Schudson challenges those who expect objectivity from the news media, arguing that "[o]bjectivity is a peculiar demand to make of institutions which, as business corporations, are dedicated first of all to economic survival . . . [and] by tradition or explicit credo, are political organs. It is a peculiar demand to make of editors and reporters who have none of the professional apparatus which, for doctors or lawyers or scientists, is supposed to guarantee objectivity."[35] Nearly half a century earlier, Walter Lippmann expressed similar ideas and, furthermore, pointed out that news and truth cannot be equated. It was Lippman's view that "[t]he function of news is to signalize an event, the function of truth is to bring to light the hidden facts, to set them into relation with each other, and make a picture of reality on which men can act."[36]

During the last decades the press has moved away from the pure objectivity ideal, an ideal that seems at odds with another, traditional role of the American press—that of a watchdog of governments and public officials. In this role, as Hallin described it, journalists see themselves "as champions of truth and openness, checking the tendency of the powerful to conceal and dissemble." Merely reporting what a president or any government official says complies with the objectivity ideal, but may not satisfy the watchdog role that requires the media to scrutinize the statements. One example of the journalist as watchdog, offered by Hallin, concerns the Vietnam War: "In 1968, when the generals were claiming a major victory in the Tet offensive, Walter Cronkite returned from his own inspection of the war to conclude that it had become a 'bloody stalemate.' "[37] Journalists and scholars have pointed to the 1950s, 1960s and 1970s as periods during which the change from objective to interpretive reporting took place. Peter Braestrup traces the roots of this change at both the *New York Times* and the *Washington Post* back to the 1950s "when some license had been given . . . to ordinary reporters (as opposed to columnists, whose independence was generally accepted)" to interpret and explain the news within so-called straight news stories.[38] Others, among them Tom Wicker and Samuel Kernell, explain the advent of interpretive reporting with the growth of television news beginning in the 1960s and the need for the print press to go beyond the "front page function" that was taken over by television news. For Wicker, the interpretive press role includes the watchdog or in his words the "adversary function" of the media.[39]

A number of media researchers, for example Leon V. Sigal, Todd Gitlin, and Edward Jay Epstein, view organizational and bureaucratic procedures as more plausible keys to understanding how every day news is reported than are other explanations. According to Sigal, "what newsmen report may depend less on who they are than how they work."[40]

One difficulty hampers the research of objectivity and bias in the news: There is simply no way to establish reality that could be used as a measuring stick to determine whether news coverage is objective or slanted with respect to specific views. Lang and Lang once compared television coverage of an event with descriptions of eyewitnesses they had stationed at the very same spots where TV cameras were recording the same event.[41] However, as Epstein has pointed out, "the fast-breaking nature of news usually defies this simultaneous surveillance of news events and news reporting over extended periods of time."[42] One can trust to overcome this problem only by comparing the coverage of different media organizations. In the case of newspapers, the political views of publishers and leading editors are regularly expressed in editorials. If the comparison of news presentations in newspapers with different editorial positions demonstrates that so-called straight news coverage consistently favors sources in agreement with the editorial stance, a relationship between press opinion and news coverage would seem to exist.

Such a relationship could even be assumed in cases in which sources in disagreement with a newspaper's editorial view are covered more often and more extensively than those in tune with the editorial policy. For example, suppose one newspaper, which expresses support for a president's fiscal policy, covers this topic over a certain time period by devoting 70 percent of its coverage of this particular topic to sources supportive of the president's fiscal program, 20 percent to neutral sources, and 10 percent to sources critical of the president's position; however, a second newspaper, which voices editorial opposition, provides 50 percent of its space covering this topic to pro-presidential, 10 percent to neutral, and 40 percent to critical sources. Clearly, in this case a relationship between the editorial positions and the news coverage of the two newspapers can be construed.

This method is useful in examining the complex questions of objectivity and bias in the news, and it is used throughout this book.

CRISES AND THE PRESS

While many politicians, bureaucrats, and scholars agree that the elaborate system of checks and balances and of competing pluralist interests in the American governmental process obstruct a president's ability to govern, it is also recognized that in times of crises political actors such as Congress, interest groups, the public and others tend to yield to presidential leadership in order to allow effective management of the particular crisis at hand.[43] According to pluralists this behavior of political actors during emergencies is the result of a broadly based consensus over the most important values of the system. The press is believed to be a special guardian of the highest American values such as equality, justice and so forth. Having studied how the news is in fact reported by leading news magazines and television networks, Gans concluded that the news they present "defends democratic theory against an almost inevitably inferior democratic practice."[44] It is this insistence on the ideals that makes for tensions between press and government and especially between press and president.

If the press is indeed the guardian of the highest values, most of all national sovereignty and life and property of the citizenry, one should expect that news coverage during crises periods reflects the tendency of political actors to support a crisis-managing president or, at least, to refrain from expressing criticism. Furthermore, one would expect that media-based opinion would be more supportive or less critical of a president's relevant policies during a crisis than before the emergency. Exactly this has been suggested by media experts. Doris Graber, for example, has observed that "the media abandon their adversary role during crises."[45] Others have concluded, "When a president seizes the initiative and appears to take strong measures to resolve or respond to a crisis, news organizations ordinarily line up behind him."[46]

Is this kind of reaction the norm in all types of crises? With respect to public reaction to crises situations a distinction has been made between international and domestic emergencies. John Mueller has linked the "rally-'round-the-flag" effect to international crises pointing out that domestic crises such as riots, scandals, and strikes "are at least as likely to exacerbate internal divisions as they are to soothe them."[47] Others, however, suggest that in emergencies no distinctions exist between those with domestic and international scopes. According to Graber, "In the American political culture, the normal feuds of politics are suspended when the nation is in danger. While this unwritten rule has been most often mentioned in connection with foreign policy . . . it applies equally as much to domestic crises."[48]

This book concerns itself with those types of crises that either directly or indirectly affect the whole nation: war or the threat of war, a military intervention, the assassination of a president or an assassination attempt that causes serious injuries, a major civil disturbance, or a major catastrophy or the threat of one, such as the one caused by the Three Mile Island nuclear accident. Those incidents fit Graber's definition of crises as "natural or manmade events that pose an immediate and serious threat to the lives and property or to the peace of mind of large numbers of citizens."[49]

Looking for patterns in the way the news media cover crisis situations,

Graber theorized that three distinct stages can be recognized: During the first stage, the press offers all the information it can get, but the first news accounts are often fragmented and incomplete. In the second stage, the crisis coverage is more complete and questions asked by the press are more probing. Finally, in the third stage, the press makes efforts "to place the crisis into its larger, long-range perspective."[50]

I, too, theorized and searched for patterns in the coverage of major crises that could be used as a valuable comparative tool. Looking closely at the time periods before, during, and after several severe emergencies, I predicted and found four phases in each one of them:

1. *A pre-crisis period* covering the days or weeks preceding the crisis in which—if issues related to the coming emergency are part of the public debate—the press tends to reflect the pros and cons of that debate.

2. *An acute crisis period* covering the most critical phase of the crisis in which the press seems to affirm a rally-'round-the-flag reaction among domestic political actors or the suspension of much opposition against the crisis-managing president. This tends to be the case, if there is agreement that the nation is indeed faced with a very serious crisis.

3. *A lingering crisis period* covering the phase following the acute emergency period during which the coverage tends to reflect some efforts on the part of some political actors to return to the old normalcy of conflictual politics. In the lingering crisis phase threat and danger are perceived to be somewhat less than during the previous acute stage. For example, once Krushchev agreed to the removal of Soviet missiles from Cuba in October 1962, the acute threat of war was ended but the danger lingered on until President Kennedy revealed that he had ordered the lifting of the naval blockade of Cuba in response to Soviet assurances that all Russian IL-28 bombers would be removed from the island as well.

4. *A post-crisis period* covering the days and weeks following the crisis during which press coverage tends to reflect more efforts by presidential opponents to return to the normal political state of conflictual politics. However, the degree to which they are successful in doing so seems to depend on the perception of a president's crisis management. A president widely believed to have managed the prior crisis very well seems to enjoy favorable post-crisis coverage based on the reluctance of opponents to criticize a chief executive still riding high on his crisis-managing success.

PRESS, PRESIDENTS, AND CRISES

Much has been written about the place of the news media in the system of government, the media's coverage of certain policy areas, the Washington press corps, the give-and-take between press and public officials, and the influence of the media on policymakers.[51] Journalists and ex–White House aides have recalled and scholars have researched the relationship between presidents and the news media.[52] Moreover, scholarly research has dealt with the question: How did the news media cover major crises periods with the presidency at center stage? Hallin, for example, examined the content of the print press and of television network news in a comprehensive study of the media and the Vietnam War, and Braestrup, in an equally monumental task, focused on the coverage of the Tet offensive by American newspapers, news magazines, wire services, and TV networks. Lang and Lang traced the connections between the president, the press, and public opinion polls during the Watergate era in a most interesting project.[53]

While each of the studies mentioned deals with one very important crisis, two recent works are based on media content analyses of several crises. Examining the three over-the-air TV networks' reports of six very different crises (from the very political terrorism drama of the Iranian Hostage Crisis to the Mount St. Helens Eruptions, a natural disaster), Dan Nimmo and James E. Combs found different coverage patterns: CBS was all in all reassuring and left the viewing audience with the impression that the experts will take care of things. ABC, on the other hand, preferred alarm and fueled the perception that things were bad and could get worse. NBC, finally, transmitted a feeling of resignation: "What happens . . . is tragic. But in the larger scale of things, a given crisis is but a crisis, not the end of the world."[54]

In another ambitious project, Montague Kern, Patricia W. Levering, and Ralph B. Levering examined the relationship between President John F. Kennedy and the press during four foreign policy crises—the Laotian Crisis of 1961, the Berlin Crisis of the same year, the Cuban Missile Crisis in 1962, and the Vietnam Crisis of 1963. Their content analyses of five newspapers and interviews with reporters, editors, publishers, and public officials led them to the conclusion that the press of the Kennedy era was reflective in its coverage of foreign policy crises. The authors found that "the literature asserting that the president dominates the press is valid under certain conditions." But they also concluded that presidential dominance depends on the presence or absence of other political actors in the public discussion of an issue. "If the forces are there," Kern *et al.* write, "then the press is like a prism. It will reflect, focus, and magnify their views. Like sunlight focused through a magnifying glass, political forces reflected in the press lens may be powerful enough to start a fire, to put constraints on a president, or, conversely, to assist him in the elimination of his opposition and the acquisition of power."[55]

While my study shares with Kern, Levering and Levering the focus on newspaper coverage of presidential crises policies, it differs from and/or adds to their and other previous research in several important respects:

1. I examined press coverage of domestic and foreign crises from the most serious type (example: The Cuban Missile Crisis) to middle-level incidents (example: The Attempt to Assassinate President Reagan) which occurred during the terms of four different presidents (Kennedy, Johnson, Carter, Reagan) over a period of twenty-one years. Although I chose vastly different cases (except for the Dominican Republic and Grenada Invasions) that occurred in three decades I observed distinctive patterns in the crisis coverage of the press.

2. Three of the chosen crises—the Cuban Missile Crisis, 1962, the Dominican Republic Invasion, 1965, and the Detroit Riot, 1967— occurred before the assumed 1968–1974 turning point in the press–president relationship while three other events—the Three Mile Island Accident, 1979, the Attempt to Assassinate President Reagan, 1981, and the Grenada Invasion, 1983—happened afterward. Thus, I was able to compare press coverage before and after the 1968–1974 turmoils, and I have found that there was no fundamental change in the way newspapers covered crises episodes.

3. Finally and most importantly, I systematically compared the so-called straight news coverage with the editorial positions of the examined newspapers and found a relationship between them in the vast majority of the time periods I analyzed.

The 1960s, 1970s, and 1980s experienced many crises. Why, then, were six incidents chosen over other, equally or more significant ones as, for example, the Watergate scandal or the Iranian hostage crisis? There were several reasons for my choices: First, my aim was to analyze press coverage of different types of crises in terms of severity, duration, and the domestic–foreign division. Second, in order to compare coverage before and after the 1968–74 watershed, this period had to be excluded. Third, long lasting crises, for example the 444 days of the Iranian hostage crisis, were simply not manageable within this undertaking. I chose the Cuban Missile Crisis as the most serious foreign crisis period since World War II while the Dominican Republic and Grenada Invasions seemed an ideal pair of similar crises for comparative purposes. The Detroit race riot was picked because it was the only one among similar violent racial outbursts during the 1960s in which federal troops were deployed. The Three Mile Island accident qualified as the worst nuclear power plant emergency in the United States and the attempt to assassinate Reagan as an incident that constituted what Graber has called "a serious threat . . . to the peace of mind of large numbers of citizens."[56]

Three daily newspapers, the *New York Times,* the *Washington Post,* and the *Chicago Tribune,* were chosen for content analyses. The selection of the first two publications was motivated by the widely accepted view that they arc the foremost leaders and agenda setters for the rest of the print and electronic news media and that they influence the news judgment of other news organizations heavily.[57] These newspapers are most widely read by the Washington community of political elites and are recognized as intragovernmental means of communication.[58] The *Chicago Tribune,* on the other hand, is neither as influential as the two East Coast newspapers in Washington political circles nor within the national media. While the *Post* and *Times* represent the so-called liberal Eastern media elite, the *Tribune* is perceived as representative of a middle-America view. Many observers assume that all three of these newspapers had different orientations during the Kennedy and Johnson presidencies in the 1960s than in the second half of the 1970s and the early 1980s with first Carter and then Reagan in the White House: The Democratic-leaning *Times* and *Post,* which were major actors in the events surrounding the Pentagon Papers and Watergate, became more critical of presidents and government overall, and the Republican *Tribune,* on the other hand, changed from a one-sided arch-conservative stance in the 1960s to a less idiosyncratic publication. The choice of these three newspapers enabled me to compare the coverage of the two East Coast publications and the Midwestern newspaper. There are several reasons why I did not examine television news coverage: A complete record of network evening news programs is available only from 1968 on, but I wanted to compare coverage before and after the 1968–74 watershed. Also, unlike newspapers, TV network news programs do no offer daily editorials and thus no opportunity to compare editorial positions with its straight news coverage very closely.

I used the following methodology to examine the manners in which the three newspapers covered major crises: For each pre-, acute, lingering, and post-crisis period of each case I examined and rigorously content-analyzed all relevant stories in the political sections of the three newspapers.[59] I focused particularly on the number of lines attributed to news sources such as the president, his White House staff, other members of the administration, members of Congress, and so forth. Adapting a method developed by Benjamin Page and Robert Shapiro, I categorized the intention of each type of source toward the crisis-related presidential policy as either supportive/ probably supportive, neutral/ambiguous, or against/probably against.[60] For example, during the acute phase of the Grenada Invasion, Republican Senator Malcolm Wallop was quoted to have said, "We are seeing an increasing level of Soviet adventuring all over the world. It's time we responded."[61] This was coded as fitting the supportive/probably supportive category. Democratic Senator Daniel Patrick Moynihan was reported to have characterized the invasion as "an act of war" that the United States did not have a right to.[62] This was coded in the against/probably against category. House Speaker Thomas Tip O'Neill's comment, "Now is not the time . . . to be critical of our government when Marines and Rangers are in action down there,"[63] was coded as neutral/ambiguous. Keeping track of separate sources enabled me to establish how different types of political actors fared in the news coverage. For example, I was interested in establishing what percentage of lines was attributable to administration sources and how much to congressional sources or whether partisans of a president were more likely to be used as sources supportive (or critical) of his crisis-related policies than members of the opposition.

The decision to focus on the amount of space (number of lines) per source was the result of some preliminary analysis during the early stage of this project. While coding articles concerning the weeks preceding the Cuban Missile Crisis in the *New York Times,* I found stories with an equal number of sources supportive and critical of President Kennedy's position, but the vast amount of space was attributable to one side. This difference in the space considerations for news sources, for example seventy-five percent of an article's linage based on pro-president sources, ten percent on sources critical of the president (the rest falling into the neutral/ambiguous category), encouraged me to concentrate on the amount of linage for various sources and not simply on the frequency with which news sources were used.

Also, the initial placement of sources in each story (in a front page headline, in the text of a front page story, in an inside article) was recorded. Placement in front page articles (even if a source is mentioned in the inside continuation of a story that begins on page one) amounts to a preferred placement because surveys have revealed that front page stories are read by more readers than stories appearing on inside pages.[64]

Editorials were also categorized in order to examine whether or not relationships between editorial positions of newspapers and their respective news coverage existed.

For the six crisis cases combined, I examined more than 3500 news items—news stories, dispatches, news analyses, editorials. The line-by-line coding necessitated a careful reading of all relevant items—from very long ones to dispatches of only a few lines. During this process, I kept track of what various sources had to say during various stages of each crisis. Thus, the six case studies, which are presented in chapters 1 through 6, are the result of both quantitative and interpretative content analyses. In chapter 7 I offer answers to questions about press hostility toward presidents, changes in the press–president relationship caused by the 1968–1974 turmoils, patterns in newspaper crisis coverage, and about bias in the mass media.

1

THE CUBAN MISSILE CRISIS

ON THE BRINK OF NUCLEAR WAR

October 22, 1962. Washington experiences a mild, clear autumn day with the temperature reaching 66 degrees. Few of those who live and/or work in the White House take notice of and enjoy the Indian summer day. Four-year-old Caroline Kennedy and some of her nursery school friends, playing carefree on the South Lawn, are perhaps the sole exceptions. Washington journalists who sense that dramatic developments are taking place behind closed doors in the presidential mansion hurry past pickets along Pennsylvania Avenue on their way to the White House press room. Few pay attention to familiar picket signs critical of the President: Liberal protesters plead that "Cuba Can Be Negotiated" while conservative critics demand, "More Courage and Less Profile." Unknown to demonstrators and passers-by is the irony that all these signs relate to the predominant topic of discussion inside the White House.[1] At one minute before 7:00 P.M. President John F. Kennedy walks across the Oval Office toward his large desk, sits down in a comfortable chair, and begins to read "the most serious speech in his life."[2] The presidential address is broadcast live on television and radio. Seventeen minutes later, when the 35th President of the United States ends his grave announcement, millions of Americans fear what the inner circle around the chief executive has known for days—that the world is "on the brink of nuclear war."[3]

Revealing the discovery of offensive missile sites as part of a massive Soviet military buildup on Cuba, Kennedy announces "a strict quarantine on all offensive military equipment under shipment to Cuba." He leaves no doubt that the naval blockade will remain in place until the Soviet Union agrees to "the prompt dismantling and withdrawal of all offensive weapons in Cuba." The President does not minimize the possible dangers of his "initial steps"; in fact he spells them out: "We will not prematurely or unnecessarily risk the costs of worldwide nuclear war . . . but neither will we shrink from that risk."[4] Clearly, the premier foes are no longer Fidel Castro and Cuba but Nikita Khrushchev and the Soviet Union.

The Cuban Missile Crisis has begun.

Within hours, printing presses all over the country ready newspaper editions marked Tuesday, October 23, 1962. Front pages everywhere are dominated by huge headlines spread across their whole width, all carrying the same message in similar wordings: "Kennedy Orders Cuba Blockade as Reds Build A-Bases on Island" *(Washington Post)*, "U.S. Imposes Arms Blockade on Cuba" *(The New York Times)* or "Quarantine of Cuba On!" *(Chicago Tribune)*. Most daily newspapers publish the complete transcript of Kennedy's speech, summaries, evaluations, background information, features, analyses, editorials, first Soviet reactions.

On one point even the two feuding superpowers agree: This is the most severe, the most serious crisis since world War II. Years later, Kennedy's close adviser Arthur Schlesinger Jr. will characterize the Missile Crisis as possibly one of the three major threats to the very existence of this nation (according to Schlesinger the others were the Civil War and World War II).[5] And longtime Soviet Foreign Minister Andrei Gromyko will call the Cuban Missile Crisis "the most dangerous crisis in international affairs since the end of World War II."[6]

KENNEDY'S "HEAVIEST POLITICAL CROSS"

The crisis did not hit unexpectedly like a bolt of lightning out of a calm sky. On the contrary, the "Cuban problem" had plagued the Kennedy administration since its earliest weeks and months. In fact, the ill-fated CIA-directed Bay of Pigs invasion by a Cuban exile brigade in April 1961 had spoiled and shortened the honeymoon period traditionally granted to every incoming president by other political actors. Although Kennedy had inherited the CIA–Cuban exile project from his predecessor, Dwight D. Eisenhower, who had authorized the plan in early 1960, he had taken full responsibility for the costly failure—rightly so, because he could have reversed the Eisenhower decision. What his own closest aides characterized as "debacle, fiasco, disaster," and the "worst defeat of his career,"[7] had haunted Kennedy because neither right nor left activists allowed him to forget it. Those who in the wake of the Bay of Pigs failure had wanted the marines to finish the Cuban job and those who had chastised the president for the U.S. role in the invasion of a small, sovereign country, made sure that Cuba remained as Theodore Sorensen put it, "the Kennedy administration's heaviest political cross."[8]

Whether a result of the Bay of Pigs incident or not, Castro's Cuba and the Soviet Union tightened their embrace. In late 1961, Castro proclaimed openly, "I am a Marxist-Leninist, and I shall be a Marxist-Leninist until the last day of my life."[9] And in 1962, Cuba emerged as the number one political issue, hotly debated even before the congressional campaigns began after Labor Day. While the conservative wing of the Republican Party especially criticized Kennedy's "do-nothing" and "soft-on-communism" stance in the face of Russian military buildups in Cuba, the administration tried its best to deny that the island was becoming a Soviet colony and fortress.

Concluding that the Bay of Pigs adventure had been a grave mistake, Kennedy seemed determined to depend on more peaceful measures in order to isolate Cuba and to weaken the regime of Fidel Castro. He placed, for example, an embargo on exports to and imports from the island.

While generally enjoying a high degree of popularity during the first eighteen months of his presidency, the White House was well aware that a growing number of Americans was "frustrated over Communist influence" in Cuba[10] and dissatisfied with Kennedy's handling of the Cuban dilemma. In August, the Gallup poll measure of presidential popularity dipped to 66 percent—the first time during his administration his approval rate had gone below the 70 percent mark.[11] At this time, the Kennedy opposition not only charged that there were shipments of vast amounts of weapons from the Communist bloc to Cuba but also began to complain about offensive missile sites on the Caribbean island. The standard administration argument that the arsenal on Cuba was strictly defensive in nature convinced the general public less and less. President Kennedy himself was not without suspicion. He personally authorized a series of U-2 reconnaissance flights over Cuba. The result of a photographic mission in mid-October stunned the leading men in the administration: The pictures proved that the Russians were preparing the deployment of surface-to-surface ballistic missiles on Cuban soil, an offensive arsenal that the President regarded as a threat to the national security of his country. Kennedy learned of the evidence on the morning of October 16. Four days later, after around-the-clock-deliberations by a high-level governmental group (called Executive Committee of the National Security Council or Ex Comm) that examined the possible courses of action, the President chose the blockade option. Still two days later, with all necessary preparations and military movements executed, the President made his response to the Soviet-Cuban threat public, using the news media —television, radio, and the print press—as vehicles to transmit his message to his own country and to the whole world.

JFK AND THE PRESS

Few politicians and few presidents before and after his short presidential term have understood the central role the news media play in the political process as well as John F. Kennedy did. Accordingly, he made great efforts to influence, use, and manipulate the press in his favor. George Reedy, one of President Lyndon B. Johnson's press secretaries, identified three twentieth-century presidents "who truly understood the working of the press. They were the two Roosevelts—Theodore and Franklin D.—and John F. Kennedy."[12]

Kennedy, like the two Roosevelts before him, was fully aware that he had to lead public opinion in order to maintain his ability to find support for his policies. At the same time, he recognized the close connection between public and elite opinion. During the 1960 election campaign Kennedy had read Richard Neustadt's *Presidential Power* with great interest. He subscribed to Neustadt's views, namely the political scientist's identification of professional reputation and public prestige as the most important sources of presidential power. Moreover, Kennedy had instinctively placed the news media into the center of Neustadt's "power connection" scheme that determines whether a president is strong or weak in his dealings with other actors in the political arena.[13] It worked to his advantage that he had some experience as a newsman working for a short period after World War II for Hearst's International News Service and, more important, that he had cultivated journalists, editors, and publishers during his fourteen years in the House and the Senate. Finally, the first televised campaign debates in history had made Kennedy aware of his gift of persuading millions of listeners and viewers. Kennedy made no secret of his admiration for Franklin Roosevelt's communication skills. According to Sorensen, nothing concerned JFK more than "public communication—educating, persuading and mobilizing that [public] opinion through continued use of the political machinery, continued traveling and speaking, and, above all, continued attention to the mass media: radio, television, and the press."[14]

During JFK's 1036 days in office, the relationship between this President and the media was both cooperative/symbiotic and adversarial/hostile. On the whole, however, Kennedy and White House reporters got along very well and each side seemed to respect and even like the other. Kennedy could not blame his press secretary when he was unhappy with media reports. Although Pierre Salinger served the President with devotion and skill, yet without losing the respect and good will of the White House press corps, Kennedy was in reality "his own press secretary. . . . He believed he could do it better than anyone else,"[15]

As congressman and senator, Kennedy had befriended several newsmen in the capital; as President, he was relentless in trying to coopt media representatives. According to one account, "during the Thousand Days of Camelot, reporters were romanced with invitations to glittering state dinners, luncheons, and receptions at the White House on a scale unmatched by previous administrations."[16]

But the press–president relationship was not all peaches and cream during the Kennedy years. Kennedy may have had more personal contacts with journalists than any other president, but there seems also agreement that he was "not only the friendliest, but the most thin-skinned of presidents."[17] His hypersensitivity to critical stories, editorials, and columns was well known to those who committed such "sins." Kennedy and his staff believed in the stick-and-carrot approach. They rewarded the authors of friendly stories; they punished journalistic critics by scolding them and denying them access to sources within the White House. According to one Washington reporter at the time, the President and his aides "were intolerant of any criticism. What was worse, reporters who wrote stories that annoyed the White House suddenly found that their sources of information were drying up. Those staffers who had been so accessible were suddenly too busy to talk. Phone calls went unreturned."[18]

The term "managed news" was coined during the Kennedy years, unjustly though, because all presidents have managed or manipulated information about their administrations to one degree or another. All presidents from George Washington on have released advantageous information and withheld items unfavorable to them. Kennedy was no exception. Yet, incidents during the Cuban Missile Crisis period earned Kennedy and his administration the reputation of having "managed" and "censored" government information in an unprecedented way and thus of violating the public's right to know what their government is doing.

During the acute phase of the missile crisis, the Defense and State departments and, of course, the White House withheld "sensitive" information. According to one White House newsman at the time, the press understood these crisis measures: "No reporter I know faulted Kennedy for managing the news while he and Soviet Premier Khrushchev were 'eyeball to eyeball' at the brink of a nuclear war. . . . But when the embargo on *all* information concerning negotiations with Moscow and the U.S. blockade of Cuba continued long after Khrushchev had agreed to remove his missiles, the press perceived, as the *New York Times* put it, that it was 'being used more often than informed.' "[19] A storm of protest in the press broke loose when Arthur Sylvester, the Pentagon's spokesman, characterized government news management in the cold war era as part of the "arsenal of weaponry." In Sylvester's scheme, the government has "the inherent right to lie" in order to save itself and its nation, when faced with nuclear war.[20] Other government officials before and after Sylvester, before and after the Kennedy administration, probably had similar attitudes, but never had anyone expressed this view so bluntly as Sylvester did. This and the decision of the Kennedy administration to deny press access to officials in the White House, at the State Department, and at the Pentagon during the lingering missile crisis alienated many in the media. The frustration grew when it became clear that a few select Kennedy friends in the press were able to speak to decision makers and to write complimentary accounts of the handling of the crisis.

All in all, President John F. Kennedy was and still is widely regarded as a gifted communicator who handled his relations with the press skillfully and sucessfully.

DOMESTIC DEBATE DURING THE PRE-CRISIS PERIOD

During a news conference on September 13, 1962 President Kennedy lashed out at his political opponents who demanded an invasion or a blockade of Cuba, criticizing their "rash" and "loose" talk. Such calls for military action, the President warned, could only help "to give a thin color of legitimacy to the Communist pretense that such a threat exists." At this time, Kennedy assured the nation, Cuba did not represent a serious threat to the United States or the hemisphere, but this country would move swiftly against Cuba if necessary to protect its security.[21] The *New York Times* ("Kennedy Hits at War Talk"), the *Washington Post* ("President Urges U.S. to 'Keep Head' on Cuba"), and the *Chicago Tribune* ("No Cuba Threat: Kennedy") carried detailed reports of the press conference on their front pages in the editions of September 14. The same day, both the *Times* and the *Post* commented on Kennedy's stand in editorials, the *Tribune* followed one day later. Supporting the President's Cuba position, the *New York Times* editorialized that the Cuban question "today is complex, delicate, dangerous—but not dangerous enough to justify rash action. President Kennedy has been firm and frank. If Premiers Khrushchev and Castro were issuing a challenge, it has been answered. They can go so far—and no further." Echoing Kennedy, the *Post* concluded in a long editorial, "Rash and impulsive military adventures, much as they may be clamored for, are to be resisted as long as direct military safety permits and so far as the integrity of the other American countries allows."

In contrast, the Chicago newspaper analyzed Kennedy's statements concerning Cuba in an editorial very critical of the President and his claim that Castro's Cuba did not represent a threat. The *Tribune* interpreted this as "hands-off" policy on the part of Kennedy that allowed the military buildup in Cuba to continue. The editorial concluded with the biting question, "When is Mr. Kennedy going to face the fact?"[22]

These editorials illustrated the opposing views on the Cuban question and furthermore revealed how the three newspapers viewed the issue in the two months preceding the Presidential announcement of a Cuban blockade on October 22. During this pre-crisis period (August 23 to October 22, 1962), the official administration line was the following: Yes, the Soviet Union was sending large quantities of armaments to Cuba, but these were identified as defensive in nature. While there was no threat to the national security of this or any other country in the hemisphere, the Kennedy administration again and again assured that the Cuban development received its constant attention. Finally, while the administration let it be known that it worked hard to isolate and hurt Cuba economically in order to hasten the expected demise of the Castro regime, the President rejected military actions. The opposition, led by Republicans, some conservative Democrats, and anti-Castro Cuban exiles charged that the Russians provided Castro with missiles and troops that represented a direct threat to the United States and Latin American countries. Their calls for military intervention grew louder during September and October.

The three mentioned editorials of mid-September were representative of the editorial pages during this period: The *Times* and *Post* gave overwhelming support to Kennedy's Cuban stand, while the *Tribune* opposed the President all the way.

Of nine relevant editorials that the *Washington Post* published in the weeks preceding the acute phase of the missile crisis, seven were supportive, one was neutral, and one somewhat critical of Kennedy's policy. The latter suggested a third alternative to deal with the Cuban dilemma—"the course of deliberately and skillfully encouraging an internal uprising within Cuba that could immediately be assisted by outside arms." The editorial page editors expressed dissatisfaction with the President for not considering this option, complaining that the failure to do so "is especially odd since the Kennedy Administration came to power with the determination to develop a capacity in unconventional warfare . . . ".[23] Otherwise, however, the *Post* editorialized clearly in favor of the administration's Cuban policy, often repeating the very same arguments Kennedy publicized in released statements or during news conferences. For example, after several Kennedy counterattacks on critics like Senators Homer E. Capehart, Kenneth B. Keating, and Barry Goldwater, an editorial in the Washington newspaper followed up by criticizing Republicans for making Cuba the "dominant issue" of the ongoing election campaign. The editorial charged, "Noisy campaign nonsense serves only to weaken confidence in American leadership, to make the country look ridiculous, and to bring joy to the propagandists in Castro's Cuba."[24]

The *New York Times*, too, editorialized in favor of Kennedy's Cuba policy. Thirteen of seventeen editorials in the pre-crisis period that had direct relevance to this issue were in favor of the administration, two fell into the neutral/ambiguous category, while two voiced criticism. The latter two dealt with Cuban exiles and their raids on Cuba and ships in the area. In both editorials, the *Times* criticized the U.S. government for not preventing these attacks. Otherwise, there was massive support for Kennedy's Cuba policy. Representative of the editorials in this period was one published on September 1, in which Kennedy's rejection of military moves against Cuba was endorsed. The *Times* wrote, "To invade Cuba under the present circumstances would—as President Kennedy indicated at his press conference this week—be the course of irrevocable folly."[25]

The editorial stance of the *Chicago Tribune* during this period was very different from that of the two other papers. All nine editorials with direct relevance to the Cuba issue were critical of the Kennedy administration's policy. In early September, for example, the *Tribune* questioned the President's will to stand up to Khrushchev. A few days later, the publication found it inevitable that Cuba had become a partisan campaign issue because "widespread dissatisfaction with government policies are the things candidates talk about in political campaigns." By the end of the month, a *Tribune* editorial attacked "the spineless administration for which [Secretary of State] Rusk speaks." In its last editorial in the pre-crisis period, the publication spoke of the Kennedy administration's "sudden flurry of activity to demonstrate that it is not caving in to the Kremlin and Castro." But instead of applauding a possible move away from the "do-nothing" policy which the *Tribune* had criticized harshly, the editorial warned, "It is to be hoped that, out of concern for election prospects, Mr. Kennedy and his associates will not embark upon some dramatic but reckless last minute course to demonstrate that they really are not fainthearted."[26]

All three publications covered the Cuban issue extensively during the pre-crisis period. As Table 1.1 demonstrates, in the overall coverage (domestic and foreign sources combined) both the *Times* and the *Post* based

TABLE 1.1   Overall Pre-Crisis Coverage, Cuban Missile Crisis:
Domestic and Foreign Sources, Directly Relevant (Editorials Excluded)

Linage	For/Probably For	Neutral/ Ambiguous	Against/Probably Against	Total Lines
TIMES	43.8%	26.3%	29.9%	11,714
POST	41.7	33.1	25.2	8,836
TRIBUNE	37.3	16.3	46.4	8,086

more lines on sources supportive of the President's Cuba stand while the *Tribune* devoted more linage to critical sources. The *Times* covered foreign news concerning the Cuban question more extensively than the *Post* and *Tribune*. In all three papers, foreign sources (especially Cuban officials) were overwhelmingly critical of the President, namely, when referring to Kennedy's repeated assurances he would move against Castro's Cuba, if there was proof of offensive weapons.

Covering the domestic debate surrounding the Cuban issue, the *Tribune* gave slightly more space to sources critical of the administration's policy than to those that voiced support for the President's Cuba stand. The *Post* and the *Times* also gave considerable space to domestic sources that voiced opposition to the President's Cuban policy but pro-Kennedy sources captured significantly more space than his critics (see table 1.2).

Clearly, the opinion of publishers and editors did not prevent sources with views different from their own to be covered by these newspapers. Yet, in all three cases, sources that expressed a Cuba line compatible with that articulated on the editorial page fared better with respect to space than those with opposite views. On August 31, for example, Kenneth Keating of New York told his colleagues in the U.S. Senate that 1200 Soviet troops had arrived in Cuba between August 3 and 15. He contradicted the President, who had claimed that there was no evidence of Russian troops on the island. Keating's revelation was made on the same day on which the White House announced that a U.S. Navy plane had been attacked by machine-gun fire from two vessels believed to be Cuban. This announcement with a firm presidential warning to Castro was front page news in all three newspapers the next day. While the *Tribune* covered Keating's latest charge concerning the Soviet military buildup in Cuba in 20 lines, *Times* and *Post* gave Keating 8 lines each. Two days later, on September 3, the *Tribune* reported that two Democratic Senators (George Smathers and Strom Thurmond) had called for military intervention in Cuba and that Senator Keating had again criticized Kennedy's Cuba policy. In this case, the anti-administration sources

TABLE 1.2   Pre-Crisis: Cuban Missile Crisis, Domestic Sources, Directly Relevant (Editorials Excluded)

Linage	For/Probably For	Neutral/ Ambiguous	Against/Probably Against	Total Lines
TIMES	49.0%	29.7%	21.3%	8,962
POST	49.3	36.4	14.3	7,273
TRIBUNE	42.6	13.7	43.7	6,584

commanded 76 lines. In its edition of the same day, the *New York Times* mentioned the Kennedy critics in 22 lines. Although over all the least accommodating to anti-Kennedy sources during this period, the *Post* in this particular instance reported the call for action against Castro by Thurmond and Smathers and new anti-administration remarks by Keating in a story that commanded about the same linage as the *Tribune* report.[27]

As revealing as the space considerations for pro and con sources by the three papers were the placement decisions of their editors. Looking at the coverage of the Kennedy opposition in the editions of September 3, the administration's critics fared best in the paper that was consistently critical of Kennedy's Cuba policy: The *Chicago Tribune* placed this story on its front page with a continuation on page 2. The *Post,* although giving considerable space to the senators opposing both Kennedy's and the newspaper's editorial line, "buried" the story on page 16. The 22 lines with which the *New York Times* reported about Kennedy's Cuba critics in the Senate were part of a lengthy front page story by Tad Szulc about Fidel Castro's efforts to modernize the Cuban army but appeared toward the article's end within its inside-page continuation on page 2. However, in some instances, the *Times* chose to grant front page and even page one headline coverage to Kennedy's opponents. In mid-September, for example, both Barry Goldwater and Richard Nixon made front page headlines in the *Times* with demands for a quarantine of Cuba and attacks on Kennedy's "do-nothing" policy.[28] All in all, domestic administration critics were more likely to be mentioned in page one articles in the *Tribune* than in the *Post* and *Times* during the pre-crisis period, while sources favorable to Kennedy's Cuba policy were often covered in front page stories published by the two East Coast papers. In the *Times* sources supportive of the President's position made front page articles in 73 cases while critical sources achieved this preferential placement in 28 instances. In the *Post,* the source placement in front-page stories was 47–25 in favor of the pro-administration side. Finally, while the *Tribune* gave sources in favor of Kennedy's Cuba policy the page one story privilege in 27 cases, anti-administration sources managed to make page one articles in 26 cases. On the other hand, foreign sources critical of the Kennedy administration's Cuban policy made the front pages and even page one headlines of all three papers regularly. This happened often when Fidel Castro or Nikita Khrushchev denounced the American President.

While all three papers reported the most important domestic and foreign developments concerning the Cuban question, they differed in what types of stories they emphasized or downplayed. The *Tribune,* for example, published a number of prominently placed articles that reported growing Russian influence and military presence in Cuba and massive dissatisfaction with Castro among his countrymen. On September 16, the Chicago newspaper printed a lengthy article by A.P. correspondent William L. Ryan who wrote, "Havana is ringed by military hardware, managed by Russians and Cubans. The Russians paid cash for former estates near Havana and the belief is the areas will be used for anti-aircraft batteries and rocket launching sites." The *Tribune*'s Jules Dubois charged that the Soviets, not Castro, were in charge in Cuba, writing, "Castro has no control over the Russian force [in Cuba]. The Russians take orders only from their own officers." Claiming to have inside information from a Cuban refugee, Dubois reported that an "overwhelming majority of the Cuban people are clamoring for the United States to liberate them." [29]

These types of alarming stories were not to be found in the other two papers. Both the *Times* and *Post* preferred stories that assured the nation that the Washington government was on top of Cuban developments and that there was no reason for alarm or military action. Whenever Kennedy or Secretary of State Dean Rusk sought Latin American or European support for its Cuba policy, the East Coast papers were more likely to allocate prime space to administration sources than the Chicago publication. On the other hand, whenever the President and other members of his administration talked tough in the direction of Moscow or Havana, the *Tribune* tended to be more generous in allocating column space and most desirable placements to administration sources.

The White House, State and Defense departments were very successful in getting the official administration line on the Cuban issue into the columns of the *Times* and *Post*. The President and his Secretary of State repeatedly made front page headlines in the two liberal papers by urging Latin American and European allies to support Washington's anti-Castro initiatives, namely in limiting trade relations with the island. Both publications also gave the administration an opportunity to demonstrate that attacks on Kennedy's alleged "do-nothing" Cuba policy and his weakness vis-à-vis Khrushchev were unjustified. On October 5, for instance, the *Times* reported under the headline "Reprisal for Cuba Trade Tougher Than Expected" that the administration had decided to deny American port facilities to vessels belonging to nations that permitted their ships to transport military equipment to Cuba. The *Post* had carried a similar story a day earlier in its edition of October 4. In an article headlined "Berlin–Cuba Deal Report Is Ridiculed" the Washington paper gave State department sources front page space to hit back at charges that Kennedy was willing to make concessions in Berlin in exchange for a Russian promise to slow down its military buildup in Cuba. [30]

Measured in column linage, Kennedy and members of his administration fared better in all three papers than members of Congress in the two months before the blockade decision was announced, but although Congress generally receives much less media coverage than the executive, the legislative branch captured a considerable amount of space in all three papers (see table 1.3). The administration captured more and the Congress less linage in the two East Coast newspapers that were supportive of the President's Cuba policies than in the *Tribune* with a critical editorial view of Kennedy's relevant positions.

With the exception of editorials, journalistic sources are included in the source data presented in this case study and in the following chapters. However, in order to examine whether or not identifiable media attitudes in journalistic descriptions, background information, and news analyses confirm the objective or biased press views, they deserve special attention. During the pre-crisis period, the overwhelming amount of lines based on media sources in the two East Coast newspapers, more than 90 percent in the *Times* and more than 80 percent in the *Post*, fell into the neutral/ambiguous category. In contrast, more than 70 percent of the media-based lines in the *Tribune* revealed critical attitudes vis-à-vis the President's Cuban policies.

THE SIX "EYEBALL-TO-EYEBALL" DAYS

Although the President and his top advisers had wrestled for seven days in complete secrecy with the Cuban threat, the acute crisis began only when Kennedy notified the Soviet Union and made his public announcement of a naval blockade. Up to then, there had not been any publicized hints of such a dramatic and potentially conflictual move. According to Sorensen, President Kennedy was "amazed as well as pleased" that there had not been a leak, and he called the secret activities on the highest level of his administration in the days before the quarantine "the best kept secret in government history."[31] However, some members of the press were not at all in the dark. Indeed, the weekend before Kennedy's crucial Monday announcement, Pierre Salinger learned that some journalists had knowledge of the "entire story, except for the actual time the quarantine would take effect."[32]

TABLE 1.3   Linage Administration and Congressional Sources: Pre-Crisis Cuban Missile Crisis

	Administration Sources	Congressional Sources	Total Lines
TIMES	74.0%	26.0%	5,281
POST	64.7	35.3	4,456
TRIBUNE	54.7	45.3	4,434

Salinger alerted the President who personally "interceded that night with both the *New York Times* and the *Washington Post* who agreed to withhold publication in the interest of national security."[33] In its first edition following the blockade announcement, the *Times* revealed that "several newspapers learned the nature of the threat that was seen by the Government. At the request of the White house the story was not carried in this morning's [October 22] editions."[34]

This cooperative stance of the two influential newspapers even before the official crisis broke out foreshadowed the coverage during the six days of the acute Missile Crisis period, when in the words of Secretary of State Dean Rusk the two superpowers were "eyeball-to-eyeball."[35] During this phase of the crisis, beginning with the editions of October 23 and ending with those of October 28, there was a fundamental change in the overall coverage: All three papers dedicated a great amount of space to the crisis; all three papers supported Kennedy's firm stand vis-à-vis the Kremlin and Havana in their editorials, and in all three papers administration and other sources supporting the crisis-managing President dominated the domestic coverage.

In a complete turnaround, the editors of the *Tribune,* who had attacked the President's Cuba policy continuously, threw their support behind Kennedy. The editorial that was published on the morning after the blockade announcement praised the President's firmness and explained the *Tribune*'s prior opposition to the administration line by observing that "many Americans believe that the President's stern declaration should have come much sooner." But the publication left no doubt where it stood now: "The President can count on the support of a united people."[36] The five editorials related to the Missile Crisis, which the *Tribune* published in the "eyeball-to-eyeball" period, were fully supportive of the President's crisis management. Not even the campaign for the upcoming congressional elections should interfere with the full support of Kennedy's Cuba stand, another *Tribune* editorial stated, pointing out, "Cuban policy was, indeed, an issue in the campaign before the President took resolute action, but now his commitments are beyond debate. On Cuba the parties are united."[37] For the time being the paper was even willing to forget its differences with Adlai Stevenson, the U.S. Ambassador to the United Nations during the Missile Crisis. Applauding Stevenson's "eloquent, fiery, and effective presentation of the case of the United States" in the UN Security Council, the *Tribune* editorialized, "We have had our differences with Adlai Stevenson in the past, as Mr. Stevenson surely has had his with the *Tribune,* but we must salute him now."[38]

Having supported the President's moderate Cuba policy during the preceding months and weeks, the *New York Times,* in an editorial on October

23, gave an explanation why those in charge of the paper's editorial policy had switched from a wait-and-see to a get-tough view. The *Times* argued that the discovery of offensive missile sites and of bombers capable of carrying nuclear weapons on the Cuban island had altered the situation. Given the new circumstances, the paper found, "Drastic action was called for; and the President announced last night that drastic action has now been taken."[39] Four days later, the paper supported the Acting Secretary General of the United Nations, U Thant, in his efforts to arrange diplomatic talks but at the same time the continuation of Kennedy's firm stand, writing, "The United States does and must continue the blockade to stop further shipment of nuclear arms. We must also continue to insist that the bases themselves are removed."[40] The six editorials in the *Times* that dealt with the Cuban conflict during this period were without exception in complete agreement with Kennedy's Cuba position.

The *Washington Post,* too, supported the new Cuba policy wholeheartedly. All seven editorials published during the acute crisis period favored the Kennedy decision in respect to the Cuban-Soviet threat. In its first editorial after the blockade announcement, the *Post* called the President's decision an "inevitable response" and characterized it as a defensive move. Referring to the Monroe Doctrine, the editorial argued, "There was no element of aggression in the Monroe Doctrine when it was proclaimed, there is none in the present use to which it has been put."[41] And in a later editorial, the paper justified the President's Cuba steps, writing, "President Kennedy had to act decisively, courageously and with unmistakable determination to avoid any fatal misunderstanding on the part of the Kremlin."[42]

The editorial positions seemed in tune with the overall crisis coverage in that sources in favor of the new Kennedy stand captured by far more column lines than his opponents (see table 1.4)—even though a very high percentage of the foreign sources used by the three newspapers were very critical of the Kennedy decision to force the Cuban issue and to risk a military, if not nuclear, conflict with the Soviet Union. In the *Post* and in the *Tribune*

TABLE 1.4   Overall Coverage: Acute Cuban Missile Crisis, Domestic and Foreign Sources, Directly Relevant (Editorials Excluded)

Linage	For/Probably For	Neutral/ Ambiguous	Against/Probably Against	Total Lines
TIMES	56.8%	29.8%	13.4%	22,893
POST	67.8	16.2	16.0	11,015
TRIBUNE	61.3	22.6	16.1	10,682

foreign sources that opposed Kennedy's blockade were used for more lines than supportive foreign sources while the *Times* based more space in its foreign coverage on supportive sources. The New York newspaper covered the foreign reaction more extensively than the other two publications both of which concentrated on the United States' major foes: Cuba and the Soviet Union.

The domestic coverage was dominated by sources who supported Kennedy's blockade decision and his management of the crisis while critics captured only a small percentage of the domestic news coverage (see table 1.5).

During the acute crisis, there were practically no dissenting voices among those who had led the Kennedy opposition during the weeks before the blockade. With the exception of some members of Congress who faulted President Kennedy for not punishing Algeria's Ben Bella for his loud pro-Castro support by breaking up economic talks to aid his country and even diplomatic relations with Algeria, there was no criticism from members of Congress, other leading politicians in both parties, the Cuban exile community, or other influential interest groups. Some church groups who articulated concern over the blockade decision and its possible consequences came closest to representing mainstream opposition. Otherwise, dissent was voiced and demonstrations were staged by more marginal peace and student groups, left-oriented organizations, and a handful of individuals. Domestic dissent was "negligible."[43]

Those who voiced disagreement with the President's Cuban blockade decision were treated differently by the three publications. The *Times* was more generous than the other two in providing space to those who opposed the President's Cuban stand, and the *Washington Post* gave even less linage to the sparse dissent than the Chicago-based paper. In all three newspapers, the opposition had a difficult time making front page stories. The *Times* used sources opposed to the quarantine move four times in front page articles, the *Tribune* twice, the *Post* once. Both space and placement decisions were

TABLE 1.5   Acute Cuban Missile Crisis Coverage: Domestic Sources, Directly Relevant (Editorials Excluded)

Linage	For/Probably For	Neutral/ Ambiguous	Against/Probably Against	Total Lines
TIMES	62.5%	31.5%	6.0%	16,035
POST	81.6	16.6	1.8	7,907
TRIBUNE	71.4	24.4	4.2	7,678

probably justified by the editors with the recognition that an overwhelming majority of Americans supported Kennedy on Cuba, while very few objected to his new toughness. Still, in a number of instances, "straight news" stories using sources disagreeing with the administration's Cuba policy revealed that writers and/or editors did not look kindly at dissenters.

The *Times,* for example, reported on October 24 under the headline "Campuses Voice Some Opposition" that Harvard professor H. Stuart Hughes had called for a peaceful settlement of the Cuban issue and that some students also objected to the blockade. This, however, was followed by the qualification that Hughes "appeared to have little impact on students in the Boston area beyond Harvard Square." Pro-blockade demonstrations at Boston University were mentioned to justify this assessment.[44] While the *Times* reported in a front page story on October 25 that the "Student Peace Union" was preparing a peace demonstration in Washington, mentioning a spokesperson for the Chicago-based organization as source, The *Washington Post* told its readers of the upcoming anti-Kennedy protest by using Washington's police chief Robert Murphy as a source and revealing that he made preparations for the "onslaught" of 750 to 1000 demonstrators.[45] During the acute crisis, the *Tribune* mentioned World War I flying ace Eddie Rickenbacker twice as criticizing Kennedy because in his view the President was still too soft vis-à-vis Cuba and the Soviet Union. On one occasion he demanded the bombing of Cuban missile bases. While the *Tribune* reported this in a matter-of-fact manner, the editors seemed to take delight in ridiculing student protesters who were probably perceived as left-leaning. Headlining an October 25 article "Cuba Pickets Get Bum's Rush at Indiana University," the newspaper reported that 15 antiblockade demonstrators found a crowd of 2000 Kennedy supporters waiting for them.[46] In the same edition the *Tribune* did grant front page coverage to the Washington protest march planned by the "Student Peace Union," which, after all, had its headquarters in Chicago. Still, quoting the national secretary of the organization as having said that about 1000 student protesters from "the entire East Coast" were expected to participate in the march on the White House, seemed to point out how unimportant a protest movement was that could muster at best 1000 partipants from a fairly large region of the country.[47] The editors paid special attention to sources in their city or region who had something to say about the Cuban crisis.

All three newspapers emphasized stories that described a President in control of a tense situation and determined to focus completely on the number-one matter at hand. They published very similar accounts of the President's disposition, his order that all cabinet members discontinue campaign activities, and the decision to cancel all social events in the White House. In one article the *Times* reported that the President "was the calmest man around the White House today." The *Post,* describing Kennedy's long working hours, assured, "Whatever may be in his heart, President Kennedy appears calm and competent in the greatest crisis of his administration." The *Tribune,* too, paid tribute to Kennedy by publishing an article with the following lead: "The calmest man in the White House tonight was President Kennedy." These reports were not based on direct observations but on sources in the White House. In his "Report From Washington," the Chicago newspaper's bureau chief in the Capital, Walter Trohan, declared that the President "has turned his profile to show the face of courage."[48]

Depending mostly on administration sources to report the status of and the developments in the crisis, namely officials in the Pentagon, State department and White House, the papers also followed closely Cuba-related activities at the United Nations with Adlai Stevenson pushing the American point of view and within the Organization of American States with Dean Rusk speaking for the administration. If there was frustration over the inability to get first-hand evidence of the actions or nonactions in the quarantine region and over the administration's news management, it was not detectable in the columns of the three papers. On October 25, the *Post* and *Times* reported that Salinger had issued a memorandum containing twelve areas of information said to be sensitive with respect to national security. The papers published all points without questioning this kind of press guidance by the White House.[49] It was obvious that the administration "fed" the press what it wanted published and withheld what it did not. For example, the White House did not reveal the news that a U-2 plane was missing over Cuba and that another U-2 had violated Soviet air space. Both incidents were kept from the press until Kennedy and Khrushchev had come to an agreement on Cuba.[50]

At times, the two East Coast papers were chosen by high administration officials to receive exclusive information which promised to make the President and his men look good. The first "now it can be told" stories began to appear. The *Post* published a lengthy description of the pre-crisis developments. And the *Times* gave a detailed account of the pre-crisis contacts between the American and the Soviet side and about the obviously untrue assurances Khrushchev and Gromyko gave Kennedy concerning the then rumored military buildup on the island. In both cases, administration sources provided this inside information. The *Post* seemed to have the edge in presenting news analyses based on what informed administration sources expected, feared, and hoped for at various times during the acute crisis. In one front page news analysis, for instance, Warren Unna revealed what the highest level of the administration thought half-way through the six tense crisis days, when he wrote, "The United States realizes it now has backed Khrushchev into a corner but does not consider that it has deprived him of the flexibility he needs to comply with U.S. demands in Cuba and still keep his job."[51]

In describing the six acute crisis days at "the grimmest of the Thousand Days of John F. Kennedy's presidency," Pierre Salinger has recalled that at the start of the crisis, the men in charge were fully aware that "every word that came out of the White House would play a fateful role in determining the course of events." Moreover, according to Kennedy's press secretary, the American and the Soviet governments decided independently of each other to communicate through the news media instead of using slower, diplomatic channels.[52] This was behind the carefully orchestrated information policy of the Kennedy administration. The press brought some of its complaints to the White House press office. According to Salinger, there was "some grumbling about our handling of the news," but there were no publicized outcries in the three papers or elsewhere in the media over what would soon be criticized as censorship and governmental news management.[53]

Members of Congress, too, either agreed with the President or withheld their criticism during the tense crisis days. The conflictual push and pull that characterizes pluralist politics in normal times yielded to the preeminence of the chief executive and his branch, and this was most obvious in the way the President and his administration overshadowed Congress, when it came to space that sources of each branch captured in the three newspapers (see table 1.6).

While it was difficult for the domestic opponents of the President's Cuba stand to make the front pages, foreign foes were given such preferred placement more often than foreign supporters of the administration. There were many more foreign than domestic Kennedy critics in this matter.

Journalistic descriptions, background information, and news analyses in no instance revealed opposition to the President's decisions, actions, and views concerning the crisis. In all three newspapers, a significant number of

TABLE 1.6   Linage Administration and Congressional Sources: Acute Cuban Missile Crisis

	Administration Sources	Congressional Sources	Total Lines
TIMES	94.7%	5.3%	7,442
POST	93.2	6.8	3,756
TRIBUNE	89.9	10.1	3,920

lines did, however, reveal support for the administration's relevant positions.

A STEP BACK FROM THE BRINK

In a triple front page headline on October 29, the *Washington Post* summarized the developments that had taken place over the last twenty-four hours: "Reds Agree to Scrap Bases in Cuba; U.S. Greets Move as Tension Eases; U.N. Aides Going to Havana Tuesday." The other two newspapers reported the Kennedy–Khrushchev arrangement to solve the Cuban crisis under similar headlines on this last Monday in October. Khrushchev had agreed to stop work on missile sites in Cuba, to dismantle the disputed weapons, and to ship them back to the Soviet Union. The U.S. President, in return, had promised to lift the naval blockade as soon as a United Nations team was in place to oversee the removal of the Soviet military equipment. Also, Kennedy had pledged not to invade Cuba, if the Soviet weapons were fully removed from the island.

On the same day, all three newspapers published editorials that commented on the change in the Cuban conflict. Applauding both leaders for giving the world "the most significant breaks in the cold war since its beginning," the *Post* paid special tribute to the American side, stating, "For this dramatic turn in the course of the cold war the Kennedy Administration merits a large measure of credit."[54] The *New York Times,* too, left no doubt that so far the President had prevailed in this conflict, pointing out, "The Soviet ruler's decision to liquidate his Cuba bases meets President Kennedy's first condition."[55] In a *Times* front page news analysis, James Reston underscored what the President had achieved with his tough stand vis-à-vis Moscow: "In his [Kennedy's] dealings with the Russians, he has probably removed the Soviet illusion that America would not fight and thus reduced the chances of miscalculation in Moscow."[56] Calling Khrushchev's willingness to remove Soviet missiles from Cuba under UN supervision an "astonishing proposal," The *Chicago Tribune* did not mention President Kennedy or the administration. Still, the *Tribune* seemed somewhat supportive of the President, claiming that in case of satisfactory solution of the dispute, "it will prove to have been an unexpected show of American firmness" that would have accomplished this.[57]

During the three weeks of the lingering crisis (October 29 to November 20, 1962), there were ups and downs in the Cuban conflict. Castro's refusal to honor Khrushchev's agreement with Kennedy prevented the UN from supervising the dismantling of missiles and launchers. Once the removal took place and was verified, the dispute centered around Russian IL-28 jet bombers, which Kennedy wanted out of Cuba as well. Until Castro finally agreed to the removal of these aircraft from the island and Kennedy lifted the naval blockade, the crisis lingered on.

Throughout this period, the two East Coast publications adhered to their editorial support for the Kennedy administration. All eight relevant editorials that the *Post* published in the three weeks of the lingering crisis were in agreement with the Kennedy position on Cuba. Typical of the pro-Kennedy stance was the editorial of November 2, in which the *Post* applauded Kennedy's refusal "to gloat over the Soviet Union's backdown in Cuba" in view of Castro's refusal to comply with the Kennedy–Khrushchev arrangement. Moreover, the *Post* denounced those who criticized Kennedy's crisis management, arguing that "serious-minded citizens have an obligation to refrain from conduct or premature conclusions that might be embarrassing to their government."[58]

Of the thirteen editorials in which the *Times* dealt with the Cuban issue during this period, eleven were supportive of the President, while two fell into the neutral/ambiguous category. When commenting on the President's role in the crisis, the New York paper was full of praise. Recalling the heights of the crisis, during which "the world escaped a nuclear Armageddon," the *Times* commented that the chief credit for the easing of the tension "belongs, first of all, to President Kennedy, who, after fumbles that go back to the Bay of Pigs disaster, took the fateful decision to confront Soviet Russia head-on as soon as he had hard evidence of the Soviet nuclear advance toward our shores."[59] The qualification in this positive appraisal was perhaps the result of some uneasiness on the part of the *Times* editorial board that it might be perceived as a cheerleading team for the President. Why else would the editorial mention the President's pre-crisis "fumbles"? Apart from the Bay of Pigs fiasco, the *Times* had, after all, supported Kennedy's moderate Cuba policy up to the blockade announcement. Aside from this critical remark, the *Times* continued to editorialize in favor of the Kennedy administration's Cuba line. In assessing the effect of the ongoing removal of Russian missiles from Cuba on world public opinion, one editorial suggested that this had "created new confidence in American leadership."[60]

During pre-crisis and acute crisis, the editorial writers of the *Tribune* had frequently commented on the Cuban dispute. However, in the three weeks of ever-new developments in the lingering crisis they restricted their editorial comments on this topic. After publishing the aforementioned initial editorial with its lukewarm support, only one other editorial with direct relevance to Kennedy's Cuba policy was published. In it, the *Tribune* did not try to hide its growing displeasure with the President's handling of the Cuban crisis. Analyzing the Cuban crisis at the time, the editorial criticized that the initial resolution shown by the White House "had run down like a clock. Apparently the blockade will soon be lifted. How do we know that more Soviet contraband will not be brought in? Is Castro to be permanently protected in his communist staging base by the President's guarantee to Khrushchev that there will be no invasion?"[61] An additional editorial during this period that dealt with the administration's news management during the Cuban crisis and thus with an indirectly relevant issue, attacked the administration harshly for having violated "the ancient right of the American people to know the truth about their government."[62] Neither the *Post* nor the *Times* commented editorially on the dispute over the administration's ongoing press censorship during this or the previous acute crisis period.

In the overall crisis coverage of all three newspapers combined, domestic and foreign sources supportive of the President's Cuban position continued to be the dominant news sources. Table 1.7 shows that there were no significant differences in the overall news reporting the three publications presented to their readers. In all three newspapers foreign sources with neutral or ambiguous attitudes toward Kennedy's Cuba policy were used for more than half the space based on news sources abroad. Critical foreign sources captured more linage in the three examined publications than foreign supporters of Kennedy's position on Cuba. The latter tended to support the President's willingness to settle the missile issue peacefully.

In the domestic realm, the change from an acute crisis with its real fears of a third world war to a lingering crisis with its focus on diplomatic solutions resulted in a different behavior of the longtime, conservative critics of Kennedy's Cuba policy. While they had either supported the administration or at least suspended public criticism during the six tense crisis days, they now made efforts to return to the pre-crisis pluralistic debate. This was especially the case during the ten-day period beginning with the announcement on October 28 that Kennedy and Khrushchev were willing to settle the Cuban dispute peacefully and ending with the congressional elections on November 7. Once again, formal political actors, i.e., conservative members

TABLE 1.7   Overall Coverage, Lingering Cuban Missile Crisis: Domestic and Foreign Sources, Directly Relevant (Editorials Excluded)

Linage	For/Probably For	Neutral/ Ambiguous	Against/Probably Against	Total Lines
TIMES	47.9%	38.9%	13.2%	18,871
POST	48.3	39.6	12.1	12,764
TRIBUNE	49.3	33.9	16.8	9,450

of Congress who had led the Kennedy opposition in the months before the blockade decision, spearheaded an attack on the President's Cuba policy.

Relative to the volume of its Cuba coverage The *Chicago Tribune,* which began to voice its reservation against the Kennedy–Khrushchev formula to settle the Cuban issue, provided more space to the Kennedy opposition than did the other two papers. Senator Capehart who campaigned for reelection in Indiana charged repeatedly that Kennedy's promise not to invade Cuba would give Communism a "deed to Cuba forever." Senator Barry Goldwater attacked the noninvasion pledge as giving Castro a free hand to continue subversive actions in Latin America. The *Tribune* reported extensively about such charges by these two senators and others, mostly Republican conservatives. And when in early November, Cuban exiles began to complain that Castro was hiding Russian missiles in caves, the Chicago paper carried these reports.[63]

The *New York Times,* too, accommodated the newly arising criticism in its coverage of the Cuban issue. When the formation of a new national "Committee for the Monroe Doctrine" was announced, the paper reported in a two-column story that the founders of this group protested the terms on which Kennedy and Khrushchev planned to settle the Cuban crisis, namely the President's noninvasion pledge.[64] The *Times* also carried stories about increasing dissatisfaction of Cuban exiles and their claims that Cuba was hiding Russian missiles underground. Senator Hugh Scott, his colleague Barry Goldwater, and other Kennedy critics were used as sources by the *Times,* and on one occasion the paper granted front page coverage to a Goldwater attack on "soft" Kennedy advisers.[65]

The *Washington Post,* unlike the other two papers, ignored the emergence of new opposition against Kennedy's Cuba policy by and large, and when critics were mentioned it was at times done in an indirect manner. For example, in one of the already cited *Post* editorials, those who criticized the President were chided.[66] When Goldwater demanded the removal of Adlai Stevenson and three other high officials in the Kennedy administration because of their timid Cuba stand, the *Post's* report focused on Stevenson's counterattack and his letter to the Senator.[67]

The results of the elections on November 7 were interpreted as a vote of confidence for the President. The Democrats increased their majority in the Senate and maintained their dominant position in the House. Senator Capehart, the most relentless of Kennedy's critics as far as the Cuban issue was concerned, was defeated by Birch Bayh. This took of wind out of the sails of those who opposed Kennedy's handling of the Cuban crisis.

As the election results demonstrated, there was much domestic support for the President and his crisis management. And in all three publications, sources in favor of the administration's Cuba policy were dominant. The administration had virtually a monopoly over information about the Cuban crisis. Selected journalists, namely those representing The *Washington Post* and the *New York Times,* were able to get an "inside view" from administration officials. The *Post* seemed to have an advantage in this respect. In the edition that reported the Kennedy–Khrushchev agreement to solve the Cuban problem, the Washington paper presented two lengthy news analyses dealing with the new situation. Both pieces were based on "top figures in the U.S. Administration connected with the Cuban crisis" and on "authoritative sources,"[68] Also, the "now-it-can-be-told" accounts of the crisis decision-making process continued in both the *Post* and *Times.* The Chicago newspaper also took note of administration revelations about decision-making considerations, but these types of stories were much more common in the East Coast papers.

The two East Coast papers continued to publish human interest items that reminded readers that the President and his advisers were working very hard during the crisis for the good of the country and that the Cuba watch was still in place. Under the headline "U.S. Forces Keep Watch On Cuba" the *Times* reported that on the first weekend in November "many leading administration officials spent the day at home or in the country with their families—for the first time in several weeks."[69] And in a story about a Presidential visit to Middleburg Estate in the *Post* it was explained that this "was the first time the President had left the White House, except to go to church, since he cancelled his campaign tour in Chicago on October 20."[70]

The domestic news coverage of the three newspapers during the lingering crisis seemed influenced by each one's editorial position: The *Post* editors, who were staunch supporters of Kennedy's Cuban stand, mostly ignored critical domestic sources. The *Times* was clearly supportive of Kennedy in its editorial policy; and although domestic sources supportive of the President commanded a significant linage advantage over critical sources in the New York publication, the *Times* did not ignore the Kennedy opposition. In fact, as far as space was concerned, *Times* and *Tribune* provided about the same linage to sources speaking out against the administration's crisis handling. However, given the by far greater amount of space the New York newspaper dedicated to the crisis coverage, Kennedy critics captured a higher percentage of lines in the *Tribune* than in the *Times.* The Chicago publication was, as mentioned earlier, the only one among the three newspapers that began to criticize Kennedy's Cuba policy editorially. In this paper the gap between pro and contra sources was somewhat smaller than in the East Coast publications (see table 1.8).

Domestic sources in agreement with the President's handling of the Cuban crisis were given preferential placement by all three newspapers. While the *Tribune* used critical sources quite often, this newspaper was the least generous when it came to mention Kennedy-critics in front page stories. Here, the pro-administration sources held a dominant 46–3 advantage. Opponents of the administration's Cuba policy did not fare much better in the other two papers. In the *Post,* the pro-Kennedy sources held a 73–10 front page story advantage while in the *Times* favored supportive sources 83–7 with respect to using them in page one stories. As far as foreign sources were concerned, there was a different placement picture: In all three publications sources critical of the President's crisis policy were more often mentioned in front page stories than supportive sources.

Although less tense than the six days of the acute crisis, the three-week-long lingering crisis period did not end the dominance of administration sources over congressional sources in the crisis coverage of the three newspapers. The coverage of all three newspapers mirrored a situation in which the administration was by far the more active and Congress the more passive branch. As table 1.9 shows the *Tribune* provided more linage to congressional sources than the two East Coast newspapers. This was the result of the attention the Chicago newspaper paid to conservatives such as Senators Capehart and Goldwater.

In spite of the dominance of supportive domestic sources there was also evidence of an underlying desire to return to normal pluralistic, conflictual

TABLE 1.8   Lingering Cuban Missile Crisis Coverage: Domestic Sources, Directly Relevant (Editorials Excluded)

Linage	For/Probably For	Neutral/ Ambiguous	Against/Probably Against	Total Lines
TIMES	62.1%	30.4%	7.5%	12,164
POST	65.0	32.6	2.4	7,872
TRIBUNE	65.1	21.5	13.4	6,573

TABLE 1.9   Linage Administration and Congressional Sources: Lingering Cuban Missile Crisis

	Administration Sources	Congressional Sources	Total Lines
TIMES	93.9%	6.1%	6,951
POST	95.4	4.6	4,528
TRIBUNE	89.2	10.8	4,616

conditions. To discover it, one must examine the coverage of issues that were indirectly relevant to the ongoing crisis, namely question of the administration's news management. The *Tribune,* for example, informed its readers in a front page story that "[a] substantial press revolt against an apparent administration policy of treating news as a government weapon" had broken out in Washington.[71] The same day, the *Times* reported that the president of the American Society of Newspaper Editors had protested against the admission by Arthur Sylvester, Assistant Secretary of Defense for Public Affairs, that "Government news releases were being used as propaganda weapons in the cold war."[72] The *Post* reported at length about a speech by Merriman Smith, White House correspondent of the United Press International, who also criticized the President for the administration's news curbs in connection with the Cuban crisis.[73] Critics who might have hesitated to attack the President's crisis management directly seemed more inclined to voice criticism in matters indirectly connected to the crisis (see table 1.10).

Journalistic descriptions, background informations, and news analyses were overwhelmingly neutral or ambiguous as far as the attitude of media sources vis-à-vis the President's crisis management and Cuban policies was concerned. In all three newspapers more than 70 percent of the lines attributable to journalistic sources fit the neutral/ambiguous category.

BLOCKADE AND CRISIS END

Two days before Thanksgiving Day, on November 20, President Kennedy revealed that he had ordered the lifting of the naval quarantine of Cuba in response to an assurance by Nikita Khrushchev that all Russian IL-28 bombers would be removed from Cuba within thirty days. Although acknowledging that important other parts of the American–Russian agreement to settle the Cuban crisis peacefully had yet to be carried out, the President clearly signaled the end of the threat to the country's national security. And

TABLE 1.10   Lingering Cuban Missile Crisis Coverage: Domestic Sources, Indirectly Relevant (Editorials Excluded)

Linage	For/Probably For	Neutral/ Ambiguous	Against/Probably Against	Total Lines
TIMES	32.4%	48.2%	19.4%	1,842
POST	37.0	53.2	9.8	887
TRIBUNE	42.6	3.8	53.6	754

he told his fellow Americans, "In this week of Thanksgiving there is much for which we can be grateful as we look back to where we stood only four weeks ago . . .".[74] A day later, over 14,000 reservists who had been called to active duty the prior month were released, and the return of 63 warships from the blockade zone to their home ports was ordered. Although it took the two superpowers several more weeks before they came around to declaring officially the end of the Cuban Missile Crisis, the threat was over when the quarantine was lifted and the military alert called off.

The end of the naval blockade was reported in front page stories in all three publications the day after Kennedy's announcement during a White House news conference.

The *New York Times,* in an editorial published the same day, applauded Kennedy's decision to lift the blockade but to continue aerial surveillance of Cuba until an international verification system could be set up. Although warning that there was no reason for euphoria, the *Times* was clearly pleased with the President, describing him to have spoken "with a sense of calmness and assurance that reflected his very great successes of the past month," when he announced the newest developments in the Cuban issue.[75] During the following weeks of the post-crisis period (November 20, 1962 through January 31, 1963) the *Times* continued to support the President editorially when expressing an opinion in matters directly related to the Cuban problem. Of its eight editorials published in the post-crisis weeks, six were supportive, one fell into the neutral/ambiguous category, one seemed somewhat critical. This latter piece dealt with a Khrushchev statement threatening to take whatever actions were necessary if the United States should fail to observe its Cuba commitments, namely the noninvasion pledge. The *Times* in this context not only expressed concern, as Secretary of State Dean Rusk had done, over thousands of Russian troops allegedly stationed on the Cuban island but also seemed to advocate a tougher stand on Cuba, arguing, "if the present number of military personnel is anything like the rumored figure of 15,000 there are certainly too many of them in Cuba now." The editorial closed with the conclusion that "conditions for that promise [not to invade Cuba] have not been fulfilled."[76] This was not very different from what Cuban exiles and conservative Kennedy critics said. An additional editorial, indirectly relevant to Kennedy's Cuban policy, chided the President for the administration's failure to get directly involved in efforts to win the release of more than a thousand Bay of Pigs prisoners still held by Castro. Although the *Times* acknowledged that the exiles invaded their homeland voluntarily, the editorial recognized responsibility on the part of both the Eisenhower and the Kennedy administrations for having trained and armed the invaders (under Eisenhower) and for having given the signal to let them go and the means to get there (under Kennedy).[77]

The *Washington Post* continued to support the President's Cuba policy completely. In its first editorial following the lifting of the blockade, the newspaper praised the progress in Cuba and supported Kennedy's latest decision, writing, "Without prejudicing our interest in any way we can calmly wait for a reasonable time for delivery on the bomber pledge and the rest of the contract."[78] All four editorials directly relevant to the Cuban problem published during this period by the *Post* were supportive of the President's position. However, the realization that the crisis had ended and a state of normality had returned was not lost on the editorial writers. While they had not taken a position on the heated issue of the administration's "news management" during the acute and lingering crisis phases, they hastened to do so immediately after the blockade had ended. In its edition of November 22, the *Post* lectured President Kennedy on press freedom, charging that his press conference statements "indicated that the President does not understand or does not admit understanding the real objections of the press."[79] Thus, while still supporting the President on his Cuba policy, the *Post* severely criticized him in an indirectly relevant issue the newspaper had avoided in the editorial department during the crisis weeks.

The *Chicago Tribune* resumed the critical editorial stance of the pre-crisis period. The five editorials directly relevant to the Cuban issue published in the post-crisis weeks were all critical of the President and his administration. In one of these editorials, the newspaper urged Congress to investigate whether a secret deal had been made with the Kremlin before Khrushchev agreed to withdraw missiles and bombers from Cuba.[80] In another editorial, the *Tribune* attacked Kennedy in matters both directly and indirectly relevant to the Cuban issue at the time. Demanding a congressional investigation of exile reports (as reported by the *Tribune*'s correspondent Jules Dubois) that not all missile sites on Cuba had been dismantled, the editorial also pointed out that the President did not deserve to be honored by recently released Cuban prisoners taken during the Bay of Pigs invasion. The Tribune wrote, "Mr. Kennedy has become the symbol to them of their liberation. Mr. Kennedy is not the symbol but the very man who got them into trouble in the first place. He gave them the go-ahead for their descent on the Bay of Pigs and then, at the last minute, withheld the air cover they needed to secure their beachhead."[81]

Editorially, then, all three newspapers returned to their pre-crisis posture: The *Post*, with the exception of the indirectly relevant dispute about the administration's "news management," supported Kennedy's Cuba policy all the way; the *Times* expressed mostly support, but also indicated where it might differ with the President, namely on matters less directly relevant to the Cuban issue; the *Tribune*, on the other hand, resumed an editorial stance as critical of the President's Cuban policy as during the pre-crisis period.

During the months that preceded the Cuban crisis, President Kennedy's approval rate had dipped for the first time since he took office under the 70 percent mark and had reached the lowest point (62 percent) in October prior to his blockade announcement. Kennedy's handling of the crisis, however, reversed this downward trend dramatically: In December, his approval rate was up a dozen points to 74 percent; in January 1963, 76 percent of the public approved of the President's performance.[82] This impressive recovery in the Presidential popularity ratings could not be separated from the Cuban issue and from the way Americans perceived the President's handling of the crisis. Clearly, a majority of Americans gave Kennedy and his administration high marks for a successful stand against Cuba and the Soviet Union. The President and members of his administration made great efforts to keep this positive momentum alive. Hardly a day went by during the weeks and months that followed the removal of the blockade that did not witness some activities, announcements, or explanations relevant to the Cuban affair on the part of the White House and/or the Departments of State and Defense.

The press coverage reflected this continued activist administration stance and the willingness of the newspapers to report to a great extent whatever information was released. Often, the newspapers carried the announcement of an upcoming presidential activity as well as a report, once that activity had taken place. For example, the *Times* reported in a front page story that Kennedy would meet with his top advisers during a Thanksgiving stay on Cape Cod in order to shape a new Cuba policy in the wake of the removal of all missiles and the upcoming withdrawal of jet bombers from the island. An article that reported on this review of the Cuba situation was also carried on the front page in the following edition of the newspaper. The same before-and-after and preferential placement pattern was adhered to on other occasions: The *Times,* in a front page article, announced the President's plan to visit military bases in Georgia and Florida to thank units that had been alerted during the Cuban crisis, and two days later the newspapers reported on Kennedy's "thank-you trip." The upcoming White House visit of Anastas Mikoyan, a Soviet First Deputy Premier, was front page news for the *Times* as was the following report on the three-hour meeting between Kennedy and Mikoyan that did not bring progress in the ongoing Cuba negotiations between the two sides.[83]

The *Tribune* was not immune to the flow of administration announcements and statements. Just like the *Times* the Chicago paper also published "before" and "after" articles about the Mikoyan visit in the White House. The publication reported extensively each time the President praised those who had supported the nation (for instance, broadcast outlets that had donated air time to beam the Voice of America to Cuba, or military units on alert during the crisis periods). Also, revelations about the preparedness of the armed forces before and during the crisis were generously published by the Chicago paper as were announcements of continued surveillance of Cuba. Thus, a Presidential announcement in mid-December that a daily aerial surveillance of the island was still in place earned front page placement in the *Tribune* as did a State Department warning that countries whose ships participated in trade with Cuba risked the loss of American aid.[84]

The *Washington Post* was at least as susceptible to administration statements and announcements as the other two newspapers and continued to make use of unnamed sources in White House and in various departments. A front page news analysis by Chalmer M. Roberts described "a new mood" of well-being and buoyancy among officials in the Capital "not evident here in a long, long time" in the aftermath of the Cuban crisis.[85] This kind of optimism was reflected in the overall coverage of the Cuban question in the weeks after the end of the quarantine.

Nevertheless, with the "rally-around-the-flag" sentiment of the crisis period fading, even a superactivist President riding on a new wave of popularity was unable to prevent the surfacing of renewed criticism and opposition. To one degree or another all three newspapers used sources critical of the President's post-crisis Cuba policy in their coverage, once those sources began to articulate their views, namely in late December and in January. When Senator Goldwater charged that President Kennedy had "watered down" his tough Cuban stand, the *Washington Post* reported this. Both the *Times* and *Tribune* gave detailed accounts of Senator Keating's claims that there were still 114 missile launchers, 24 bases, and 500 antiaircraft missiles on Cuban soil. Also, renewed complaints by Cuban exiles that Castro had stuck away Russian weapons in underground hiding places were reported.[86]

In the relevant domestic coverage, pro-Kennedy sources captured two-thirds or more of the total linage in all three newspapers (see table 1.11). Nevertheless, critical sources were used for a considerably higher percentage of the space than during the acute and lingering crisis periods. There

TABLE 1.11   Post-Crisis Coverage, Cuban Missile Crisis: Domestic Sources, Directly Relevant (Editorials Excluded)

Linage	For/Probably For	Neutral/ Ambiguous	Against/Probably Against	Total Lines
TIMES	69.0%	18.4%	12.6%	4,221
POST	74.5	15.5	10.0	3,696
TRIBUNE	66.6	13.5	19.9	3,411

seemed to be a relationship between editorial positions and news coverage in that the editorially critical *Tribune*'s reporting was less favorable to the President than that of the editorially supportive East Coast papers.

Not unaware of opinion polls that showed overwhelming public support for President Kennedy following the Missile Crisis, critics opposed to the administration's policy in matters directly related to the crisis issue may have hesitated to criticize the President outright. There was less restraint when it came to issues indirectly relevant to the then current Cuban problem. And the leading issue in this category was once again the Bay of Pigs invasion. When Barry Goldwater demanded a Senate inquiry into the U.S. government's role in the Bay of Pigs invasion, all three newspapers covered his initiative. While the *Tribune* preceded the Senator's formal inquiry request by a report that the Republican Policy Committee in the Senate had thrown its support behind the Goldwater initiative, the *Post* followed up with an article reporting that a Republican Senator (Jacob Javits) and one of his Democratic colleagues (Hubert Humphrey) were highly critical of "partisan Bay of Pigs inquiries."[87] Those sources who were critical of Kennedy's Cuba policy in late 1962 and early 1963 used the controversial handling of the invasion in 1961 as a convenient crisis-related substitute to attack the President and administration. The *Tribune* gave about the same amount of lines to supporters and opponents of the President in issues indirectly related to the crisis while the coverage in the *Times* and in the *Post* was more favorable from the administration's point of view (see table 1.12).

In the aftermath of the crisis, the number of foreign sources used and the lineage reserved for covering them declined dramatically. Internationally, the Cuban question was no longer a topic that preoccupied the international and domestic community.

Table 1.13 shows that as a result of the dominance of domestic pro-Kennedy sources in the coverage, the President fared very well in the overall news reporting (combined domestic and foreign sources).

All three papers gave preferential placement to domestic sources in favor

TABLE 1.12　Post-Crisis Coverage, Cuban Missile Crisis: Domestic Sources, Indirectly Relevant (Editorials Excluded)

Linage	For/Probably For	Neutral/ Ambiguous	Against/Probably Against	Total Lines
TIMES	56.0%	25.5%	18.5%	2,098
POST	63.0	15.7	21.3	2,267
TRIBUNE	42.1	15.0	42.9	1,010

of the President's Cuba policy much more often than to critical sources. The *Times* used pro-administration sources in 73 front page stories, critical sources in 4 page one articles. In the *Post,* the pro-Kennedy sources had a 36–1, in the *Tribune* a 43–2 front page story advantage. Foreign sources did not make the front pages very often during the weeks following the end of the blockade: in the two East Coast papers critical foreign sources had an edge over supportive sources as far as front page placement was concerned (3–2 in the *Times,* 4–2 in the *Post*). The *Tribune* used foreign sources in only 4 front page stories during this period and in all instances the intentions were of a neutral or ambiguous nature.

Finally, administration sources held an overwhelming linage advantage over congressional sources during this period (see table 1.14). One reason for this administration dominance was the fact that after the congressional elections in November little was heard of the lame duck legislative chambers until members returned to Washington for the convening of the 88th Congress in the second half of January.

As far as journalistic sources in descriptions, background information, and news analyses were concerned, in the *Times* more than 90 percent and in the *Post* over 70 percent of the lines in this category were of a neutral or ambiguous nature. In the *Tribune,* less than half of media-based lines fit the

TABLE 1.13 Overall Post-Crisis Coverage, Cuban Missile Crisis: Domestic and Foreign Sources, Directly Relevant (Editorials Excluded)

Linage	For/Probably For	Neutral/ Ambiguous	Against/Probably Against	Total Lines
TIMES	56.5%	30.1%	13.4%	5,570
POST	65.5	20.6	13.9	4,281
TRIBUNE	57.7	20.5	21.8	3,937

TABLE 1.14 Linage for Administration and Congressional Sources: Post-Crisis Cuban Missile Crisis

	Administration Sources	Congressional Sources	Total Lines
TIMES	89.0%	11.0%	3,269
POST	87.8	12.2	2,866
TRIBUNE	90.6	9.4	2,166

neutral/ambiguous category while a similar amount of lines based on journal-istic sources revealed either support for or opposition to the President's crisis-related policies.

SUMMARY

Faced with the most serious crisis since World War II and at the brink of a war against the Soviet Union, the nation supported President Kennedy and his attempts to manage the most pressing affair of state. Not only conserva-tive politicians, who had relentlessly attacked Kennedy's Cuba policy before the blockade decision, but also critical editorial writers switched to pro-Kennedy positions. The newspapers reflected this wave of support. It was as classic a "rally-'round-the-flag" reaction among the overwhelming majority of domestic actors as could be expected during very serious crises.

Domestic sentiment was very different during the weeks before the blockade: Active opposition to Kennedy's Cuba policy provoked conflict and a sharp debate with the administration and its supporters. The press re-ported extensively about these political disagreements.

Once the critical phase of the crisis was over, some opposition was again voiced against Kennedy's Cuba policy, but an impressive victory by Demo-crats in the congressional elections in early November took much of the steam out of these attacks. This development during the lingering crisis phase was mirrored in news coverage and in editorials.

Finally, after the removal of the blockade and the end of the crisis, news coverage took note of a pluralist debate in matters related to the Missile Crisis that was beginning to take shape. However, Kennedy's opposition did not come close to regaining the strength it had mustered during the weeks before the blockade. Kennedy benefited from the widespread belief among Americans that he had managed the crisis skillfully. The President and his aides exploited this success by mounting a clever public relations campaign that resulted in ample positive press coverage. Under these circumstances, opponents of the President's Cuba policy were more inclined to attack him in matters indirectly related to the Missile Crisis, such as the Bay of Pigs fiasco.

These findings confirm Kern, Levering, and Levering's conclusion that during the Kennedy era the press was "reflective" with respect to foreign crises coverage. This case study demonstrates furthermore that newspa-pers did not present their readers with identical news coverage. Kern et al. found that the dominance of a president in press coverage depends on the presence or absence of other political voices.[88] Newspapers did indeed take note of both Kennedy's supporters and critics in Cuba-related matters. More important, however, is the following finding: The extent to which the President's domestic proponents or opponents were highlighted or downplayed in the news depended on the editorial view of each newspaper. During all phases of the Cuban crisis there was a relationship between so-called straight news reporting and editorial positions of each news organization.

2

THE DOMINICAN REPUBLIC INVASION

THE MARINES HAVE LANDED

Wednesday, April 28, 1965. Sometime in the afternoon, the State department receives an urgent cable from Washington's Ambassador in Santo Domingo informing the Johnson administration that "the time has come to land the marines."[1] The request is made four days after yet another coup in the Dominican Republic, a country of about three million inhabitants on the Caribbean island of Hispanola. U.S. Ambassador W. Tapley Bennett's call for military action does not come as a surprise to President Lyndon B. Johnson. Having followed the developments of a bloody civil war in the island state since it began the previous weekend, he now is determined to act. He invites the congressional leaders to the White House to inform them of his decision.

Shortly after meeting with the legislators, the 36th President of the United States walks into the White House television theater to address the nation. It is shortly before 9:00 P.M. Washington time, when Americans learn that their President has ordered "to put the necessary American troops ashore in order to give protection to hundreds of Americans who are still in the Dominican Republic and to escort them safely back to this country." Johnson also reveals that "400 Marines have already landed."[2] Fearing for the safety of the 2000 or so Americans in the Dominican Republic, the USS *Boxer* had been moved closer to the country's shore two days earlier. More than a thousand American citizens had been evacuated from the troubled area and flown to Puerto Rico on Tuesday and Wednesday. Nevertheless, as the President speaks, additional hundreds of Americans are waiting to be evacuated from Santo Domingo. Johnson promises help to them and to all foreigners who want to leave the country. The President mentions only one reason for ordering American soldiers to intervene in a Latin American country for the first time since the Nicaraguan intervention in 1927—to protect Americans and other nationals.

With United States Marines deployed in a combat area and given the permission to fight in order to protect their own lives and those of American civilians, the President's announcement is in fact his public acknowledgment that the nation is faced with a crisis.

Two days later, in a second live television broadcast, the President informs the nation, "In the last 24 hours violence and disorder have increased [in the Dominican Republic]." Again justifying American military involvement with the need to protect American citizens, he also claims, "Meanwhile, there are signs that people trained outside the Dominican Republic are seeking to gain control. Thus, the legitimate aspirations of the Dominican people, and most of their leaders, for progress, democracy and social justice are threatened."[3] Earlier in the day, in a discussion with his Secretary of State and others, the President had expressed himself even clearer, stating, "The last thing we want to have happen is a Communist takeover in that country."[4] Still two days later, in his third television address within six days, the President tells fellow Americans that the revolt in the Dominican Republic has been seized by a "band of Communist conspirators" many of which have been trained in Cuba. During the same speech Johnson announces that 14,000 United States troops have been committed to the Dominican Republic to protect lives and to prevent the establishment of "another Communist state in this hemisphere."[5]

Beginning with the news of the first Marines landing in the Dominican Republic, the crisis is the number one news topic in the American media.

AT THE END OF THE SECOND HONEYMOON

When American helicopters touched down on a polo field a few miles west of downtown Santo Domingo to land 405 U.S. Marines who immediately made their way to the United States Embassy, President Johnson enjoyed a reassuring degree of popularity at home. As his second "First Hundred Days" drew to a close, 67 percent of his fellow Americans approved of the way LBJ was handling the presidency.[6] There was growing criticism of the President's Vietnam policy in some quarters but a major foreign policy speech on April 7, 1965, at Johns Hopkins University managed to mute his Vietnam critics with the announcement that the United States government was willing to negotiate. One national news magazine reported, "Few U.S. foreign-policy declarations of recent years have met with such an immediate and overwhelmingly favorable response."[7]

In the weeks and even months following the assassination of President John Kennedy his successor Lyndon Johnson had enjoyed a great deal of good will on the part of a mourning nation. The new President had pushed the fallen predecessor's agenda, namely major civil rights legislation, and he had succeeded where Kennedy had been obstructed by Congress. The Civil

Rights Act of 1964 and the Tax Reduction Bill of the same year had been sought by Kennedy but accomplished by Johnson.

Conscious that he had not been elected by the American public to the highest office in the land and that he had moral obligation to take care of Kennedy's unfinished business, Johnson had begun to articulate and to push his own agenda as well. In a commencement address at the University of Michigan on May 22, 1964, Johnson had unveiled his Great Society vision and program in an effort to present his equivalent to the New Deal of Franklin Roosevelt, the Fair Deal of Harry Truman, and the New Frontier of John Kennedy.[8]

In November 1964, Lyndon Johnson had been elected to the presidency in his own right with 61 percent of the total vote, beating Republican Senator Barry Goldwater in 44 states and the District of Columbia. This landslide victory had given him a mandate of his own to keep pushing his agenda. During the "second honeymoon" following his inauguration on January 20, 1965, Johnson laid the groundwork for the Voting Rights Bill, which was enacted in August of 1965. Assessing Johnson's second "First Hundred Days" as a "stunning legislative achievement," *Newsweek* marveled: "The $1.3 billion school-aid bill swept through the Senate, the medicare rolled to an overwhelming victory in the House, and both branches of Congress were well on their way to the toughest voting-rights bill since the adoption of the Fifteenth Amendment 95 years ago."[9]

Clearly, at the end of April 1965 and at the end of his second presidential honeymoon, the first in his own right, Lyndon Johnson had popular and legislative support. This was the political situation when the American intervention in the Dominican Republic began.

LBJ AND THE PRESS

Succeeding a president whose violent death had left deep scars on an emotionally wounded nation, Lyndon Johnson was the beneficiary of an outpouring of sympathetic feelings for the new man in the White House. In a way, Americans granted the former Vice-President who had taken over from their fallen leader a prolonged honeymoon period. The press was no exception. George E. Reedy, the second of Johnson's four White House press secretaries, observed that during his first six months as President LBJ had the media "eating out of his hand."[10] Others felt that the President's honeymoon with the media lasted twelve months or so. Thereafter, however, the relationship between President and press was less harmonious. Long before the American involvement in Indochina resulted in massive protest movements and growing media criticism, Johnson had begun to astonish, frustrate, and alienate many members of the White House press corps.

Johnson's difficulties with the media were rooted in his inability to understand journalists as individuals and the press collectively. According to Carroll Kirkpatrick who covered the White House under Johnson and under Nixon, "He [Johnson] understood the Senate like no other. He knew how the bureaucracy operated in a very detailed and expert way. He knew where the lobbyists were and how to make use of them. But he did not understand the press."[11]

Kirkpatrick and others came to the conclusion that Johnson's earlier experiences with the Texas press and with a small group of journalists who covered the Senate caused his misconception of how to deal with the White House press. Convinced that the press had significant influence on the public at large and on politicians in Washington, LBJ "tried to crowd everybody else out of the paper." This desire to "blanket the newspapers" was in the opinion of Johnson's press secretary Reedy the reason for LBJ's "horrible Saturday morning press conferences."[12] Deep in his heart Johnson felt that the White House media could be controlled in the same way as he had gotten his will with the press in Texas years ago—by winning the cooperation of the most influential publishers. Also, as Senate leader, he had been able to deal effectively with reporters who covered the congressional beat by "bully[ing] them into submission or, if that did not work, seduc[ing] them with favors."[13]

As President, Johnson made great efforts to co-opt and to seduce White House journalists to report favorably. He invited individual reporters or groups for lunch, granted exclusive interviews, asked them to accompany him to his ranch in Texas. In return, he expected that those he singled out would write positive stories about him. George Reedy quickly learned that Johnson's idea of a good story was one that began, "Lyndon Baines Johnson is a calm, collected statesman who is the finest representative of the American dream."[14]

White House correspondents during the Johnson era still recall LBJ's efforts to co-opt them by promising to "make big men" of those who became part of the Johnson entourage. Frank Cormier was one of the White House journalists approached by President Johnson in this manner. On one occasion, Cormier and four other journalists were told by LBJ, "I need your help. There is no reason why the members of the White House press corps shouldn't be the best informed, most respected, highest paid reporters in Washington. If you help me, I'll help you and make you all big men in your profession."[15] These efforts to "buy" the press failed. Johnson blamed individual journalists, the press as a whole, even the Kennedys and other Eastern intellectuals who in his mind were more successful in influencing press coverage. According to Reedy, Johnson believed that "there was some mysterious art here that he couldn't quite dominate, that he couldn't quite master. I think he believed it had something to do with the Ivy League —that the Kennedys had gone to Harvard, whereas he had only gone to Southwest State Teachers College." [16]

Obsessed by the alleged power and influence of the media, Johnson had a super TV console with three screens put into the Oval Office and into his bedroom, which enabled him to view the network news simultaneously and to switch on and off the sound of the various programs. In addition, the Oval Office was equipped with three wire service tickers that provided Johnson with the news bulletins of AP, UPI and Reuters. [17] Although LBJ had the service of capable press secretaries (Pierre Salinger, George Reedy, Bill Moyers, and George Christian), Ben Bagdikian believes that "[o]ne trouble with Lyndon Johnson was that he was his own press secretary." [18]

While Johnson enjoyed a prolonged honeymoon with the press in the wake of the Kennedy assassination and through the 1964 presidential campaign, the relationship turned to a more adversarial stance about one year after he had moved into the White House. Thus, when Johnson sent American troops into the Dominican Republic, the press–president relationship had normalized. In Bagdikian's judgment, "in early 1965 the President came upon normal journalistic times and he, like every President before him, didn't like it." [19]

NO DOMINICAN ISSUES BEFORE THE COUP

Although plagued by instability since the assassination of longtime dictator Rafael Leonidas Trujillo in May 1961, the Dominican Republic had not been in the news in the United States during the first months of 1965 until a coup was attempted on April 24. Neither the *New York Times,* the *Washington Post,* nor the *Chicago Tribune* published articles about the political situation in the Caribbean state in the period from January 1 to April 24, 1965. Growing dissatisfaction with the government in Santo Domingo, headed by Donald Reid Cabral, seemed nothing extraordinary in a country that had experienced seven overthrows of governments since the death of Trujillo.

Trujillo had ruled the country for 32 years. After his assassination in 1961, there had been hope for the establishment of a democratic system. President John F. Kennedy had encouraged efforts to transform the Dominican Republic into "a showcase for democracy" and "thus showing up the Communist government of Fidel Castro." [20] The beginning of such a "showcase" had been achieved in 1963, when Juan Bosch had been inaugurated as the first freely elected president of the country. Then Vice-President Lyndon Johnson had been President Kennedy's representative at Bosch's inauguration. Seven months later, a military coup had overthrown Bosch who had been forced to flee to Puerto Rico.

The Reid government, in power before the eighth coup since 1961 occurred, had the support of Washington. However, there was growing dissatisfaction with Reid within his own country. Perceived as a moderate, Reid was opposed by political groupings both to the left and to the right of his middle-of-the-road position. Reacting to deteriorating economic conditions, Reid had imposed tough austerity measures, a move that had cost him much of his prior popularity among his countrymen. Bosch supporters had never forgotten that it was Reid who had followed Bosch into office. The political right was unhappy because Reid had recently removed some military officers who were known to be holdovers from the Trujillo reign. Finally, Reid's opponents accused him of stalling preparations for elections in September of 1965.[21]

President Johnson was at Camp David when he was informed that "there was once again trouble in the Caribbean: this time in the Dominican Republic." The news did not come as a complete surprise to the Johnson administration because intelligence sources had reported that a minimum of four different uprisings were planned for May or June. Indeed, Washington was well enough informed about the likelihood of yet another impending coup to ask U.S. Ambassador W. Tapley Bennett to come home for consultations. Bennett had traveled North and was in Washington when the first news of a coup attempt was received on April 24; he had come to participate in discussions about "what should or should not be done when one or another of them [uprisings] occurred."[22]

The American media and public took notice of the developments in the Dominican Republic only after a coup was attempted on April 24 and 25. Because there was no reporting either on developments in Santo Domingo or on relevant discussions within the Johnson administration prior to the rebellion against the Reid government, the pre-crisis coverage consisted of only four days, beginning with the first reports of an attempted coup and ending with President Johnson's revelation that he had ordered the deployment of U.S. troops in the Dominican Republic in order to protect the lives of American citizens.

None of the three newspapers had a correspondent in Santo Domingo, when the anti-Reid forces moved to overthrow the government. Reports that originated in Santo Domingo and were published by the *Times, Post,* and *Tribune* from April 24 to 28 were compiled by the wire services (AP, UPI, and Reuters). These articles described what was happening in the island state and what was uncertain about the quickly changing developments. Americans who read any one of the three newspapers received much of the same information from Santo Domingo, often stemming from the same wire service stories.

Although early reports considered the coup against the Reid government to have collapsed, the accounts that followed made clear that the American supported government had been overthrown by Army insurgents who wanted the reinstatement of Juan Bosch as head of government. Jose Rafael Molina Urena was named Acting President by the coup leaders. However, Air Force, Navy, and some parts of the Army fought the pro-Bosch forces under the leadership of Brigadier General Elias Wessin y Wessin. There were reports of people having been killed and injured as a result of heavy fighting in the Dominican capital.

Besides wire service reports from Santo Domingo, there was a second set of reports about the developments in the Dominican Republic written by the three newspapers' own journalists outside the troubled country. *Times* newsman Tad Szulc reported from San Juan utilizing telephone conversations with sources in Santo Domingo. He also described the reaction of Juan Bosch who lived in exile in Puerto Rico. The *Post*'s Dan Kurzman interviewed Bosch and wrote of Bosch's appeal to the United States to give support to pro-Bosch forces in the Dominican civil war.[23] While the *Times* and *Post* used Bosch, who had the reputation of a liberal politician, as source, the *Tribune*'s Jules Dubois utilized first coup-target Reid Cabral and thereafter General Wessin y Wessin as sources. Dubois characterized those behind the coup against Reid "leftist-oriented young officers."[24] Dubois reported of a phone conversation with General Wessin who had told him that he was fighting "against leftist rebels to prevent the Dominican Republic from becoming a second Cuba."[25] Moreover, reporting from Puerto Rico, Dubois clearly sided with the troops led by Wessin and took a position against the pro-Bosch forces whom he described as leftists and Communists or influenced by Communists. In one instance, for example, Dubois reported, "The anti-communist forces claimed victory today over the leftist rebels who are striving to return former President Juan Bosch to power in the Dominican Republic."[26]

While the Johnson administration kept a very low profile during the days preceding the intervention and did not reveal its view on the waring factions in the Dominican Republic, the DuBois position that leftists had caused the turmoil in the island state was a few days later publicly adopted by President Johnson.

During the days before Washington acted, little news related to the developments in the Caribbean country was based on sources in Washington and in the administration. On April 27, Johnson voiced concern about the Dominican situation during a press conference.[27] It seemed that the administration had but one objective at this time: to demonstrate that the developments in the Caribbean were closely observed and that there was reason for concern in the United States. The *Times* reported of a "day-long conference on the situation" in the State department with Secretary of State Dean Rusk participating.[28] And the same newspaper referred to State department sources assuring that there was no plan to intervene in the Dominican situation.[29] The news that a naval task force was being moved closer to the coast of the Dominican Republic and that Americans were being evacuated from the country originated mostly in the American Embassy in Santo Domingo.[30]

The Dominican coverage during the days before the American intervention was overwhelmingly factual "straight news" reporting. This was especially true of the wire service dispatches from Santo Domingo. The difference in the exclusive reports by each publication's own reporter was in their source selection: Both the *Times* and *Post* gave "liberal" Juan Bosch an opportunity to explain his views on the struggle in his homeland while the *Tribune* made first use of "moderate" Reid Cabral and thereafter of "conservative" General Wessin. However, while the reporters for the two East Coast newspapers did not reveal their own views in their articles, the *Tribune*'s Dubois left little doubt that he sided with the Wessin-led "anti-Communist forces" and was against the "leftist" pro-Bosch "rebels."[31]

The *Times* reported from Havana that a Cuban "propaganda broadcast" had charged that "United States forces were preparing to land in the Dominican Republic . . . ."[32] This was the only foreign criticism which one of the three newspapers took notice of.

The New York publication was the only one of the three to publish an editorial concerning the Dominican situation in the days before the intervention. Perhaps knowing of the belief in the White House "that the Dominican Republic was in the process of becoming 'another Cuba' and [that] no American President could allow that" to happen,[33] the *Times* may have anticipated a military move by the Johnson administration in spite of assurances that no intervention was under consideration. Pointing out the difficulties at hand in Santo Domingo, the editorial concluded with the warning, "Meanwhile, Washington had better sit back and wait."[34]

Table 2.1 shows that the coverage of the turmoil in the Dominican Republic in all three newspapers was dominated by sources whose intent fell into the neutral/ambiguous category. This is no surprise because the bulk of published material was based on reports from journalistic sources in Santo Domingo who described what was going on in the Caribbean country.

The domestic coverage of the developments in the Dominican Republic was a carbon copy of the overall reporting in that it was mostly based on seemingly objective accounts of what was going on in the island state. Sources with neutral/ambiguous intent dominated in the coverage of all three newspapers. There was no opposition to the administration's assurances of concern, of no intention to intervene, and of making arrangements for the evacuation of American citizens from the war-torn area. Table 2.2 illustrates this lack of disagreement over the U.S. position toward the Dominican development prior to the President's announcement that Marines had landed on Dominican soil.

FROM RESCUE ACTION TO INTERVENTION

When President Johnson told the American people that he had ordered a contingent of Marines into the Dominican Republic to protect the lives of American citizens and to assist in their evacuation, he let it be known that his administration's previously expressed concern over the situation in the Caribbean island state had changed to a decision to act. Americans were in danger and American soldiers, with the permission to fight "to protect themselves and American civilians," were in the middle of another country's civil war.[35]

All three newspapers made the landing of U.S. Marines the lead story on their front pages in the editions of April 29. The same day's editions carried

TABLE 2.1   Overall Pre-Crisis Coverage: Domestic and Foreign Sources, Directly Relevant (Editorials Excluded)

Linage	For/Probably For	Neutral/ Ambiguous	Against/Probably Against	Total Lines
TIMES	10.8%	87.4%	1.8%	1,053
POST	3.4	96.6	—	702
TRIBUNE	20.2	79.8	—	642

TABLE 2.2   Pre-Crisis Coverage: Domestic Sources, Directly Relevant (Editorials Excluded)

Linage	For/Probably For	Neutral/ Ambiguous	Against/Probably Against	Total Lines
TIMES	14.7%	85.3%	—	775
POST	4.4	95.6	—	546
TRIBUNE	18.9	81.1	—	530

reports of Americans who already had been evacuated from the Dominican Republic and who, as the *Times* put it, landed at Kennedy Airport "with tales of shooting and terror."[36] Those who read in the two East Coast newspapers and the Midwestern publication what the President and other officials of his administration said, had to get the impression that the U.S. Marines were involved in a mission intended only to protect and to safely evacuate Americans and other nationals eager to leave the uproar in and around Santo Domingo.

However, many of the articles published during the short acute crisis phase (April 29 to May 5) contained hints and even outright accusations of a Communist role in the Dominican unrest. Jose A. Bonilla, the Ambassador of the Dominican Republic in Washington, charged according to the Associated Press "that the strife in his country was a result of a Communist attempt to take over the nation."[37] Charles Mohr of the *Times* learned from administration officials "that some Communist leaders had been clearly identified as among the rebel forces."[38]

The *Tribune*'s Latin America correspondent Jules Dubois, who was the first journalist to enter the Dominican Republic since the outbreak of fighting, described the conflict he witnessed as being fought between "leftists" and "loyal troops." In doing so, Dubois continued to prepare the ground for President Johnson to widen the rescue mission into one to prevent a second Cuba. For the time being, however, the Dubois dispatches of fierce fighting and looting in Santo Domingo supported the rescue and protection line of the administration. In fact, if anyone had any doubt about the danger Americans faced in the Dominican capital, Dubois made efforts to lay those to rest when he described how he himself had been under fire by rebel troops. The correspondent of the *Tribune* wrote, "Communist rebels shot at me today —but missed—as I toured on foot alone thru the business district of this war-torn capital."[39] In another dispatch Dubois reported from Santo Domingo that the Dominican situation had arisen because the "Communists have put into operation their long-standing plan to take over this [Dominican] republic, and thus have a second base of operation in the Caribbean for a final blow against Venezuela."[40]

Reports in both *Times* and *Post* revealed that the fear of "another Cuba" had led to the Johnson administration's military response to the rebellion in the Dominican Republic.[41] These disclosures were based on unnamed sources in the administration, who, like the President himself, officially upheld the rescue explanation and tried to pacify critics of the intervention, especially Latin Americans.

In the first editorial the *New York Times* published during the initial phase of the acute crisis the newspaper supported the President—although with reservations. While chiding the Johnson administration for ignoring the Organization of American States and unilaterally deciding to make a Dominican move, the *Times* acknowledged, "There was a solid reason for the United States to put a Marine landing force into Santo Domingo. This reason was to protect Americans and to evacuate those who desire to leave."[42] Two days later, a *Times* editorial again gave qualified support to the American intervention, suggesting now that it had a humanitarian as well as a political end. Affirming the "need to protect lives in a state of anarchy . . .", the *Times* warned that the reinforcement of the Marines suggested "an intention to stay in the Dominican Republic after the function of getting American nationals out has been completed."[43] Still, as far as the rescue line of the administration was concerned, the *Times* did not dispute it.

The editorial stance of the New York newspaper remained reluctantly supportive after the President's announcement that the original rescue mission was now a commitment to "prevent another Communist state in the hemisphere."[44] The *Times* suggested that Johnson's determination not "to see another Communist state established in this hemisphere will command national support." The same editorial criticized the President for not articulating this reason behind his intervention earlier. Also, the *Times* wondered whether the military in the Dominican Republic had exploited the American "fears of Communism to preserve its power."[45] Still, as far as the President's foremost policy goals in the Dominican action were concerned the newspaper again was somewhat supportive of the crisis manager. Increasing reservations were evident in the last editorial the *Times* published during the acute crisis. The opinion piece ended with the observation that it might have been the American intervention that "brought the Communists to the forefront [of the Dominican uprising]."[46] On the whole this editorial was somewhat ambiguous vis-à-vis the President's crisis policies.

The *Washington Post* published three crisis-related editorials during the acute crisis, beginning with one that concerned itself with Domestic politics in the Dominican Republic. Headlined "Unhappy Republic," this opinion piece was neutral regarding the American military action.[47] A day later, the Washington newspaper published an editorial under the headline "Back to 1916?" that commented on the deployment of Marines in the Dominican Republic and referred to the declared presidential goal to protect and evacuate American citizens, but there was neither an expression of support nor of opposition. Discussing a possible role of Communists in the Dominican uprising, the *Post* agreed that "the United States does not want to see the Dominican Republic become another Communist Cuba." But the editorial went on to suggest, "Certainly either the OAS itself or the U.N. would appear preferable to the U.S. Marine diplomacy of 1916."[48] While critically mentioning a possible parallel between Johnson's action and the Dominican intervention of 1916 under President Woodrow Wilson, the *Post* did not deny the need to stop Communist expansion in the hemisphere. On the whole, this editorial was ambiguous toward the crisis policy of the President. Finally, in its third editorial published during the acute crisis period, the *Post* seemed to support the rescue part of the American intervention while admitting that a possible Communist threat represented a dilemma for the United States government. According to the *Post,* "If it [the American government] is overly apprehensive and takes prompt action to forestall a possible Communist coup it will be accused of intervention and violation of the OAS charter. If it is too slow to act, it will find Communists installed in some country."[49] Overall the editorial left the impression of being probably supportive of Johnson's Dominican action.

Both the *Times* and the *Post* seemed supportive of the non-Communist pro-Bosch forces and critical of the military establishment led by Wessin y Wessin. Also, both newspapers favored a leading role of the OAS in solving the Dominican crisis.

The one editorial in which the *Chicago Tribune* commented on the landing of U.S. Marines in the Dominican Republic endorsed the President's rescue action wholeheartedly, reminding the reader that "historically, it has been American policy to protect American lives and interests in strife-torn areas of the Americas." Pointing out that the Dominican revolt was "believed to have been animated by communist elements," the editorial suggested that the Dominican rebellion might be "a mask for an attempted takeover" by agents of Fidel Castro. "If that is so," the editorial concluded, "the marines may find they have a further mission."[50] Clearly, the *Tribune* stood firmly behind Johnson's Dominican decision.

President Johnson and members of his administration took a very active role in assuring the public via the press that the intervention was necessary and well-managed by Washington. Three times in six days LBJ used television to address the nation. In the first speech he characterized the American military action as a rescue mission only, his second address charged that Communists played a role in the Dominican civil disorders, and finally he argued that the United States had to prevent the establishment of a second Cuba in the hemisphere. The Secretary of State and other State department officials and Adlai Stevenson as the U.S. Representative at the United Nations were among other leading administration officials who also helped to publicize this official American line.

In spite of early indications that "red fear" on the part of the American administration had inspired the military measures, there was practically no domestic opposition to the U.S. involvement in the island state, especially not before President Johnson announced that the original goal of protecting and evacuating American citizens had changed into one aimed at preventing

Communists from taking over the Dominican Republic.[51] One of the few critical voices in Congress, the one belonging to Senator Wayne Morse, did not find its way into the *Tribune* but was mentioned in both the *Times* and the *Post*. However, the Chicago newspaper did mention Senator Morse's initial reaction to the landing of Marines, when it still looked as if the protection of American citizens was the only purpose of the original force of but a few hundred Marines. In a longer article describing the supportive stance of both Democratic and Republican senators, the *Tribune* reported that "Morse said he approved the President's action."[52] While neither of the two East Coast newspapers published this supportive Morse remark, the *Times,* a few days later in an article about congressional reaction to the Dominican intervention, quoted Senator Morse as saying in reference to the Dominican intervention, "Have we lost our minds. . . . Have we become military power-drunk?"[53] The same article mentioned critical remarks Senator Allen Ellender had made on the Senate floor. The *Post* also took note that "the strongest congressional criticism [against the U.S. military move into the Dominican Republic] came from Sen. Wayne Morse."[54] All in all, however, in its early stage the Dominican invasion enjoyed domestic support similar to the blockade of Cuba under President Kennedy.

While treating the few openly critical domestic voices differently, the three newspapers reflected the overwhelming supportive or at least neutral/ambiguous reactions within the nation. In the *Tribune,* the huge amount of lines based on pro-Johnson sources were partially the result of the *Tribune*'s Dubois who openly supported Johnson's Dominican moves (see table 2.3). What was the reason for the nonexistent or tiny space for critical sources in the *Tribune* and *Times* respectively and comparatively more critical linage in the *Post?* The difference was the result of two longer pieces—one a news analysis, which was not identified as such, the other a feature that painted a rather sympathetic, idealistic picture of pro-Bosch rebels at a time when Johnson claimed that Communists had infiltrated rebel ranks.[55]

TABLE 2.3   Acute Crisis Coverage:
Domestic Sources, Directly Relevant (Editorials Excluded)

Linage	For/Probably For	Neutral/ Ambiguous	Against/Probably Against	Total Lines
TIMES	60.9%	37.6%	1.5%	4,921
POST	33.8	56.9	9.3	3,356
TRIBUNE	90.8	9.2	—	3,280

As far as the relationship between editorial positions of the newspapers and their overall domestic news coverage was concerned, there seemed to be somewhat of a connection: In the *Tribune* with its unconditional, strong support for Johnson's decision to deploy the Marines, supportive sources captured an overwhelming amount of space: critics were not mentioned at all. The *Times* with three probably supportive editorials and one ambiguous piece during this period had a space distribution heavily in favor of pro-Johnson sources and only minimal linage for critics. Finally, the *Post,* with two editorials falling into the neutral/ambiguous category and one piece of probably supportive nature, gave the greatest amount of space to neutral or ambiguous sources, less space than the other two publications to the President's supporters, and more linage than the *Tribune* and *Times* to critical voices.

Given the overwhelming supportive or neutral/ambiguous reaction of domestic actors, it comes as no surprise that supportive sources enjoyed preferred placement in front page headlines and page one stories. The *Chicago Tribune* mentioned sources supportive of Johnson's crisis policy in 32 front page stories. The *Washington Post* gave a 22–1 front page placement advantage to supportive sources over critical ones, and in the *New York Times* sources in favor of Johnson's crisis handling had a 25–1 placement advantage in front page stories.

Most domestic news sources the press relied on came from the three major beats in the executive branch: the White House and the Departments of State and Defense. Surprisingly, the Midwest newspaper based a higher percentage on its linage on congressional sources than either the *Times* or the *Post* (see table 2.4).

In all three newspapers, foreign sources critical of the President's Dominican move captured the greatest amount of space—over 50 percent of the linage dedicated to foreign sources. This was not surprising, given the fact that not only unfriendly governments led by those in Cuba and in the Soviet

TABLE 2.4   Linage Administration and Congressional Sources: Acute Crisis, Directly Relevant

	Administration Sources	Congressional Sources	Total Lines
TIMES	95.8%	4.2%	2,546
POST	97.7	2.3	1,190
TRIBUNE	87.0	13.0	1,594

Union, but also friends and allies in Latin America and Europe were very critical of the Dominican move. Officials and the public in Latin America were especially outraged that the United States had acted unilaterally instead of consulting with and involving the OAS.

The *Times* covered foreign news sources more extensively than the other two newspapers and based a higher percentage of its foreign coverage on critical sources than *Post* and *Tribune*. In both the *Times* and *Post* critical foreign sources had a better chance making front page stories than those supportive of the President while the *Tribune* gave this placement preference more often to foreign supporters of the Johnson crisis policy than to opponents. In the *Times* the front page placement advantage was 21–9 in favor of sources critical of the administration's Dominican move, in the *Post* critical sources had a placement advantage of 9–3 as far as front page stories were concerned. However, the *Tribune* gave 7–4 front page placement edge to foreign sources sympathetic to Johnson's crisis handling.

The overwhelmingly favorable domestic sources and the mostly critical foreign sources added up to an overall acute crisis coverage that made more use of sources in favor of the Johnson policy than of critical sources. The combined coverage in the Chicago newspaper was the most favorable from the point of view of the Johnson administration and the least favorable in the *Post* (see table 2.5).

As far as journalistic descriptions, background information, and news analyses were concerned, these media-based sources fell overwhelmingly into the neutral/ambiguous intent category in the *Times* and the *Post*, even though the Washington newspaper published several articles that conveyed, as described earlier, a critical attitude toward Johnson's crisis policy. In the *Tribune* many of the lines based on journalistic sources supported the President's crisis management; this was especially true for many stories that were published with Jules Dubois's byline.

TABLE 2.5   Overall Acute Crisis Coverage:
Foreign and Domestic, Directly Relevant (Editorials Excluded)

Linage	For/Probably For	Neutral/ Ambiguous	Against/Probably Against	Total Lines
TIMES	46.9%	31.4%	21.7%	7,804
POST	31.0	45.7	23.3	4,810
TRIBUNE	66.1	16.6	17.3	4,981

OAS AGREES TO TAKE OVER PEACE EFFORTS

On May 5, a cease-fire agreement was signed in Santo Domingo. More importantly, the same day, the Organization of American States agreed to the American request to take over the peacekeeping efforts in the Dominican Republic and establish and command an OAS peacekeeping force. At this time, the acute crisis phase gave way to a lingering crisis period that lasted through June 21. More than 3000 Americans and foreign nationals from 41 other nations had been evacuated, and although the various cease-fire agreements were violated by the feuding Dominican factions, this much was clear: Those Americans who wanted to leave the Caribbean country had been evacuated. And although American troops were at times caught in the cross fire between the two sides in the Dominican struggle, they were not officially involved in the fighting. Finally, by agreeing to put American soldiers under OAS command, Lyndon Johnson seemed to have retreated from his claim that U.S. forces had to prevent a "second Cuba." Still, an estimated 35,000 American troops were in or close to the Dominican Republic when the OAS agreed to take the lead in the Dominican emergency.

The situation in the Dominican Republic during this period was quickly changing and at times confusing—and so was the Johnson administration's crisis policy in that it proclaimed publicly to be neutral in the domestic Dominican struggle while, in fact, vacillating between support for the Wessin-led conservative forces and efforts to oust Wessin and other right-wing military leaders in order to include the Pro-Bosch rebels in a united front attempt to establish democratic conditions in the Dominican Republic.

Given this seesaw type of crisis management and policy, the three newspapers reacted by moving back and forth between support and criticism in either their editorial opinions or in their news reporting or in both. Indeed, this period with no consistent Washington policy concerning the Dominican involvement had an extraordinary amount of reporting and analyzing in the "straight news" sections, which revealed either support for the American policy in Santo Domingo or, more often, a critical attitude toward the Dominican stand of the Johnson administration.

The only consistent stand was taken by the editorial page of the *Chicago Tribune:* Its editorials published during this period were critical of Johnson's Dominican policy that the newspaper had endorsed during the acute crisis days. How did this complete turnaround come about? The Chicago newspaper had applauded Johnson for dispatching Marines to protect American citizens caught in the Dominican war and, even more so, for preventing a Communist takeover of the Caribbean country. However, the moment the OAS agreed to a joint peace force and Johnson pledged to put American troops under OAS command, the *Tribune* switched to an editorial stance very critical of the President. All four editorials the newspaper published during the lingering crisis phase were opposed to Johnson's handling of the crisis.

In an editorial reaction to the news that the OAS was taking charge of peace efforts in the Dominican Republic, the *Tribune* complained that the American forces were sent to the Dominican Republic but not allowed to move against the leftist rebels. The newspaper advocated that the United States should make it clear "that, whatever the opinion of the UN, the OAS, or anybody else, we are going to do all that must be done to halt the spread of communist infection."[56] A few days later, the *Tribune* attacked the Johnson administration for allegedly pressuring General Wessin y Wessin to resign from the Army. Praising the General as "staunchest anti-communist on the island," this editorial again accused Washington of favoring a peace-bringing "deal" with the "communist-tainted rebels."[57] Under the headline "Appeasement?" yet another editorial in his period faulted Johnson for turning against the anti-Communists led by Wessin and listening to the voices "of the so-called democratic left of Latin America."[58] Repeating the appeasement theme, an editorial in the *Tribune* suggested that "the voice of appeasement, of compromise with communism, continued to be heard among another Presidential advisory group on hand in Santo Domingo."[59]

Not only the growing role of the OAS, sought by Johnson, but also efforts by American officials to move away from the right-wing military led by General Wessin and a junta headed by General Antonio Imbert and to communicate and work with moderate rebel leaders had moved the *Tribune* from firm editorial support in the acute crisis period to a harshly critical stand during the lingering crisis.

The editorial positions of the two East Coast newspapers were not as consistent as the editorial stance of the *Tribune*. Of nine editorials published in the *Times* during this period, two were somewhat supportive, one was ambiguous, and six expressed considerable misgivings about the Johnson crisis policy. The New York newspaper was in favor of the OAS taking over from the U.S.A. in Santo Domingo and thus editorialized favorably on this shift that the Johnson administration had sought.[60] Also, the *Times* applauded the President's crisis policy when it appeared that Washington was moving away from its support for the right-wing military and toward an open mind vis-à-vis the rebels. "This [changed American approach] will presumably clear the way for installation of a more representative Government," the newspaper concluded.[61] However, the New York newspaper wanted less of an American role in the peace negotiations and less American partisanship in favor of the military junta, now led by General Antonio Imbert. In one of its critical editorials the *Times* predicted that the "partisanship Washington already has shown toward the Imbert junta has imperiled chances for establishment of a coalition government of the type President Johnson recommended this weekend."[62]

In its four editorials during this period the *Washington Post* split its editorial expressions evenly between support for and opposition to Johnson's management of the Dominican crisis. The newspaper was in agreement when the OAS officially took the lead in the peace efforts in the Dominican Republic, a step the U.S. administration had actively promoted.[63] In addition, the *Post* seemed satisfied that an American intervention in the Dominican Republic was justified, when it stated: "Release by United States Government sources of the American version of Dominican events leading up to our military intervention last night put onto the record the information on which this country's action was based. . . . The version made public should allay the anxieties of those who have feared that action was taken impulsively."[64] On the other hand, the *Post* expressed disapproval in two editorials that criticized American support for the right-wing forces in the Dominican Republic and the failure of the United States to remove itself from the efforts to settle the crisis in Santo Domingo and let the OAS take over completely.[65] In particular, the *Post* wrote, "If the United States officials in Santo Domingo should succeed in setting up a regime satisfactory to themselves, it would doubtless fall apart as soon as the U.S. troops were withdrawn because of the resentment over this country's unilateral intervention. The only safe and feasible solution is by way of the OAS."[66]

Domestically, there was more support for the President's ongoing crisis management than criticism. Ex-President Dwight Eisenhower and Senator Barry Goldwater as well as Labor Union Leaders were among those who expressed their pro-Johnson stands in this matter.[67] The critical remarks by politicians such as Senators Robert Kennedy (Democrat of New York) and Stephen Young (Democrat of Ohio) remained exceptions.[68] Most of the criticism that was expressed in the news coverage as far as domestic sources were concerned came from the media itself—at least as far as *Times, Post,* and *Tribune* were concerned. As the uncertainty about the reasons behind the American intervention and about the vacillating U.S. position grew, journalists seemed to recognize the need to explain and evaluate and, at times, to dispute American policies and actions.

Jules Dubois of the *Tribune* kept on filing dispatches from Santo Domingo favorable to the official American line as long as he was convinced that Johnson had managed the crisis in support of the right-wing military around Wessin and the Imbert-led junta. Even when the editorials in the *Tribune* criticized the U.S. policy in the Dominican Republic, Dubois continued to praise the American role in fighting Communism in the island state. In one instance, the *Tribune* correspondent described the high and idealistic spirit of young American soldiers—his own son among them. With parental pride,

Dubois reported that his son "arrived early this afternoon, leaving behind at Shawn air force base, Sumter, S.C. his wife Ann and their new-born son, Shawn Mitchell, my first grandson."[69] However, Dubois changed to a critical stand toward the American position in the Dominican crisis when American negotiators tried to promote a broad coalition of military "loyalists" and "rebels" by pressuring for the ouster of hardline right-wingers such as General Wessin. Thus, Dubois wrote with great disapproval of the U.S. role, "The United States today forced Brig. Gen. Wessin y Wessin, the man who blocked a communist takeover of this country on April 26, to accept retirement from the army in order to try to end the civil war."[70]

While not quite as overtly as in the case of the *Tribune*, the two East Coast newspapers, too, published criticism of the administration's role in the Dominican crisis attributable to journalistic sources. Doubts about the original reasons for the Dominican intervention were expressed in journalistic descriptions and background stories; also, correspondents in Santo Domingo wrote about the gap between Washington's declared Dominican position and the actual behavior of American negotiators and troops in the island state.

In the *Tribune*, 14.8 percent of all lines based on journalistic sources (editorials excluded) were supportive, 57.3% neutral/ambiguous, and 27.9 percent critical vis-à-vis Johnson's Dominican role. Of the linage based on journalistic sources the *Times* published, 73.5 percent fell into the neutral/ambiguous and 26.5 percent into the critical category. 79.0 percent of the media-based sources in the *Post* were neutral/ambiguous, 20.8 percent critical, and 0.2 percent supportive as far as Johnson's Dominican policy was concerned.

All during the lingering crisis period Lyndon Johnson continued his campaign to explain and defend the reasons behind his decision to intervene in the Dominican Republic. He did so in press conferences as well as in speeches before various groups. In an address to a Home Builders conference in Washington, for example, he promoted his Dominican policy. The same was true for a speech before editorial cartoonists that was nationally televised because it was known in advance that the President was going to address the U.S. role in the Dominican Republic. The President and other administration officials seemed tireless in their efforts to persuade both domestic and international audiences of the rightness of their positions.

To this end, the administration released what officials called evidence of Communist involvement in the Dominican situation, namely a list with the names of persons who according to the administration had been identified as Communists active in the events in Santo Domingo. Secretary of State Dean Rusk made himself available to be interviewed and took the opportunity to detail Johnson's Dominican position. Moreover, three other officials were major domestic news sources who articulated full support for the official

American line: At the United Nations, Adlai Stevenson; at the OAS Ellsworth Bunker; and in Latin America Averell Harriman, LBJ's Ambassador at large, who traveled to capitals in the Western Hemisphere in order to calm anger over the unilateral U.S. intervention in the Dominican Republic.

Because of this activist role of leading administration officials, sources supportive of the President's handling of the Dominican situation captured more than double the space as compared with critical sources in the relevant domestic news coverage. Still, all three newspapers devoted a significant percentage of relevant lines to cover critics of the President in this matter (see table 2.6).

As far as the placement in front page stories was concerned, domestic sources supportive of the Johnson policy in the Dominican crisis fared best in the *Post* where they had a placement advantage of 23–2 over critical sources. In the *Times* pro-Johnson sources were mentioned in 37, critical sources in 7 cases in page one stories. In the *Tribune*, however, the placement advantage in front page stories was only 15–6 in favor of supportive sources. This was the result of the critical posture that correspondent Dubois switched to a few days into the lingering crisis; his dispatches made the *Tribune* front page frequently.

While administration sources were used very frequently and given a great amount of linage, congressional sources were rarely mentioned (see table 2.7). However, in the two Eastern newspapers, sources originating on Capitol Hill captured somewhat more linage in comparison with administration sources than they did during the acute crisis. In the *Tribune*, on the other hand, congressional sources fared worse than during the preceding crisis period, perhaps because there were no congressional voices that took the same line as the Chicago newspaper.

In the foreign coverage, critical non-American sources remained dominant. France's Charles De Gaulle expressed his opposition to the U.S. moves toward Santo Domingo, and Cuba's Fidel Castro and the Dominican Ex-President Juan Bosch explained their anti-Johnson stands in this matter

TABLE 2.6   Lingering Crisis Coverage:
Domestic Sources, Directly Relevant (Editorials Excluded)

Linage	For/Probably For	Neutral/ Ambiguous	Against/Probably Against	Total Lines
TIMES	39.6%	42.9%	17.5%	8,020
POST	38.4	46.4	15.2	5,504
TRIBUNE	42.3	39.3	18.4	4,569

repeatedly. In the Dominican Republic itself, the pro- and contra-attitudes of the two rivaling sides switched back and forth, depending on the American posture during the ongoing negotiations. In addition, much of what sources in the the Dominican Republic said in all three newspapers fell into the neutral/ambiguous category. Latin Americans expressed their anger and charged that by ignoring the OAS in the initial phase of its Dominican move, the U.S. had again opted for a "big stick" policy in the hemisphere.

The three newspapers mentioned foreign sources critical of U.S. policies and actions concerning the Dominican conflict more often in front page stories than sources supportive of the American crisis role. In the *Times* critical sources had a 33–9, in the *Post* an 18–3, and in the *Tribune* an 18–2 advantage.

Given the great amount of coverage foreign critics of the American Dominican role received, the overall crisis-related coverage (domestic and foreign sources) was not very favorable from the administration's point of view (see table 2.8). While supporters of the President had a slight space advantage over opponents in *Times* and *Tribune*, there was a slight linage advantage for anti-Johnson sources over supportive ones in the *Post*. All in all the differences in the way the three newspapers provided space to sources with various attitudes toward the Johnson crisis handling were insignificant. In spite of their editorial differences, the three newspapers

TABLE 2.7   Linage Administration and Congressional Sources:
Lingering Crisis, Directly Relevant

	Administration Sources	Congressional Sources	Total Lines
TIMES	91.4%	8.6%	2,875
POST	93.7	6.3	2,150
TRIBUNE	98.3	1.7	1,565

TABLE 2.8   Overall Lingering Crisis Coverage:
Foreign and Domestic, Directly Relevant (Editorials Excluded)

Linage	For/Probably For	Neutral/ Ambiguous	Against/Probably Against	Total Lines
TIMES	31.3%	39.2%	29.5%	11,935
POST	28.2	41.8	30.0	8,381
TRIBUNE	31.2	40.6	28.2	7,205

presented also a reasonably similar domestic coverage in terms of numbers. However, while the criticism in the two East Coast newspapers came from sources expressing a liberal view, the anti-Johnson view in the Midwestern *Tribune* was mostly a conservative one.

AMERICAN TROOP WITHDRAWALS BEGIN

With the U.S. announcement on May 21 that the first contingent of American soldiers would be withdrawn from Dominican soil, the administration signaled that there was no longer a threat against U.S. citizens and against American interests in the hemisphere although the Johnson administration still defended its line that Communists had tried to take over in Santo Domingo. However, a peaceful and lasting solution of the crisis was very much on the mind of international negotiators from the OAS, the United Nations, and Washington. While the Johnson administration tried to convey the message that it was deferring to the Organization of American States, when it came to OAS peacekeeping troops and peace negotiations, reports from Santo Domingo revealed that American officials continued to play leading roles in both areas. Still, with the announcement of troop withdrawals and the beginning of a step-by-step decrease of the American military presence in the Dominican Republic, the post-crisis phase began (the relevant news coverage in this period was examined over a fifteen-day period beginning with the editions of May 22, the day the news of the withdrawal announcement was published by the daily print press). What followed was a time characterized by various truce agreements, violations of cease-fire arrangements, and tireless negotiating efforts. American policy now had a clear goal: Washington's envoys encouraged a coalition government in Santo Domingo led by Antonio Guzman, a former cabinet member of the Bosch government.

Washington's move away from the military junta and toward moderate elements in the rebel forces was received differently by the editorial boards of the three newspapers. Consistent with their previous views, the *Tribune* was very critical of Washington's stand; the *Times* remained critical of the whole military enterprise the United States had conducted in the name of fighting Communism but applauded Washington's new efforts to encourage democratic Dominican forces; the *Post* was mostly sympathetic to the American position once Washington rejected a rule of military right-wingers in Santo Domingo.

Under the headline "How to Make Life Safe For the Reds" the *Tribune* published an editorial very critical of an American agreement to let the OAS representatives in Santo Domingo pay salaries to Dominican civil servants regardless of what side they supported in the civil war. The editorial in the Chicago newspaper was very much opposed to paying out money to members of the rebel force or to their sympathizers, lamenting, "We went into the Dominican Republic to prevent the Communists from taking over as they did in Cuba; and now, it seems, we're paying them."[71] In a second editorial, the newspaper endorsed President Johnson's warning remarks concerning Communist expansionism but questioned whether his claim that the American intervention in the Dominican Republic had defeated the Communists' goals was valid or "perhaps prematurely" assumed. The *Tribune* editorial found it "disturbing" that Johnson discovered his new realities about Communism only after "having been maneuvered by circumstances into a position which he once professed to abhor."[72] On the whole, this editorial was somewhat critical of Johnson's and the Democrats' understanding of the Communist threat.

Of six editorials in the *Times* three were critical, two were ambiguous, and one was supportive as far as the American position in the Dominican situation was concerned. The New York newspaper continued to attack the Johnson administration's efforts to justify the massive intervention. On one occasion, the *Times* repeated a previous charge that the American military action had indeed strengthened the position of Communists in Latin America. The newspaper argued that "Latin American Communism never had such a resounding boost to its collective ego as when the United States sent 30,000 troops into Santo Domingo to foil 53 asserted Communists and Communist sympathizers."[73] Defending the OAS against critics complaining about the organization's hesitance in getting involved in the Dominican crisis, the *Times* stated, "The role the organization was asked to play was essentially to pull the Johnson Administration's chestnuts out of the fire. There could hardly be enthusiasm for this, especially when United States marines had been hastily sent to prevent a popular, anti-militarist and anti-oligarchical solution of the crisis."[74] Questioning President Johnson's renewed efforts to justify the Dominican intervention, the *Times* concluded, "The contradictions between what Washington said and what was being done in Santo Domingo were bewildering—and still are."[75] Another editorial in the *Times* did express support for efforts to encourage the establishment of a coalition government in Santo Domingo, but blamed Washington's previous support of the Dominican right wing for making the forming of a coalition government more difficult. On the whole, this particular editorial fell into the ambiguous category.[76] Commenting on the stalemate between the military junta and the rebels that stood in the way of a coalition government under the leadership of Antonio Guzman, the *Times* reminded its readers of the irony that the American goal of a coalition government in Santo Domingo was blocked by a military right-winger (General Imbert) "who came to power because the

United States chose and supported him."[77] While supporting the current U.S. goal in the Dominican capital, the *Times* continued to blame the United States for creating such a difficult situation there. This editorial, too, was ambiguous overall. Commenting on Secretary of State Dean Rusk's revelation that the United States would support a plebescite on a constitution in the Dominican Republic in still another editorial, the *Times* expressed support for the administration, explaining that "the important point is that, as Mr. Rusk suggests, the Dominicans must be permitted to decide for themselves what kind of constitution and what kind of government it is that they want."[78]

Of six editorials the *Washington Post* published in the period following the crisis weeks, five were supportive of the U.S. administration's stand and one fell into the ambiguous category. The *Post* endorsed the Johnson administration's moving away from the Dominican right and toward the moderate rebel elements. In one editorial the newspaper listed "the firm stand taken by the United States officials in Santo Domingo against the continuation in power of any dictatoral regime" as one of the reasons for a better outlook in the whole Dominican situation.[79] In another editorial the Washington newspaper acknowledged that "President Johnson has gone a long way toward taking the sting out of the United States' intervention in the Dominican Republic." The piece praised Johnson because he had "clearly identified himself with the aspirations of the Dominican people."[80] Underlining the President's assurance that the United States had "no interest in imposing any particular kind of regime on the Dominican people," the Washington newspaper allied itself with the Johnson administration in assuring that "[t]he interest of this country in our small Caribbean neighbor is not imperialistic."[81] These editorial remarks were representative of the *Post*'s position in the aftermath of the acute and lingering crisis. The only editorial not expressing support for the U.S.–Dominican position was one that discussed the difficult role of OAS Secretary General Dr. Jose Mora in the Dominican negotiation without explicitly referring to the American position.[82] There was no doubt that now the Washington publication stood firmly behind Johnson's U.S.–Dominican policy.

With the beginning of troop withdrawals from the Dominican Republic, the administration intensified its campaign to defend its intervention decision and its belated support for a negotiated, democratic solution in the Dominican Republic. The President, and Secretary of State Dean Rusk, personally pushed their Dominican view in press conferences, interviews, and speeches. Dean Rusk held his first press conference in two months, and in one instance Lyndon Johnson made two public appearances in one day to counter criticism of his Dominican policy. These initiatives resulted in ample news coverage. For example, when the President encouraged an OAS machinery to deal

with Communist subversion in Latin America and assured that the Dominican people yearned for a democratic government, the two East Coast
newspapers took note of his speech in front page articles while the *Tribune*
chose to place this report on an inside page.[83] When the Secretary of State
proposed a plebescite in the Dominican Republic on a new constitution, he
made the front pages of *Times* and *Post* and page three in the *Tribune*.[84]
Even though the Chicago newspaper did not always place the highest administration sources prominently on page one, a treatment these sources received frequently in the *Post* and in the *Times,* the administration's public
relations "blitz" was covered regularly in all three newspapers.

The Pulitzer Prize–winning poet Robert Lowell drew attention to his
opposition to the U.S. policy in the Dominican Republic (and in Vietnam),
when he rejected an invitation to participate in a White House art festival.
The same was the case when twenty leading scholars, writers, and artists
expressed their support for Lowell.[85] The *New York Times* reported that
"Arthur Schlesinger Jr. criticized the unilateral United States intervention in
the Dominican Republic."[86] And there was even a report that the director of
the Community Relations Service within the Johnson administration had
warned in a speech in San Juan "that force is not always the answer to
Communism but even can become its greatest incubator."[87] Once the acute
and lingering crises were over, criticism was voiced mostly by academics,
writers, and artists. Not much was heard from or written about politicians
inside and outside of Congress. Most conservatives seemed satisfied that
Communism had been stopped in the Dominican Republic and most liberals
seemed satisfied that Washington was now supporting a democratic solution
to Santo Domingo.

The *Tribune*'s Latin America expert and correspondent on the scene in
Santo Domingo, Jules Dubois, remained critical of the Johnson policy as he
had been during most of the lingering crisis period. In one of his reports
Dubois complained, for instance, "It is apparent here that the United States
has decided to force Brig. Gen. Antonio Imbert-Barera to fight a war of
attrition with Col. Francesco A. Caamano rather than let the armed forces
of the government of national reconstruction quickly wipe out the Communists. Caamano is the rebel leader."[88] While Washington no longer claimed
that there was still a Communist threat in the Caribbean country, Dubois
reported otherwise and claimed, "Fidel Castro had plans to be welcomed
here as a conquering hero of a second Cuba on June 14, it was learned
today. Those plans have been dashed, but the communist danger re-
mains."[89] On the other hand, some journalists reporting for *Times* and *Post*
seemed critical of the Dominican right wing and sympathetic to the moderate
rebel faction. In a news analysis, Tom Wicker of the *Times* identified the
U.S. administration's early support for the Dominican right wing as an

obstacle to a satisfactory solution in Santo Domingo. His article closed with the warning that any solution "acceptable" to Washington was unlikely to be seen "as much more than a creature of Washington" in the Dominican Republic, in Latin America, and in the world.[90] An article in the *Post,* carrying the dateline Santo Domingo, denied administration claims that the OAS was searching for a settlement of the Dominican situation. Staff Writer John Goshko of the *Post* judged otherwise, writing, "Despite Washington's carefully orchestrated campaign to cloak the political negotiations in the trappings of the Organization of American States, they remain very much a U.S. managed operation."[91]

More than 75 percent of lines based on journalistic sources (editorials excluded) in the *Post* and in the *Times* fit the neutral/ambiguous category; in the *Tribune,* however, 47.6 percent of all lines attributable to journalistic sources expressed critical attitudes toward Johnson's crisis-related policies. Still, more than half of the *Tribune*'s media-based lines fell into the neutral/ambiguous category.

Mostly as a result of the reporting by correspondent Dubois, the *Tribune*'s coverage was by far more critical of the President than that in the *Times* and the *Post.* In the Chicago newspaper, which was editorially in complete disagreement with Johnson, critical domestic sources were used for significantly more space than supportive ones. In the East Coast papers that agreed *(Post)* or in some points agreed *(Times)* with Johnson's post-crisis policies, supportive domestic sources captured far more space than did critics of the administration's Dominican positions (see table 2.9).

As far as placement was concerned, domestic pro-administration sources fared better in the East Coast newspapers than in the Midwest publication with its critical editorial line. In the *Times,* domestic sources supportive of Washington's Dominican policy had a 25 to 5 advantage over critical sources, when it came to front page stories. In the *Post,* this kind of placement advantage was 20 to 4 in favor of supportive domestic sources. However, the *Tribune* gave only a slight 6 to 5 advantage to pro-Johnson sources.

TABLE 2.9   Post-Crisis Coverage:
Domestic Sources, Directly Relevant (Editorials Excluded)

Linage	For/Probably For	Neutral/ Ambiguous	Against/Probably Against	Total Lines
TIMES	49.6%	35.4%	15.0%	4,535
POST	32.3	61.0	6.7	4,409
TRIBUNE	25.1	38.9	36.0	3,429

While administration sources were very much in the news, congressional sources were used sparingly in the coverage of all three newspapers (see table 2.10).

In all three newspapers foreign sources critical of the American Dominican policies captured a greater percentage of the linage than sources in favor of U.S. policy. While the negotiating efforts were going on in Santo Domingo, some foreign actors such as De Gaulle, Castro, and other Latin American officials remained very critical of the U.S. role in the Caribbean country. Within the Dominican Republic support for and opposition to the U.S. line by the competing sides in Santo Domingo changed repeatedly.

In the *Tribune* critical foreign sources, namely those in agreement with the newspapers position, made front page stories six times, supportive foreign critics twice. The editorially supportive *Post* used critical and supportive foreign sources twice each in front page articles, while in the *Times* critical foreign sources had a slight 19–18 placement advantage in front pages over foreign supporters of the President's Dominican policy.

The *Washington Post,* which supported the President's handling of the Dominican situation editorially, provided an overall Dominican coverage (domestic and foreign sources) in which sources supportive to the American policy commanded nearly three times as much linage as critical sources. The linage advantage of pro-Johnson sources was smaller in the *Times* where supporters of the administration's Dominican efforts captured nearly twice as many lines as opposing sources. Thus, the New York newspaper, whose editorial stand was mixed but clearly more critical of the President's Dominican policy than was that of the *Post,* presented its readers with an overall Dominican coverage somewhat less favorable to the administration than that of the Washington newspaper. The *Tribune,* which remained critical of Johnson's handling of the Dominican problem, was the only one of the three publications to publish more linage attributable to critical sources than to supportive ones (see table 2.11).

TABLE 2.10   Linage Administration and Congressional Sources: Post-Crisis, Directly Relevant

	Administration Sources	Congressional Sources	Total Lines
TIMES	99.6%	0.4%	2,338
POST	95.4	4.6	1,516
TRIBUNE	94.6	5.4	852

SUMMARY

One of the best known American columnists, Walter Lippmann, praised the U.S. press for the way it covered the Dominican crisis explaining that "[r]eporters on the scene and editors back home who printed the news saved that situation from becoming a moral disaster for the United States." Lippmann believed that "reports from correspondents in Santo Domingo gave a more accurate account of the Dominican situation than did Washington announcements."[92] This praise was directed toward the liberal media, the *Times* and the *Post* among them, that had strongly opposed Johnson's initial support of the right wing in Santo Domingo. However, both the liberal and the conservative press expressed much of this journalistic opinion outside of the editorial pages—in news reports and news analyses. The press coverage of the Dominican invasion period seemed to indicate that the absence of a coherent administration policy and the hesitation on the part of domestic actors to voice their criticism was conducive to increased interpretive journalism.

While the coup and the developments surrounding this event in Santo Domingo were reported in the American press, no one outside the administration debated American intervention during the days before the landing of U.S. Marines. There were simply no crisis-related issues to be reported.

As soon as U.S. troops were on Dominican soil and President Johnson spoke of the need to rescue hundreds of Americans stuck in the civil war zone, the news coverage reflected a strong "rally" reaction by domestic political forces. Even when Johnson hinted that U.S. forces needed to prevent a Communist takeover in the Caribbean state, little criticism was voiced as long as American citizens waited to be evacuated and American soldiers got caught in the crossfire of fighting Dominican factions.

Once the acute crisis had given way to a lingering phase, much of the

TABLE 2.11   Overall Post-Crisis Coverage:
Domestic and Foreign, Directly Relevant (Editorials Excluded)

Linage	For/Probably For	Neutral/ Ambiguous	Against/Probably Against	Total Lines
TIMES	42.9%	34.3%	22.8%	6,718
POST	27.8	62.6	9.6	5,938
TRIBUNE	19.4	43.8	36.8	5,090

domestic criticism expressed and reported in print were journalistic descriptions and news analyses that questioned Johnson's Dominican policies and actions.

When the crisis was over, the President's critics at home were more willing to speak out against the way Johnson had handled the American involvement in the Caribbean conflict. The growing criticism was countered by administration officials who defended the U.S. role in Santo Domingo. Newspaper readers at the time were presented with the pro- and con-arguments in the public debate concerning Johnson's Dominican policy.

There was a relationship between the editorial positions of the newspapers and their news reporting in the acute, lingering and post-crisis phases. During the days preceding the American involvement in the Dominican Republic there were no political issues related to the subsequent crisis and therefore neither editorials nor relevant news coverage available for a comparison.

3

THE DETROIT RIOT OF 1967

"IT IS LIKE BERLIN IN 1945"

July 23 , 1967. Early Sunday morning in Detroit. At the corner of 12th Street and Clairmont, a crime-plagued area with mostly black residents, a Vice Squad officer leads a raid on a "blind pig," one of those after-hours drinking and gambling clubs that have survived from Prohibition days. Expecting but a few patrons in the United Community and Civil League shortly before 4:00 A.M., the police raiders are surprised to find 82 persons who are still partying in honor of several servicemen, two of whom have recently returned from Vietnam. There is indignation over the police intrusion, and there are expressions of protest, when police officers begin to transport the club patrons from the scene. It is a humid summer night, and surprisingly large numbers of citizens are moving in the streets. Hundreds of blacks gather in front of the club while the police action is in progress. The protest shouts grow louder. Rocks are thrown. Stores are looted. Still, even though Police commissioner Ray Girardin, Mayor Jerome Cavanagh, and black leaders such as U.S. Representative John Conyers Jr. are notified quickly, the disturbance around 12th Street does not look like the beginning of "the most devastating race riot in U.S. history—and a symbol of a domestic crisis grown graver than any since the Civil War."[1]

However, in the early afternoon, what one witness would later describe as a "carefree mood with which people ran in and out of stores, looting and laughing, and joking with the police officers,"[2] changes into a destructive, deadly racial war. Blacks, upset by rumors of police brutality, crowd into the streets, fires are set, fire fighters attacked with rocks and bottles. Still a few hours later, Mayor Cavanagh asks that the National Guard be immediately sent into the city. He also orders an overnight curfew beginning at 9:00 P.M. A few minutes thereafter, the first sniper fire is reported. Having surveyed errupting areas of the city, Cavanagh expresses shock: "It is like Berlin in 1945."[3] Looking at the city from the air, Michigan Governor George Romney gets the same impression. He declares a state of emergency.

At this point, Cavanagh and Romney, having requested federal troops to assist in efforts to restore order very early Monday morning, have grown impatient, if not angry over the President's hesitation to employ paratroopers who, on Lyndon Johnson's direct orders, have been flown to an Air Force base near Detroit earlier in the day. Thus far Cyrus Vance, who has been rushed to Detroit as the President's special representative, and Lt. General Throckmorton, the commander of the federal troops sent to Michigan, have not seen the need for deployment of these forces. A few hours later, however, Vance and Throckmorton change their minds—they inform the White House that federal troops should be used.

Five minutes before midnight on July 24, President Johnson, flanked by Defense Secretary Robert McNamara, Attorney General Ramsey Clark, FBI Director Edgar Hoover, and a number of other high officials, stands in the movie theater of the White House and begins to read a ten-minute live television address to the nation. The message is grave, indeed: He has ordered the deployment of federal troops within Detroit in a situation that can no longer be controlled by city and state police and National Guard. "The Federal Government should not intervene, except in the most extraordinary circumstances," the President says—surely aware that this is the first time in nearly a quarter century that federal troops are involved in fighting a racial riot in the North.[4] Ironically, the last time this happened was during race riots in Detroit in 1943. This long hot summer with earlier deadly riots in several cities has exploded into a crisis of national proportion. With federal troops fighting in the worst of all riots, there is the instant realization that this kind of urban war can happen elsewhere, anywhere in the country.[5]

A TROUBLED PRESIDENCY

When Lyndon Johnson learned that Detroit city police, state troopers, and the Michigan National Guard were unable to restore order in the streets of Detroit, he had to add another—for the time being the number one burden—to the growing troubles of his presidency. The consensus of his stunning landslide victory of November 1964 had given way to ever-growing discontent over America's role inside and outside the country. Anti-Vietnam protests, radical student actions, black power activists, nonconformity-preaching hippies were expressions of alienation. The "doves" who resisted the U.S. role in Vietnam were no more frustrated with their country than the "hawks" in Middle America who witnessed the war against the war in their own country. In a way they all saw in the President the symbol for everything that had gone wrong—that was wrong with the country—from brutal police force against hippies and peace marchers to draft-card burners waving Vietcong flags.

With less than a year-and-a-half left in his first full term in office, Lyndon Johnson's presidency was so greatly troubled that some of his own partisans began to express what many of them had come to believe—that this President had little chance to win reelection some fifteen months into the future. The pollsters seemed to affirm what members of Congress and other politicians claimed to learn from their constituents: Johnson's popularity was down, his approval ratings had dramatically dropped from the high standings of his first months and years in the White House. Republicans began to prepare for the presidential race the following year, and several likely candidates began to position themselves for the intra-Republican fight for the nomination. Former Vice-President Richard Nixon, California's Governor Ronald Reagan, and George Romney, the governor of Michigan, were among the GOP's early contenders. In April, Romney had a 53–47 percent lead over Lyndon Johnson in a Harris poll testing a possible Johnson-Romney pairing. A month later, another poll showed the two politicians in a head-to-head even race.[6] This strong competition and Johnson's rapidly fading influence in Congress, even among his own partisans, were signs of the President's growing problems.

Over the July 4 holiday Johnson had enjoyed a short visit to his Texas ranch to meet his recently born first grandchild—Patrick Lyndon, son of his younger daughter, Luci. A proud grandfather now, he had but a few rare days of relaxation until, as *Newsweek* put it, "he returned to his worries in Washington."[7] This was the political position of Lyndon Johnson, when an urban war broke out in Detroit.

THE PRESIDENT AND THE MEDIA

What had begun with a prolonged, happy honeymoon for President Johnson and the media, and eventually changed into a normal mixture of cooperative and adversarial relations, deteriorated by 1967 into a troubled, hostile press–president relationship. Journalists who covered the President and his administration had changed their minds about Johnson, the man, and Johnson, the politician and statesman.

George Reedy, who served Johnson as press secretary after Pierre Salinger's departure and before Bill Moyers's appointment, observed that Johnson had a "good press" in the early part of his term. According to Reedy, "Journalists were fascinated by him and they regarded him as a highly able man. Their stories, at least in my judgment, reflected considerable admiration and even a degree of affection." Reedy also came to believe that Johnson brought the "bad press" of the latter part of his presidency upon himself.[8]

Clearly, by 1967, many members of the White House press corps and of the media in general were turned off by Johnson's never-tiring efforts to manipulate, seduce, and punish them. Moreover, the press had begun to write about the "credibility gap" between what Johnson said and what he did. This was particularly the case as far as the ever-escalating American involvement in Vietnam was concerned.

Just as the President alienated members of Congress, members of his own administration, the nation at large, and allies abroad, he widened the gap between himself and the media. In fact, some observers came to believe that journalistic President watchers were especially aware of Johnson's "credibility gap" and of his growing detachment from realities and that, therefore, "[m]ost alienated of all, perhaps, was the press."[9] When Bill Moyers left the White House and the office of press secretary, James Reston of the *New York Times* wrote that this Johnson aide "was a casualty of the war, that he had been wounded at Credibility Gap."[10] Aware that Moyers had come to doubt the American Vietnam policies, the President was hurt and angered by his departure. By this time, Johnson was unable to stomach criticism. As David Halberstam described it, "Critics became enemies; enemies became traitors; and the press, which a year earlier had been so friendly, was now filled with enemies baying at his heels."[11]

George Christian became his fourth press secretary to serve during the last two and most difficult years of Johnson's White House terms. Even though well regarded by most White House reporters who believed that he served the President and the press well, Christian was unable to stem the rising tide of hostility between Johnson and the press. John Tebbel and Sarah Miles Watts, after examining all press–president relationships beginning with George Washington concluded: "His [Johnson's] relationship with the press combined all the worst elements of what had gone before, leaving scarcely one redeeming feature to permit a charitable conclusion. And the press responded by fighting him as it had not fought anyone else since Lincoln."[12]

A LONG, HOT SUMMER

Around the middle of July, the map of the United States in the small riot-alert room in the U.S. Justice department in Washington showed an ever-growing number of cities and towns circled in red: the areas that had suffered or were at the time experiencing urban unrest and violence in this long, hot summer of 1967. Until the *Washington Post* revealed the existence of such an information-gathering center for violence in the ghettos, only those involved with this project knew about the workings of what some of them called "The War Room."[13] However, as one official of the department told the *Post*, the intent to prevent violent outbursts with the help of what it had hoped would be an early-warning post did not quite work out.

On the contrary, the country had been plagued by violence since spring. Omaha, Houston, Chicago, Nashville, Boston, Tampa, Cincinnati, Atlanta, Buffalo, Des Moines, Kansas City, and Hartford, as well as Newark, Plainfield, and New Brunswick, New Jersey were among the places that experienced violent eruptions. In Newark alone, 23 persons were killed—21 of them blacks. Yet, in spite of growing unrest among both blacks and whites throughout the country, President Johnson had not gotten involved in antiriot measures. His first public statement concerning the troubled inner cities was the result of a question posed to him during a White House press conference on July 18. The President warned that the nation was "going to be confronted with unpleasant situations," until education, employment, and housing conditions of the poor were improved.[14]

During the weeks preceding the Detroit crisis, the President's posture in dealing with urban unrest and violence was a hands-off approach as far as direct federal involvement in dealing with local riots was concerned. Thus, the administration was not in favor of an antiriot bill before Congress that was designed to curb militant blacks suspected of encouraging riots. One intent of the get-tough measure was to make crossing state lines with the intent to incite violence a federal crime. The Johnson administration pushed for a civil rights bill aimed at improving minority rights and conditions and racial integration, for example, by forbidding discrimination in housing.

Among Johnson's opponents were conservatives in both parties who criticized the antipoverty programs of his "Great Society" policies as ineffective and demanded a tougher stand against those who provoked and participated in riots. While liberals were on the President's side on some riot-related issues such as the antiriot bill and an administration bill supposed to make it more difficult to buy handguns, they faulted Johnson for not having done enough to improve conditions in the slums. Many black leaders—not only the most radical ones—were critical of the President for fighting a costly war in Vietnam and therefore not spending enough to improve the lot of the poor at home. Only some moderate black leaders continued to support Johnson as a champion of civil rights.

In an editorial headlined "Subsidized Riots" the *Chicago Tribune* criticized Sargent Shriver, director of the Office for Economic Opportunity in the Johnson administration, for not reacting to a message by Newark's police director six weeks before the outbreak of riots in the New Jersey city warning that federal antipoverty funds were being used to foment violence. Attacking not only Shriver but more broadly Johnson's antipoverty war, the Chicago newspaper warned that people such as Shriver should listen to the complaints from Newark or they would risk "find[ing] themselves in the business of subsidizing local 'wars of liberation' in cities all over the country. And in time the professional agitators and rioters who are being nurtured by federal programs will turn on the government itself." Although Shriver was the immediate recipient of the harsh editorial attack, Lyndon Johnson, his Great Society programs, and his alleged soft stand on militants were its true targets. Both relevant editorials the Chicago newspaper published during the weeks before the Detroit riots expressed criticism of Johnson. In one instance, the editorial looked to Congress to do a better job. Referring to the antipoverty efforts of the administration, the newspaper suggested, "Congress should go over the whole establishment with a fine-toothed power saw."[15]

The President and his administration fared better in the editorials of the two East Coast newspapers during the pre-crisis period. Of four relevant pieces on the editorial page of the *New York Times,* one was supportive, two were neutral or ambiguous, and one editorial was somewhat critical. The *Times,* like the administration, was critical of the antiriot bill and supportive of a civil rights bill proposed by the Johnson administration. In one editorial, the newspaper pointed out that "[i]n the effort to reach riots at their source, an 'anti-riot' bill is no substitute for a civil rights bill, It is—at least this one—simply a gesture of frustration, quite apart from the questionable constitutionality of a bill that would attempt to stop free speech somewhere in the air between states."[16] In the second part of the editorial, the *Times* supported an administration bill that would adopt stricter gun-control measures. While warning of "black racism" as demonstrated at a Black Power conference in Newark as an answer to "justified reasons for discontent" among black Americans, the New York newspaper pleaded for "the walls that block Negro opportunity [to] come down."[17] On one occasion the *Times* editorial page expressed dissatisfaction with the President (and others) for not paying enough attention to the nation's most serious problem —racial tensions and violence. According to the *Times,* "[t]he situation is already serious enough to demand the President, Congress, and the responsible local leadership in every community to give it top priority claim on their time, their energies, and their own and the nation's resources. What is disheartening is the business-as-usual attitude in Washington and much of the rest of the country." This criticism implied lack of leadership on the part of the President in what the editorial's headline called "The Gravest Responsibility."[18]

Of five relevant editorials in the *Washington Post* during the weeks before the Detroit riots, three were supportive of the administration positions, one opinion piece was ambiguous, and another one was somewhat unfavorable. The publication editorialized three times against the antiriot bill which was favored by a majority in Congress but not by the Johnson administration. Criticizing the initiative as the result of a sentiment of panic in this long, hot summer, the *Post* wrote, "Panic is never a wise counselor. And in this instance it has more than measured up to its reputation as propagator of folly."[19] In one editorial the *Post* was indirectly critical of the Johnson administration, when it hailed public housing proposals by Senators Robert Kennedy, Abraham Ribicoff, and Charles Percy and suggested that "[t]he most imaginative and useful new ideas for urban housing are currently coming from the Senate." Suggesting that in this "off year for the Administration" the Department of Housing was "wisely" concentrating on the organization of the Model Cities program, the *Post* praised the Senators for putting forth new and potent ideas for a "national policy to rebuild the slums."[20] The proposals were not embraced by the Johnson administration.

In their news coverage of riot-related issues, the newspapers gave administration officials opportunities to explain their views. The *Times,* for example, reported about efforts by officials of the Community Relations Service to convince media representatives to exercise restraint when reporting about riots.[21] The *Post* published an article revealing that Defense Secretary Robert McNamara had criticized congressional inaction on the administration's gun control proposals, calling such an attitude "an open and permanent invitation to violence and disorder."[22] And when the *Tribune* covered a clash between Charles Percy and Housing Secretary Robert Weaver over federal housing policies, the Chicago newspaper gave more space to administration official Weaver than to the liberal Republican Senator from Illinois. The latter had proposed a program that would help the poor to buy low-cost housing, a plan the Johnson administration had rejected.[23] Criticizing the existing antipoverty programs harshly, the Chicago newspaper presumably did not favor additional initiatives such as the one Percy promoted. The three newspapers also covered moderate black leaders such as the executive secretary of the National Association for the Advancement of Colored People (NAACP), Roy Wilkins, and Republican Senator Edward Brooke. During the annual convention of the NAACP in Boston, Wilkins rejected riots as a means to achieve better conditions for blacks and spoke out against the antiriot bill in Congress. The *Times* suggested that "[b]y implication Mr. Wilkins gave strong support to President Johnson's civil rights program."[24]

The *Post* and the *Times* gave a considerable amount of space to liberals not satisfied with Johnson's efforts to alleviate poverty in the slums, which was seen as the deeper cause of the riots. Senator Kennedy's proposal for new housing and job initiatives for the benefit of slum-dwellers was covered extensively by the Washington newspaper, which reminded its readers that "the President and other officials reacted sharply last year when Kennedy suggested during Senate hearings that existing Federal programs are not reaching the majority of slum dwellers."[25] In fact, Kennedy repeated his criticism of Johnson's antipoverty program by labeling it during a speech on the Senate floor, as the *Times* reported, as "ineffective, inefficient and degrading."[26] While paying little attention to liberal "antipoverty warriors" like Kennedy and Percy, the *Tribune* did cover conservative critics of the administration more extensively. Thus, Illinois Senator Everett Dirksen was repeatedly covered when he articulated his support for the antiriot bill. When Senator Winston Prouty, a Vermont Republican, revealed during a Senate hearing that Newark police commissioner Dominick Spina had warned OEO director Shriver weeks before the outbreak of riots in his city that federally funded antipoverty workers were "agitating" against the democratic government of Newark, this was reported in a longer article in the *Tribune*.[27]

During the weeks preceding the Detroit crisis, the *Times* tended to cover Johnson's radical critics more extensively than the *Post* and much more so than the *Tribune*. Thus, the New York newspaper reported about a forth-coming "New Left" convention, quoting Michael Wood, one of the organizers, who charged that President Johnson "symbolized the political set of priorities that favors destruction in Vietnam over civil and human rights of the disadvantaged minorities at home."[28] In a lengthy front page article about a "Black Power" meeting in Newark, the *Times* quoted H. Rap Brown who charged that "President Johnson brought no help for Negroes during the Newark rioting. The only help that came was for the hunkie whites. This will cost him Negro votes in 1968."[29]

The news coverage of issues surrounding the outbreak of violence in many urban areas was fairly similar in the three newspapers in terms of space distribution for sources supportive and critical of the President. In all three newspapers, critics of Johnson's relevant policies captured more space than did supporters (see table 3.1). Even though the *Tribune* was one-sidedly critical of Johnson, its coverage was not quite as unfavorable from the President's perspective as that of the East Coast papers with their mixed editorial position. In spite of this, an argument can be made that there was a relationship between editorial positions and so-called straight news coverage: While the *Tribune* shared the view of conservative Johnson critics in these issues and favored them in terms of source selection and space consideration, the newspaper was quite opposed to the very active liberal and especially radical critics and covered them less generously than the East Coast newspapers, whose editorial posture was more compatible with liberal and perhaps even radical Johnson critics.

The *Tribune* treated pro and con sources equally when it came to the placement in front page stories; in the East Coast papers critical sources had front page placement advantage.

During the pre-crisis period congressional sources captured considerably more space than administration sources (see table 3.2). While this gap between sources of the two governmental branches varied in the examined publications, in each case it reflected the fact that Congress was more active and more outspoken than LBJ, when it came to riot-related issues during this time.

As far as journalistic descriptions, explanations, and interpretations in news articles and news analyses were concerned, there was no slant detectable either for or against Johnson's positions on riot-related issues.

FEDERAL TROOPS FIGHT DETROIT RIOTERS

Shortly before midnight on July 24 President Johnson stood before TV cameras and microphones in the White House theater to announce that he had ordered federal troops into Detroit to restore law and order in the riot-torn city. Describing the events of the day, he told the nation: "I advised

TABLE 3.1   Pre-Crisis Coverage: Detroit Riots of 1967 (Editorials Excluded)

Linage	For/Probably For	Neutral/ Ambiguous	Against/Probably Against	Total Lines
TIMES	20.1%	49.8%	30.1%	2,041
POST	21.6	41.3	37.1	1,088
TRIBUNE	30.4	37.6	32.0	713

TABLE 3.2   Linage Administration and Congressional Sources: Pre-Crisis

	Administration Sources	Congressional Sources	Total Lines
TIMES	31.4%	68.6%	682
POST	19.1	80.9	591
TRIBUNE	13.2	86.8	433

Mr. Vance and General Throckmorton to proceed immediately with the transportation of Federal troops from Selfridge Air Force Base to places of deployment within Detroit, a movement which they had already provisionally begun pursuant to their authority." Calling on all Americans to "show by word and deed that riot, looting and public disorder will just not be tolerated," the President closed his statement with an urgent message: "I appeal to every American in this grave hour to respond to this plea."[30]

Most Americans learned the next morning that the deployment of paratroopers in this city, the first use of federal troops in such a situation since the Detroit riots of 1943, had changed one more deadly and frightening local urban outburst into a national crisis. Johnson had made it clear in his midnight speech: His appeal was not only addressed to Detroiters but to citizens all over America.

In the *Chicago Tribune* the headline "Paratroopers Fight Riot" spanned the whole width of the front page in the edition of July 25. The two East Coast newspapers, as did the press in general, gave the involvement of federal troops equally prominent coverage. With the ghettos of Detroit in flames, the many incidents of the long, hot summer had overnight exploded into an acute emergency that lasted three days and nights (reported in the newspaper edition of July 25, 26, and 27).

In the editorials that the *New York Times* published during this crisis phase, the publication backed the use of federal troops to end the lawlessness in that city. "The fires must be extinguished, the rifles taken from the hands of rioters, and punishment meted out to fit the crimes," the *Times* stated.[31] In another editorial piece, the New York newspaper supported the President's view that the anguish of the cities would be relieved only when already initiated "social, economic, and educational programs . . . and additional programs on a huge scale, are pressed to the point where they begin to fulfill the hopes they have rightly engendered." Like Johnson, however, the publication made clear that in the "meantime, the absolute, prime requirement is the restoration of order."[32] Also, by praising well-known, influential civil rights leaders—Dr. Martin Luther King among them—for having joined the President's plea to restore and maintain public order and to condemn radical calls for violence, the *Times* echoed Johnson's sentiments.[33]

Three out of four editorials fell into the supportive or probably supportive category; one was critical of Lyndon Johnson's "nervous political posturing at this critical time."[34] The *Times* referred to the fact that even after the President had initiated the airlift of troops from Fort Bragg, North Carolina, to Selfridge Air Force Base near Detroit, the White House had refused to follow Michigan Governor Romney's and Detroit Mayor Cavanagh's urgent requests for federal troops. Also, when LBJ had finally given orders to send paratroopers into the city, he had harshly criticized a strong, potential rival for 1968, George Romney, explaining that "the Federal Government in the circumstances here presented had no alternative but to respond, since it was called upon by the Governor of the State, and since it was presented with the proof of his inability to restore order in Michigan."[35]

The President's behavior was cause enough for the *Times* to criticize Johnson harshly, writing: "Because he holds the highest office and therefore bears the highest responsibility both to act and to set an example, President Johnson offended most conspicuously in his pussyfooting response to the debacle in Detroit. He shilly-shallied for several hours in ordering the Army units into action in the city despite the pleas of local officials that troops were urgently needed. And when he did act, Mr. Johnson issued a proclamation and a personal statement both of which were clearly designed to place the entire political responsibility on Governor Romney." While the same editorial characterized a statement by the Republican Coordinating Committee that had blamed the President for race riots as "a flagrant outrage," there was no doubt that the *Times* found no excuse for the President's conduct, which the editorial labeled "strangely lacking in the quality of leadership."[36]

The *Washington Post,* too, remarked in an editorial that "[i]n the present riots, the nation's leadership has not distinguished itself." While primarily criticizing the Republican accusation that the riots were a product of the Johnson administration's policies, the Washington paper also noted critically: "The President, in his long minuet with Governor Romney on Monday, brought to mind nothing so much as the picture of one presidential candidate sparring with another. Much time was lost while one candidate maneuvered to put the largest responsibility on the other. The President's midnight speech was devoted mainly to saying, with lawyerish repetition, that Governor Romney had lost control of events."[37] In another editorial, however, the *Post* defended Johnson's antipoverty programs against anticipated attacks on those policies designed to improve the conditions of the poor. The *Post* argued that "[t]he country needs steady hands in this moment, and cannot let itself to [be] baited or distracted by black insurrectionaries or the white reactionaries who are, not for the first time, singing in harmony."[38]

Two days later, however, the Washington publication wondered whether in view of the riot in Detroit and prior urban explosions the President was right in suggesting that the nation was capable of dealing with both an urgent crisis at home (riots) and an urgent crisis abroad (Vietnam).[39] Of four editorials in the *Post* during the acute crisis, two fell into the neutral/ ambiguous category, one piece was supportive, another one mostly critical.

During the acute crisis the *Tribune* upheld its one-sided critical editorial stance vis-à-vis the President's crisis-related policies although the publication was in agreement with his decision to use federal forces to deal with rioters in Detroit. Agreeing with Republican leaders, who had noted that the protection of life and property was the most basic civil right, the publication noted that Johnson, "very late in the day, has shown some consciousness of this." But this as well as another editorial blamed the President's antipoverty programs and the unwillingness of Great Society advocates to "condemn the lawless."[40] According to the *Tribune,* the war on poverty had raised hopes too high among the poor: "Because they had expectations, there was supposed to be some obligation on Uncle Sugar to satisfy them. But whatever was doled out was never enough. Resentment was generated and brought open hostility." The publication left no doubt that, as some prominent Republicans charged, there was a causal relationship between domestic "handouts" and rioting, namely in the case of Detroit. Thus, the *Tribune* editorialized, "When the prospectus calls for manna from heaven, the tendency is to wait for it to fall. That makes for idle hands, and the devil will find work for them to do."[41] All three *Tribune* editorials related to the crisis were critical of the President.

However, in spite of the anti-Johnson line in the editorial stance of the *Tribune* and the critical editorial comments by both *Times* and *Post* concerning his political maneuvers vis-à-vis Republican Governor Romney, the three papers agreed with Johnson's deployment of federal troops in the Detroit crisis. Also, while the two East Coast newspapers expressed distaste for the President's political posturing in an emergency situation, they also affirmed their support for Johnson's war on poverty as a means to cure the underlying causes for the ghetto violence.

With the attention of the nation on the Detroit crisis, the newspapers published lengthy descriptions of what was taking place in the streets of the city. Many of the articles filed from Detroit were based on journalistic descriptions and on reports by local and state officials as well as on accounts provided by ordinary citizens. Most sources in these stories fell into the neutral or ambiguous category concerning their positions toward the President's riot-related actions and policies.

Contrary to the pre-crisis weeks, when the administration and especially the President had taken a passive stance toward urban troubles, Johnson's decision to use federal troops to restore order in Detroit cast him suddenly in the role of the central crisis manager. While the White House referred questions about the timetable of federal involvement and about the actual status in the riot-torn city to Cyrus Vance, the President's special envoy in Detroit, LBJ worked, as the *Times* reported, "in public and in private to dampen racial disorder." It was reported that Johnson was in continuous contact with Vance and in touch with administration officials involved in the federal role in Detroit as well as with civil rights leaders. Addressing a group of young Americans invited to the White House, Johnson took the opportunity to plead for an end of racial violence.[42] Johnson's Detroit stand-in crisis managers Cyrus Vance and General John Throckmorton were sought out by the press as information sources. Also, favorable articles were published about Johnson's "sleepless night" as crisis manager and about General Throckmorton, a veteran of three wars.[43]

On the other hand, news reports also reflected criticism both from Johnson's Republican opposition and from some fellow Democrats. For example, Mayor Cavanagh of Detroit, a Democrat, was critical of Johnson's hesitant response to the request to send troops.[44] Republicans blamed the President for racial riots in what the *Washington Post* characterized a "slashing attack" on Johnson.

Still, with the exception of the fierce, partisan attack by Republican leaders and a few less drastic critical remarks by some Republicans and Democrats (for example, Senator Robert Byrd, Democrat from West Virginia, demanded that "insurection should be put down with brutal force"[45]), there was a quick cooling off on the part of LBJ's critics. Also, support was voiced for the President. For example, when several prominent civil rights leaders, among them Dr. Martin Luther King, joined the President's pleas for an end to racial violence, they made front page headlines in the two East Coast newspapers as well as in the Midwest publication.[46]

With the Detroit violence expanding into a national crisis there was a dramatic change in the riot-related coverage. In contrast to the weeks preceding the acute emergency, when more news lines were based on sources critical of LBJ's relevant policies, the situation was now reversed: Pro-Johnson sources were used for more linage than were critics in the coverage of all three newspapers. There was a relationship between editorial positions and news coverage in that the *Times* with an editorially more supportive stand vis-à-vis the President presented the most favorable and the *Tribune* with the most critical editorial position the least favorable coverage of the three papers. The news coverage of the *Post*, which took an ambiguous editorial line, fell in this respect in between that of the two others (see table 3.3). The most outspoken critics during the acute crisis days were conservative Republicans whose views in riot-related and other matters were shared by the *Tribune.*

There was quite a turnaround in the placement of sources in front page stories during the acute crisis in comparison with the pre-crisis weeks, in that sources supportive of the President were much more often mentioned in page one articles than critics of LBJ. Regardless of the editorial positions of the papers, during the acute crisis the President's side dominated as far as the prominent placement was concerned.

With President Johnson and his administration resuming an active and visible role in the management of the riot crisis, administration sources captured more news lines than congressional sources in the East Coast newspapers. This was a significant change from the pre-crisis weeks. However, in the *Tribune,* more linage was based on congressional than on administration sources. In this respect the *Tribune*'s editorial claim of a causal relationship between Johnson's antipoverty programs and slum violence, which coincided with the view of conservatives in Congress, seemed to have affected the space considerations for sources from the two branches of government (see table 3.4).

Journalist descriptions, background information, and news analyses were overwhelmingly neutral or ambiguous as to attitudes toward Johnson's crisis policies.

RIOTS GIVE WAY TO OCCASIONAL SNIPER FIRE

Four days after the devastating riots broke out and three days after President Johnson sent federal troops into Detroit to restore law and order, the situation in the inner city had changed enough for the *New York Times* to report in a front page headline that "Detroit Riots Seem at End; Sightseers Evoke Curfew." The article, dateline Detroit, quoted President Johnson's personal representative in the riot-torn city, Cyrus Vance, as saying,

TABLE 3.3   Acute Crisis: Detroit Riot of 1967 (Editorials Excluded)

Linage	For/Probably For	Neutral/ Ambiguous	Against/Probably Against	Total Lines
TIMES	27.1%	64.1%	8.8%	3,309
POST	25.9	64.0	10.1	2,944
TRIBUNE	19.0	71.0	10.0	2,277

TABLE 3.4   Linage Administration and Congressional Sources: Acute Crisis

	Administration Sources	Congressional Sources	Total Lines
TIMES	56.2%	43.8%	682
POST	58.9	41.1	749
TRIBUNE	38.6	61.4	471

"It's pretty much over."[47] However, while the conditions in the motor city had dramatically improved, they were not yet safe and back to normal. Instead, the *Chicago Tribune* reported that "sporadic sniper fire rang thru *[sic]* the ravaged streets of Detroit."[48] Still, the acute emergency had given way to a lingering crisis that was to last four days (reported in the editions of July 28 through 31).

With the all-out Detroit rioting under control, the *Times* moved away from its cautiously supportive editorial posture and placed part of the blame for what one editorial headlined "Sickness of the Cities" at the doorstep of the White House. Referring to the expensive war in Vietnam, this particular *Times* editorial lectured, "They [the urban problems causing rioting] need to be attacked with at least the same free-spending determination that the Administration and Congress so far have reserved for the war in Vietnam."[49] In a follow-up editorial the next day, the New York publication singled out Lyndon Johnson for harsh criticism, stating, "Whenever a crisis has arisen in Vietnam, President Johnson has not hesitated to call on Congress and the nation to allocate additional men and money to meet the need. All the more surprising is the President's failure to demand a substantial escalation of the wars on poverty and urban decay in response to the current crisis in the cities of America." The *Times* also noted, "It is ironic that the most forceful call to action so far has come not from the champion of the 'Great Society,' but from Republican Senator Thruston B. Morton of Kentucky, who advocates a special $1 billion 'anti-riot chest' to finance crash social programs."[50] Of the three editorials the *Times* published during the lingering crisis period, two were critical of Johnson's crisis-related policies, one was neutral/ambiguous.

Two of the three editorials in the *Washington Post* during the lingering crisis days commented on the need for a thorough investigation of the Detroit and other urban riots, and on the Commission on Civil Disorders named by the President. While the newspaper editorialized in favor of a second investigative body to deal with the fundamental problems behind violent urban outbreaks and Congressional involvement, both seemed ambiguous in their position vis-à-vis Johnson's crisis-related stand. However, in the third relevant editorial published during this period, the *Post* was somewhat critical of LBJ and his administration, stating that the "Johnson administration, more instantly responsive to new social ideas than any of its predecessors, has temporarily run out of inspiration. It has come upon a moment of immobility. The nation now requires another great turn in policy." The *Post* made clear that it looked to Congress and members like Senator Robert F. Kennedy, mentioned in the editorial by name, to be the architects of a new antipoverty policy.[51]

The *Chicago Tribune* in the one relevant editorial it published during the lingering crisis period was bitingly critical of President Johnson's crisis management and his social policies. Even the appointment of a commission to investigate urban riots failed to impress the Midwestern publication. "We don't know what Mr. Johnson's commission to investigate the cause of riots is expected to accomplish," the *Tribune* editorialized. "The appointment of a commission is just another move in passing the buck." Referring to the President's declaration of a national day of prayer for peace and reconciliation, the editorial closed with stating sarcastically, "Prayer is always a good idea. Perhaps the appropriate text for Sunday is: 'Father, forgive them; for they know not what they do.' The rioters, arsonists, and looters have disgraced themselves and their country. It is they who ought to be praying for redemption."[52]

While the two East Coast newspapers expressed increasing editorial criticism of the President's failure to counter the urban explosions in Detroit and elsewhere with innovative federal aid programs, the *Tribune* retained its oppositional stance blaming LBJ for being too soft on rioters and for having caused the troubles in the first place, namely by putting too much emphasis on antipoverty programs. However, politicians inside and outside of Congress, from either the liberal or the conservative side, were less willing to go public with their criticism than the editorial writers.

. One of the exceptions concerned the GOP leadership in the House of Representatives. When publishing a newsletter editorial under the headline, "LBJ: A President Who Couldn't Lead," in which President Johnson's leadership in riot-related issues was characterized as being weak, unpardonable, and indifferent, they drew the attention of the news media.[53] By and large congressional and other mainstream politicians remained mostly neutral or ambiguous vis-à-vis Johnson's riot-related policies in statements relevant to the lingering crisis in Detroit and to the whole issue of urban problems. Others, Republican Senator Morton among them, chided GOP leaders for critizing the President during the acute crisis.[54]

Militant black leaders attacked the President fiercely in the context of the riots in Detroit and in other cities. All three newspapers covered a press conference by H. Rap Brown during which the "Black Power" advocate called rioting blacks "patriots" and President Johnson "a white honkie cracker," and "a wild, mad dog."[55] Nevertheless, the *Tribune* was much less likely than the *Times* and *Post* to report on more radical anti-Johnson statements. The *Times*, for example, publicized Stokely Carmichael's appeal to fellow blacks in Detroit and New York "to wage a conflict such as that in Vietnam."[56] Also, the *Times* published a lengthy article about a new book on urban problems quoting author Jeanne R. Lowe as criticizing Lyndon Johnson: "Instead of waiting to fight lawlessness, President Johnson should be fighting helplessness; instead of sending in Federal troops, he should send more Federal aid."[57] The *Post* gave front page coverage to a pastoral letter by Patrick Cardinal O'Boyle, Roman Catholic Archbishop of Washington, when he demanded—in the context of urban riots—"reparations for our past failures and past sins of omission," and called for the "immediate enactment of sweeping and costly Federal programs aimed at bettering the lives of the Negro poor."[58]

The President made efforts to demonstrate his involvement in the Detroit emergency and in efforts to end the racial violence. During the four days of the lingering period, his initiatives, statements, and even spare-time activities made the front pages of the *Tribune* and of the *Post* on three, and of the *Times* on all four days. For example, much attention was given to the appointment of a panel to probe the riots in Detroit and in other urban areas, the President's meeting with members of the commission, and his church visit on the Sunday he had proclaimed as a national day for racial conciliation. In addition, there were statements and assessments by Johnson's personal representative in Detroit, Cyrus Vance, which emphasized the President's ongoing concern for and involvement in the situation in Detroit.

Most of the articles reporting the developments in Detroit were based on journalistic descriptions that fell overwhelmingly into the neutral/ambiguous category. Also, the publications began to publish background information recounting the events surrounding the Detroit riots and, in particular, the decision to deploy federal troops in the emergency. While both *Post* and *Tribune* concentrated their background articles on sources in Detroit, the *Times* published long accounts with Detroit and Washington datelines, and one of these articles used White House sources to reconstruct the timetable of the debate between Detroit and Washington officials concerning the use of paratroopers to fight rioters.[59]

In the news coverage sources supportive of the President in this matter were used for significantly more lines than were critical sources (see table 3.5). While both East Coast newspapers switched to critical and ambiguous editorial positions, the *Tribune* still expressed the most critical editorial position. Yet, from the President's view point, the *Tribune*'s coverage was

TABLE 3.5   Lingering Crisis: Detroit Riots 1967 (Editorials Excluded)

Linage	For/Probably For	Neutral/ Ambiguous	Against/Probably Against	Total Lines
TIMES	45.8%	43.2%	11.0%	3,928
POST	23.8	62.5	13.7	3,042
TRIBUNE	23.8	70.9	5.3	2,800

more favorable than that of the East Coast papers. In terms of numbers, there seemed to be no relationship between editorial positions and news coverage. However, if one considers that liberal politicians and even more so radical activists were the leading anti-Johnson voices while conservatives mostly suspended public criticism, a connection between editorial policies and source selection emerges: The *Tribune* was in total disagreement with liberals and militants who attacked Johnson's riot-related policies for other reasons than conservatives. Thus, the conservative anti-Johnson stance of the *Tribune*'s editorial page was in fact compatible with the news coverage that paid little attention to presidential critics to the left who also happened to be in disagreement with the *Tribune*'s support for Johnson's Vietnam policy. On the other hand, the East Coast newspapers, which criticized Johnson from a liberal point of view, covered the most vocal Johnson critics during this phase more generously than the Chicago newspaper. The *Times*, although editorially more critical than the *Post*, presented a more favorable coverage than the Washington newspaper because it used in its background articles far more Washington-based administration sources than the other two papers.

Supporters of the President's crisis handling and his riot-related policies made front page stories much more often than his opponents during this period. In fact, in the *Tribune* anti-Johnson sources were not used at all in front page articles.

Both the administration and the Congress continued to be active in crisis-related issues. The *Times* covered both branches more extensively than did the other two newspapers. Also, the New York publication used administration sources for twice as many lines as congressional sources. While the *Tribune* based more lines on administration than on congressional sources, the *Post* provided about the same amount of linage to sources of both branches (see table 3.6).

Journalistic descriptions, background information, and news analysis did not reveal bias for or against Johnson's crisis-related stand.

TABLE 3.6   Linage Administration and Congressional Sources: Lingering Crisis

	Administration Sources	Congressional Sources	Total Lines
TIMES	66.9%	33.1%	1,371
POST	49.9	50.1	736
TRIBUNE	54.1	45.9	740

WITHDRAWAL OF PARATROOPERS SIGNALS END OF CRISIS

When President Johnson's stand-in crisis manager in Detroit, Cyrus Vance, told a news conference that three battalions of paratroopers, who had helped to quell the riots, were leaving the city; when Michigan National Guardsmen took over patrol duty in areas devastated by the racial disturbances, and when Governor George Romney lifted the total ban on liquor and shortened the curfew to a precautionary measure assuring that the streets of Detroit remained calm; the riot was, for all practical purposes, over. There was no more violence, nor the occasional sniper fire of the lingering crisis period (the post-crisis phase was the month of August).

Once federal troops were removed from the areas that had witnessed the most devastating race riots in this long summer, Governor Romney abandoned his restraint toward the President and challenged the White House chronology of the negotiations between Michigan and Detroit officials on one side and the Johnson administration on the other. In what the *New York Times* termed his "first open or public criticism of the President on the way the riots were handled," George Romney accused LBJ of playing politics during the hours between the first request for federal troop assistance and their actual deployment on Detroit streets.[60] While the two East Coast newspapers reported the Romney attack in front page stories, the *Chicago Tribune* chose to publish it on an inside page.[61] Perhaps the decision by the Chicago editors to "bury" Romney's very harsh criticism of the President inside the newspaper had to do with the fact that the same day's edition reported on its front page Johnson's assurance that the United States could afford to fight both the war in Vietnam and the war on poverty at home. While attacking the antipoverty programs fiercely, the *Tribune* was a firm supporter of Johnson's commitment to the fighting in South East Asia and thus gave this particular story the preferred placement Romney did not get.

Romney's outburst was just the beginning of a return to the acrimonious debate of the pre-crisis period. While militant black leaders had continued to express hostility toward Johnson's riot-related policies during the Detroit emergency, especially during the days of the lingering crisis, establishment politicians and interest group leaders had not voiced much criticism and disagreement with the President in public. Now, conservatives, liberals, and radicals seemed to feel free to resume their political infighting in this matter. Presidential hopeful Romney repeated his initial attack on LBJ during the following weeks, and other Republicans, such as New York Governor Nelson Rockefeller, Senator Barry Goldwater, Representative Gerald Ford, and Senator Everett Dirksen, expressed their opposition to the administration's crisis-management during the Detroit emergency and/or Johnson's riot-related stances. Most of these critics repeated the "playing politics" charge and demanded tougher measures against those who provoked urban disturbances and against rioters themselves. All three newspapers reflected this opposition.[62]

There was also opposition to Johnson among the President's liberal partisans in Congress, namely Senators Robert Kennedy, Abraham Ribicoff, and William Fulbright who advocated more attention to and funding for the war on poverty at home and less to Vietnam. While the *Times* seemed to pay more attention to these Democratic critics of the President, the other two newspapers also took note of these opponents.[63] The *Times* was also more inclined than either the *Post* or *Tribune* to cover the attacks on Johnson by black militants such as Stokely Carmichael, H. Rap Brown and Floyd McKissick. When, for example, H. Rap Brown called the President the "greatest outlaw in history," advocated "lynching Johnson," and warned that the recent urban riots were just "dress rehearsals for revolution," the *Times* reported on the event in an extensive front page story.[64] In this particular case, Brown made his statements in New York, which may explain why the *Times* —unlike the *Post* and *Tribune* paid a great deal of attention to the outburst.

The newspapers reported about charges by a Nashville police official that federal antipoverty funds were subsidizing a "liberation school" run by militant blacks who had fomented riots in Nashville. But the *Tribune* reported far more extensively on these charges and on claims by Newark officials that antipoverty workers had played a significant role in bringing about the riots in that city. Also, the press covered various initiatives by Republican governors, Republican and Democratic mayors, and a new Urban Coalition of a whole range of groups and civic-minded individuals who pushed for renewed activities and fresh approaches to heal the urban ills and thus the underlying causes for the riots. All these initiatives were undertaken with the explicit or implicit assumption that there was a lack of leadership on the part of the President (and Congress) in this area.

Lyndon Johnson, perhaps stung by charges of inadequate leadership on his part, continued to speak out on the administration's management of the Detroit crisis, on antipoverty programs, and on the ability of the nation to support both the war in Vietnam and the war on poverty in America. The President prodded Congress to adopt his proposed programs for urban areas in order to prevent a repeat of "the tragic events of this summer."[65] He pushed especially for the model cities, rent supplement, and research and development programs. When the Presidential Advisory Commission on Civil Disorders urged the recruitment of more blacks in the National Guard and better training in riot-control, LBJ responded by forwarding the Commission report to Secretary of Defense Robert McNamara as a matter "of the highest urgency."[66]

Vice-President Hubert Humphrey, Attorney General Ramsey Clark, Cyrus Vance (the President's representative in Detroit during the crisis periods), FBI Director J. Edgar Hoover, and various Pentagon officials were among administration members who carried the President's line, defended his decision concerning the Detroit emergency, and contributed to conveying the impression that the executive branch was very active in handling crisis-related issues in the aftermath of the happenings in Detroit. At one point, Vice-President Humphrey got carried away by his own impressions and emotions during a visit to Detroit immediately after the withdrawal of federal troops: In a speech before a convention of the National Association of Counties, Humphrey called for an all-out effort to help the impoverished areas of America and for a plan he compared to the Marshall Plan, urging that "Whatever it will take to get the job done, we must be willing to pay the price."[67] In subsequent speeches on the same subject Humphrey refrained from mentioning the American version of the Marshall Plan again because, as the *Washington Post* reported, the Vice-President's remarks had "aroused the Johnson's ire [sic] when the President was preparing a tax-increase measure and trying to cut domestic spending."[68]

The President also had some supporters outside the administration. For example, Democratic leaders in Congress pushed for relevant legislation proposed by the Johnson administration. Thus, Emanuel Celler, chairman of the House Judiciary Committee defended the administration's version of a major anticrime bill. He argued in vain, since Republicans and Southern Democrats altered and passed a bill that gave most control to the states and allowed strong antiriot measures.[69] But when the Senate Appropriation Committee approved the President's request for a $40 million rent-supplement program and funded the model cities and the research and development program Johnson had pushed for, Republican Senator Jacob Javits praised the measure as the reflection of "an objective desire to do something about the cities."[70] While this was surely meant to congratulate fellow senators, it was just as much a tribute to the President's efforts on behalf of the programs he was pushing for.

Half of the relevant sixteen editorials the *New York Times* published in the weeks following the end of the Detroit crisis were critical of the President's crisis-related policies. Of the remaining eight editorials four were supportive and four fell into the neutral/ambiguous category. The New York based newspaper attacked Johnson for not demonstrating leadership in fighting against what caused the ghetto outbursts, for doing nothing or for not doing enough. Thus, in an editorial that praised "outstanding citizens" for "taking the lead in spurring the country to positive action," the *Times* noted that this new Urban Coalition was active while investigative commissions were proliferating in Washington.[71] In another editorial the *Times* commended Republican governors for an action plan to improve housing, education and job opportunities in the nation's slums. The editorial closed with the observation that these governors "have provided leadership that the GOP members of Congress, the Democratic majority, and the Johnson Administration could all heed."[72] Again applauding the initiative of the Urban Coalition, another editorial in the *Times* warned, however, that these efforts could succeed only if "the President seizes this opportunity to lead."[73] Finally, the New York publication charged that the Johnson administration was fighting poverty only with slogans. Recalling that Hubert Humphrey had called for a Marshall Plan for America when he gave a speech in Detroit, the editorial sarcastically described how the Vice-President had reinterpreted his prior remarks warning now "against 'checkbook solutions' which 'haven't always worked.' "[74] The harshest comment during this period was made in an editorial under the headline "A Vote for Jobs" in which the *Times* charged that "President Johnson's rigidity in clinging to his own inadequate proposals is based on a topsy-turvy set of priorities, in which military needs alone have no ceiling." The editorial went on to charge that a more adequate concept put forth by the Senate Labor Committee had "not yet penetrated the war-obsessed White House."[75]

The *Times* gave editorial support to the President on issues in which he was opposed by conservatives in both parties. For example, in one instance the *Times* editorialized in favor of gun-control legislation pushed by the administration.[76] In another editorial, the newspaper sided with the Johnson administration's version of a crime-control bill and questioned the House decision to strengthen, among other features, antiriot measures available to state governments.[77] Also, the *Times* supported the President and administration in their efforts to reform the National Guard, for example, better training for antiriot control and the recruitment of more blacks for Guard units.[78]

At first glance, the *Washington Post* seemed much more supportive of LBJ than the New York newspaper: Of ten relevant editorials seven were mostly supportive, two were critical, and one piece was ambiguous toward the President's riot-related positions. However, in examining the content of these editorials closely, one discovers great similarity between the positions of the *Post* and *Times*—both supported the President against his conservative opponents, namely in issues such as the antiriot bill, civil rights measures, and reform of the National Guard. Both newspapers were unhappy with what they saw as the lack of leadership on the part of Johnson in attacking the urban problems with massive antipoverty programs and expenditures. That the *Post* published many more editorials critical of conservatives in Congress, and either explicitly or implicitly supported Johnson's position, had to do mostly with the choice of topics: Four of the supportive editorials concerned the debate surrounding reform proposals for the National Guard that in the view of Cyrus Vance, General Throckmorton, and other witnesses of the Detroit events had proved to be "trigger happy" and thus unprepared for antiriot duty.[79] The *Post* and the *Times* supported the position of the President and his administration on this issue. The other supportive editorials attacked congressional Democrats and Republicans for rewriting the administration's anticrime proposal into an imprudent antiriot bill, and they recommended instead the civil rights measures that the Johnson administration pushed for in Congress.

While dedicating fewer editorials to the charge of inadequate leadership and initiative on the part of Johnson than the *Times,* and while not quite as outspoken as the editorial writers of the *Times* in their criticism of Johnson, the *Post* nevertheless got a critical attitude toward the President across in two editorials during this period. In one instance, the Washington newspaper criticized those in the administration (and although not mentioned—the President was among them) who had argued that rioters should not be rewarded by granting special aid to the particular urban areas. The *Post* lectured, "It is as though the slum were one perverse person now being called before the bar of judgment to plead guilty. In fact, if there were thousands who rioted there were tens of thousands who suffered terror and great loss in the holocaust."[80] In another editorial that praised the initiative of a new Urban Coalition, the *Post* was especially critical of Congress for ignoring a thousand delegates of that coalition that was meeting in Washington. However, in speaking of a "lackadaisical" response in the capital and in seconding Detroit Mayor Cavanagh's complaint of not discovering any "sense of urgency" in Washington, the *Post* implicated the President and his administration as well. The editorial stated that "National drive, national leadership must match local efforts and give it sustenance."[81] This touched on the charge that this leadership was not provided by the President—even without explicitly saying so.

Unlike the two East Coast newspapers, which opposed LBJ in some and supported him in other riot-related matters, the *Chicago Tribune* remained all the way critical. Eight of nine relevant editorials published during this period were critical of the President, the remaining piece was of ambiguous nature. The Detroit paper sided with critics of efforts by the administration to reform the National Guard, and it continued to attack the alleged use of federal antipoverty funds to incite riots, sarcastically calling Sargent Shriver "Generalissimo of the Great Society war on poverty."[82] An editorial headlined "The Harvest" blamed President Johnson along with Hubert Humphrey and Robert F. Kennedy for the violence in the slums. The *Tribune* summed up its view in the conclusion of the piece, stating: "when Mr. Johnson said in 1964, 'We are going to try to take all of the money that we think is unnecessarily being spent and take it from the "haves" and give it to the "have nots" that need it so much,' what kind of expectations did he think he was arousing? He can look about him and find the answer."[83] Warning of black militants such as Stokely Carmichael and H. Rap Brown, the *Tribune* demanded that it was "time to drop the permissive doctrines which condone the acts of rioters and seek to shift their guilt to the law-abiding majority which has not heaped rewards upon them."[84]

The East Coast newspapers based about the same amount of lines on supporters and critics of the President in riot-related matters with supporters having a tiny edge in both publications (see table 3.7). In the news coverage of the *Tribune*, however, critical sources had a space advantage over supporters of Johnson. With many conservative, liberal, and left critics as well as supporters of the President to choose from, the coverage reflected the pluralist debate of this period. The editorially completely critical *Tribune* had a news coverage that was less favorable from the President's point of view than that of the East Coast papers with their not quite as one-sided editorial positions.

Johnson and members of his administration were very active in the post-crisis debate, but congressional actors were not far behind in taking the initiative in riot-related issues. While administration sources were used for more lines in the three newspapers, congressional sources captured nearly

TABLE 3.7   Post-Crisis: Detroit Riots 1967 (Editorials Excluded)

Linage	For/Probably For	Neutral/ Ambiguous	Against/Probably Against	Total Lines
TIMES	33.7%	34.1%	32.2%	7,353
POST	28.7	43.1	28.2	4,651
TRIBUNE	26.5	42.4	31.1	4,562

TABLE 3.8   Linage Administration and Congressional Sources: Post Crisis

	Administration Sources	Congressional Sources	Total Lines
TIMES	67.3%	32.7%	3,081
POST	50.2	49.8	2,107
TRIBUNE	55.8	44.2	1,583

the same amount of space as administration sources in the *Post* and significant amounts in the *Tribune* and *Times* (see table 3.8).

While pro-Johnson sources made front page stories more often than
critics of the President in all three newspapers, the placement advantage
was much less dominant than during the crisis periods.

Finally, most of the journalistic descriptions, background information, and
news analyses did not reveal pro or con bias on the part of the media
sources.

SUMMARY

Even before Detroit's inner city exploded in a bloody riot, the summer of
1967 had experienced racial disturbances and a tense debate concerning the
causes and the handling of urban violence. Press coverage reflected significant opposition to the President's riot-related positions. Johnson's opponents
on the right and left of the political spectrum were very active and very
successful in gaining news coverage during a period in which the President
and members of his administration took a low-key wait-and-see attitude.
This was very costly in terms of news coverage: The print press covered
Johnson's opponents more extensively than the President and his supporters
with respect to riot-related issues.

With federal troops deployed in Detroit and a severe national crisis at
hand, news coverage changed dramatically, becoming much more favorable
from Johnson's standpoint. News sources who were clearly in the President's corner dominated compared with Johnson's opponents. This was the
result of both the administration's efforts to get the Detroit riot under
control and a sudden reluctance on the part of many of Johnson's opponents
to criticize the President during an acute crisis.

Once it was clear that the acute emergency in Detroit had subsided into
a lingering crisis period, Johnson's critics began to express their opposition
and to appear in the news again. This was especially the case for militant
black leaders and some liberal politicians in contrast to other establishment
politicians who remained mostly on the sidelines.

As soon as the crisis was declared over, the news coverage reflected a
quick revival of the conflict and debate that had characterized the weeks
before the Detroit riot. Although for very different reasons, conservatives
and liberals in both political parties and moderate and radical black leaders
readily expressed their dissatisfaction with the President's riot-related positions.

While readers of any of the three newspapers may have gotten a fairly
good picture of the political lineup for and against the President's policies

during the four pre-through post-crisis time periods, there were significant differences in the newspaper coverage regarding source selection and space considerations. These differences were consistent with the riot-related positions expressed in the newspapers' editorials.

4

THE THREE MILE ISLAND ACCIDENT

THREAT OF THE UNTHINKABLE: NUCLEAR MELTDOWN

March 28, 1979. Most people living in the shadow of the huge cooling towers of the Three Mile Island nuclear power plant are sleeping, when at 3.53 A.M. the burst of venting steam disturbs the tranquillity around the 600-acre island just eleven miles southeast of Pennsylvania's capital, Harrisburg. Neighbors of the plant are used to this kind of noise, and so are those 60 employees of Metropolitan Edison who are working the current night shift. At 4 A.M., seven minutes after the burst, the technicians in the control room of Unit Two are alerted: Red warning lights begin to blink, a siren sounds its alarm. There is no panic, not even excitement. An alarm like this one is not unusual. And on all previous occasions, the technicians on duty have been able to solve the problems at hand. Thus, the men understandably assume that the present situation is no different than any of the other "events" before.

Technicians begin to push and pull buttons trusting that the computer-guided backup system will take care of whatever the trouble is. However, soon there are signals that this is not the case: the computer begins to print out a flow of question marks indicating that the machine, supposed to have the answers, is not programmed to deal with whatever is wrong. Some time later, workers find radioactive water that has leaked onto the floor of the containment building around the nuclear reactor. Still later, radioactive gases escape into the fresh morning air of the Susquehanna Valley.

Neither the regular night shift members in the plant nor the hastily assembled high-level Metropolitan Edison executives and technical experts know at this moment the full extent of the problem. With the cooling system malfunctioning, the reactor core heats up rapidly and dangerously, and, as B. Drummond Ayres Jr. will weeks later observe, "The unthinkable is beginning to happen in the bowels of one of this country's 72 nuclear reactors, and no one realizes it."[1] The "unthinkable" is the threat of a catastrophic nuclear meltdown of the reactor's core.

Although Metropolitan Edison (Met Ed) notifies state officials and the

Nuclear Regulatory Commission (NRC) in Washington and although the NRC
dispatches a team of investigators and technicians to the site of the accident
and, at the same time, informs the White House, by Wednesday's end
neither the power company nor state or federal officials have expressed
alarm over the accident. Met Ed Vice-President Jack Herbein assures, "I
wouldn't call it a very serious accident at this point." And NRC investigator
Charles Gallina affirms, "The reactor is stable. . . . It is in a safe condition."[2]

The news media report the accident, but based on the information provided by Metropolitan Edison and the first assessment given by NRC specialists at the scene, none of the broadcast and published accounts are
alarming. The next day, Thursday, seems to bear out the low-key approach
of the previous day. Governor Richard Thornburgh advises residents of the
area that "there is no cause for alarm nor any reason to disrupt your daily
routine."[3]

There is a dramatic change on Friday, when early in the morning, and
again shortly before noon, more radiation is discharged into the air. Governor Thornburgh, no longer assured by the information provided by the
power company, cautions those persons residing within a ten-mile radius of
the power plant to stay indoors, until it can be determined whether an
evacuation is needed. Soon thereafter traffic jams demonstrate that many
persons have begun to flee the area. President Jimmy Carter rushes Harold
Denton of the NRC as his personal representative and crisis manager to the
scene. In Washington, Dr. Roger Mattson of the NRC tells a Senate subcommittee that the Three Mile Island accident poses "some risk of meltdown."[4] Experts are concerned that a large hydrogen bubble that has formed
in the reactor could interfere with efforts to cool the unit down. If that
proves to be the case, a nuclear catastrophe lies ahead—a meltdown of
nuclear fuel through the steel floor of the containment building and, eventually, the release of radioactive gases into the atmosphere. In the CBS
Evening News broadcast of this "Black Friday," Walter Cronkite gives his
audience the bad news, observing, "The world has never known a day quite
like today. . . . And the horror tonight is that it could get much worse."[5]

The emergency in the Pennsylvania power plant has become a national
crisis.[6]

A PRESIDENT UNDER ATTACK

When "Black Friday" sent a shock wave through America and the rest of
the world, when the U.S. President acknowledged the national character of
the Three Mile Island accident by dispatching Harold Denton to the scene of

the emergency and by assuring Pennsylvania Governor Thornburgh all possible federal assistance, the presidency of Jimmy Carter had been in trouble for some time. In early March, in an article characterizing the state of affairs, *Time* magazine summed up Carter's dilemma in one single sentence: "There is a pervasive sense at home and also abroad that Carter is not in command."[7] At the same time, *Newsweek* came to the conclusion that a "worldscape of troubles stretching from Mexico to Indochina ha[s] brought him [Carter] under attack, unmatched since Harry Truman's day, for ineptness and irresolution in pursuing America's interests abroad."[8]

Although the President rightfully countered that events and changes within other countries could and should no longer be managed according to American patterns, he was unable to regain the trust of his fellow Americans. There was turmoil in the Middle East and growing worries about the Khomeini revolution in Iran, where gunmen had kidnapped and released a U.S. embassy guard. There was trouble in Afghanistan, where U.S. Ambassador Adolph Dubs had been assassinated. There was unease over Vietnam, where a Chinese invasion had taken place causing Moscow to threaten military retaliation against China.

The alleged "do-nothing" role of the President, his growing image as a weak leader, had already encouraged presidential hopeful Ronald Reagan to remark sarcastically, "I'm beginning to wonder if the symbol of the United States pretty soon isn't going to be an ambassador with a flag under his arm and climbing into the escape helicopter."[9] Other Republicans such as John Connally, George Bush, and Howard Baker, getting ready for the presidential election year 1980, were not kinder in their attacks on the President.

In the weeks preceding the Three Mile Island accident, Jimmy Carter scored one stunning foreign policy success: Recognizing that the negotiated peace treaty between Egypt and Israel was in jeopardy, the President undertook a spontaneous and risky six-day journey into the Middle East. Miraculously, Jimmy Carter returned with the agreement of both sides to sign the historic peace pact. For a change, there was praise and applause for his achievement. However, the positive reaction to his personal Middle East success did not translate—as the White House had hoped—into a lasting and broad support for the President. While 44 percent of the public gave President Carter high marks for his handling of foreign policy at this point, a nine-point increase within one month, his overall approval rate remained at a dismal 43 percent.[10]

Many Americans considered the President to be a poor manager of pressing domestic problems—the economy and the energy crisis. With a rapidly climbing inflation rate and growing signs of a severe oil shortage, Jimmy Carter was unable to shake his reputation as a weak leader. Even with the dream-come-true spectacle of Menachem Begin and Anwar Sadat signing the Israeli-Egyptian peace treaty in the White House, most Americans were unwilling to forget that their pocketbooks were hurting.

Not only Republicans criticized the President harshly; many fellow Democrats did not look kindly upon the Carter presidency in the early months of 1979. Looking ahead to the election in the fall of the following year, "dump Carter" movements began to form, and there was much talk about the possibility of Senator Edward Kennedy challenging the President in the Democratic primaries.

Such was the troubled political predicament of the 39th U.S. President when he learned of the worst nuclear reactor accident up to that date at Three Mile Island.

PRESIDENT CARTER AND THE MEDIA

In May 1977, the Sunday magazine of the *New York Times* published a cartoon on its cover that depicted a broadly smiling President Carter in front of a TV studio control console with his picture on each one of the screens. The accompanying text—"Maestro of the Media"—summarized the perception of the press–president relationship during the first few months of the Carter presidency.[11] Like most chief executives, this President, too, was enjoying a honeymoon period with other political actors—among them the press—at the outset of his term. Viewed from the White House, this cooperative relationship seemed to work especially well as far as the electronic media were concerned. Television had been very helpful in transforming "Jimmy who?" into the winner of the Democratic primaries and the presidential election of November 1976, and television continued to cover the fairy-tale story of the southern peanut farmer turned president, once the Carters had settled in the White House. Tebbel and Watts have pointed out that "[a]lthough they later came to revise their opinion, the network people at the beginning thought they had a natural—'a sensational performer' as one of them termed it."[12]

After leaving the White House Jody Powell, who served as Carter's press secretary, complained bitterly about his experiences with what he perceived as an unfair press. What galled him especially was the observation that members of the press, although predominantly identifying themselves as Democrats, treated conservative Republican Ronald Reagan better than the Democrat Jimmy Carter.[13] Actually, complaints about the press not laying a glove on the President were voiced early on in the Carter term, too.[14] However, in late summer of 1977 there was an abrupt change in the press–president relationship as a result of the Burt Lance affair, which eventually led to the resignation of the Budget Director, one of Carter's close friends. The revelations about Lance's alleged wrongdoings resulted in a flood of stories the White House did not appreciate, while the President's decision to stubbornly defend his longtime friend made matters worse. It was during this period that the relationship between the White House and the media turned sour; and that remained more or less the state of affairs for most of what remained in Carter's term.

Hedley Donovan, who for a year worked as a senior adviser in the White House, found Jimmy Carter "not exceptionally thin-skinned about the press."[15] Yet, after having lost the presidency to Ronald Reagan, neither Jimmy Carter himself nor his closest aides hid their disappointment, regret, and anger over the way the media covered the Carter presidency. Looking back at his years in the White House, Carter blamed his status as an outsider in Washington for his troubles with the establishment actors in the capital, observing: "Nowhere within the press, Congress, or the ranks of the Washington power structure were there any long-established friends and acquaintances who would naturally come to our defense in a public debate on a controversial issue."[16] Having observed the White House from within, Donovan concluded that "the President and his inner circle had a basically low opinion of the press, a mistrust of its motives and a misunderstanding of its role."[17]

It seems that Carter and the young Georgians who had plotted his candidacy and had masterfully executed their own blueprint for the presidential campaign did not manage the President's relationship with the press all that well once they moved into the White House. Jody Powell's remark that the press did not grant President Carter a honeymoon but merely "a one-night stand" was contrary to what more objective observers concluded.[18]

Increasingly plagued by problems and crises at home and abroad and by a growing perception that President Carter was a weak leader, the White House was more and more faced with press coverage it resented. Instead of resorting to the clever media exploitation of primary and election campaigns, those in the White House grew bitter and testy vis-à-vis the press, and Powell did not hide his feelings toward the end of Carter's term.

Once the damage was done, even efforts to improve the relationship did little to change the basic discontent on both sides. Neither White House suppers for publishers, editors, and selected reporters nor the decision to bring communications expert Gerald Rafshoon into 1600 Pennsylvania Avenue improved the situation much. And it did not serve the President well when he heeded the advice of aides to curtail the number of press conferences. This was the one format in which Carter put his best foot forward. Years after the 39th President had left Washington, White House correspondents recalled his good command of facts in the question-and-answer format of news conferences. Asked why Carter hadn't held more of them, Jody Powell answered, "We just didn't think they were good for us."[19]

Finally, during 1979—the year before the presidential election—the White House was resentful of what it perceived to be a bias on the part of the influential liberal Eastern press in favor of the presumed challenger Senator Edward M. Kennedy. In a way, what the Carter White House felt in this respect in 1979 was very similar to President Johnson's view of the supposedly close ties between the media and Robert F. Kennedy, especially during the preelection year 1967.

MORE NUCLEAR POWER AND MORE SAFETY

In the spring of 1977, the White House released the Carter administration's "National Energy Plan," which outlined ways to deal with and solve the growing energy crisis in the United States. In an introduction to what he called "The Plan" President Carter warned that the energy problem "grows steadily worse—even when it is not in the news." "The Plan" included, among other energy sources, the further development of nuclear power. Acknowledging that there are risks involved in the operation of light-water reactors, "The Plan" proposed "additional actions" to improve the safety of nuclear power plants. The Carter administration wanted both more nuclear power and more safety. According to the energy plan, "Today [April 1977], 63 nuclear power plants provide about 10 percent of U.S. supply of electricity. By 1985, an additional 75 nuclear plants already planned or in construction could be in operation, and nuclear power could provide as much as 20 percent of electricity supply."[20]

During the months preceding the Three Mile Island accident, two measures taken by the Nuclear Regulatory Commission fueled the ongoing discussion over safety and risk of nuclear plants: In January of 1979, the NRC revoked a "Reactor Safety Study" by Dr. Norman Rasmussen, and a few weeks later, in March, the agency ordered the shutdown of five nuclear plants. In each case, proponents and opponents of nuclear energy debated the NRC decisions.

Although it was an independent agency, the Nuclear Regulatory Commission—formerly the Atomic Energy Commission—reflected the nuclear power policy as articulated in the Carter administration's "National Energy Plan." While encouraging an increase in nuclear energy, there was also more emphasis on safety precautions. Indeed, as Richard Halloran pointed out in a *Times* news analysis, there was a division within the Carter administration concerning this issue: While Energy Secretary James Schlesinger and officials in his department advocated the increase of nuclear energy from light-water reactors, influential Carter advisers within the White House opposed the rapid expansion of nuclear energy.[21]

While the President supported the development of more nuclear energy, his "Plan" had explicitly directed the NRC to take a number of measures to improve the overall safety of light-water reactors.[22] Having appointed three of the five NRC commissioners—among them Commission chairman Joseph M. Hendrie—as well as the NRC director of nuclear reactor regulation, Harold Denton, the President could be confident that his approach to the question of nuclear energy was carried out by the regulatory agency.

By promoting both more nuclear energy and improved safety regulations the Nuclear Regulatory Agency and the Carter administration were often the targets of criticism by proponents and opponents of nuclear power plants. While the advocates of nuclear energy were critical of certain safety measures such as the precautionary shutdown of plants, foes of nuclear energy opposed the President for supporting nuclear energy and for demanding a drastic shortening of the time it took to put a new nuclear plant into operation. Given this policy, the administration and the NRC seemed never able to please either side completely during the months before the Three Mile Island crisis.

The three newspapers covered the two mentioned NRC measures (the revoking of the Rasmussen Study and the shutdown of five nuclear plants) but the *New York Times* and the *Washington Post* provided a much more extensive and prominent coverage of these decisions and the debate they provoked than did the *Chicago Tribune*. For example, both East Coast newspapers carried the news that the Nuclear Regulatory Commission had repudiated the findings of Dr. Rasmussen's report of 1975 on their front pages while the Chicago newspaper published this news in a short article on page five.[23] The earlier study had concluded that a reactor accident was as unlikely as a meteor falling on a city. While not claiming that there was a higher risk of a reactor disaster, the NRC now let it be known "that the bounds of error were greater than initially believed."[24]

While the *Times* and the *Post* published a number of articles that detailed the positions of the regulatory agency and of advocates and critics of nuclear energy inside and outside of Congress, readers of the *Tribune* had little opportunity to learn about the opposing positions concerning the issue of nuclear energy. The East Coast newspapers used sources representing advocates and opponents of nuclear power, for example, the "Atomic Industrial Forum," the lobbying arm of the nuclear industry, and the "Union of Concerned Scientists," an antinuclear expert group. Also, friends and foes in Congress were frequently quoted in the East Coast publications. Aside from reporting about the NRC measures in January and March, the *Tribune* published only one short article as a follow-up to the shutdown of five nuclear plants by the NRC. The headline of this piece, "A-Plant Shutdown Rapped," revealed its content: Advocates of nuclear energy criticized the plant closings as unnecessary. Antinuclear scientists who complained that the NRC should have acted much earlier were mentioned at the end of the story in a few lines.[25]

This was the state of affairs in the debate and coverage concerning the question of nuclear energy's safety, when the accident in Reactor 2 of the Three Mile Island power plant occurred on March 28, 1979. In their editions of March 29 and 30, the newspapers carried accounts of the nuclear calamity on their front pages, but none of the publications treated the radiation leak in Pennsylvania as a major crisis or as the number-one news story of the day.

While much of the reporting during the two days preceding the acute crisis was based on sources at the accident site near Harrisburg—namely officials of Metropolitan Edison and of the state government, NRC sources at the Three Mile Island plant and in Washington were cited as well. All of these sources seemed to follow the line of Met Ed spokesman Jack Herbein who assured the public, "We didn't have any 'China Syndrome' possibility with the events at Three Mile Island."[26] "China Syndrome" was a reference to a motion picture in release at the time which depicted the meltdown of a nuclear reactor core. NRC officials Hendrie and Denton in Washington conveyed the impression that the emergency in Pennsylvania was understood and under control—surely acting on behalf of the White House, which had been informed by the agency shortly after the NRC had been informed of the mishap.

The *Times* and *Post* publicized the reactions of two prominent Democrats to the crisis in Pennsylvania: Senator Edward Kennedy and California Governor Jerry Brown. The New York newspaper mentioned a letter Kennedy had written to Energy Secretary James Schlesinger in a front page story. Probably referring to President Carter's and Schlesinger's initiative to shorten the licensing process for nuclear plants, Kennedy pointed to the Three Mile Island accident and argued, "It is more important to build these plants safely than to build them quickly."[27] And Jerry Brown, who like Kennedy was preparing to challenge the President in the 1980 primaries, lashed out at the proponents of nuclear energy, assuring that he considered "this [the risk of a disaster in connection with a nuclear power plant] as a major issue in the decade ahead."[28]

However, these statements with implicit criticism of Carter's position on nuclear energy were made and publicized at a time when the Three Mile Island event had not yet blown up into a major crisis.

Relevant editorials in the *Times* during the pre-crisis weeks assessed the pros and cons of nuclear energy. Commenting on the NRC's change of mind concerning the Rasmussen study, the *Times* concluded, "Repudiation of the Rasmussen report does not mean that the nation should shut down all reactors, or even slow nuclear growth. It does put a heavier burden on regulators, manufacturers and utilities to insure that reactors are built and operated safely."[29] This was pretty much in line with Carter's "more and safer nuclear energy" stand. Assuming that the NRC, with a majority of Carter appointees in its top positions, acted according to the President's request for more safety measures, another *Times* editorial seemed somewhat supportive of the administration's line, when it stated that "the commission [NRC] took the only responsible course [in ordering the shutdown of five nuclear plants]."[30] Under the headline "The Credibility Meltdown" a third, ambiguous editorial offered a first assessment of the Three Mile Island accident that at this moment seemed about over. According to the *Times* the event in Pennsylvania had raised many questions about safety and risk of nuclear energy that needed to be answered.[31] Of three editorials published during the weeks before the crisis, two were somewhat supportive of Carter's policy and one piece was ambiguous.

Commenting on the NRC decision to order the shutdown of five nuclear plants, the *Post* supported the NRC decision to order the closing down of the reactors. Having done that, the newspaper drove home the point that other energy sources were risky as well, concluding that "it's curious to think that, if the same health standards [as in nuclear safety] were applied to coal and the power plants that burn it, half the country would be dining by candlelight tonight—and not voluntarily."[32] It seemed that this conclusion weakened the earlier agreement with the shutdown order. A second editorial looked at the possible consequences of the accident at the Three Mile Island plant before the full extent of the emergency was known. The *Post* concluded, "Since there are no risk-free solutions, the most sensible course is to continue to rely on a variety of different sources of power, including nuclear—and keep developing them slowly and cautiously."[33] The first part of this statement sounded very much like Carter's position as described in "The Plan," which endorsed nuclear energy while not denying the risks involved. However, considering that the repeated reference to the necessity to expand nuclear energy "slowly and cautiously" was possibly an implicit criticism of the Carter administration's effort to adopt a shorter licensing process for nuclear pants, this editorial apparently took an overall ambiguous stand toward Carter's policy. Thus, the *Post* published two somewhat ambiguous editorials during the months preceding the acute crisis.

While agreeing that any uncertainty in the area of nuclear plants "must be resolved on the side of safety" the *Chicago Tribune,* in its only relevant editorial of this period, cited Senator J. Bennett Johnson of Louisiana who had called the shutdown of five nuclear plants "absolutely asinine."[34] Obviously agreeing with Johnson, the *Tribune* was critical of the NRC decision and implicitly of the Carter administration's request for more safety measures in the field of nuclear plants.

Although those in charge of the editorial pages at the three newspapers reacted somewhat differently in case of the NRC decision to shut down five plants, they all recognized the priority of safety considerations. The *Times* clearly came out in favor of the decision, the *Post,* in spite of agreeing with the regulators, was more ambiguous, and the *Tribune* sided with those who believed that safety concerns had led to an overreaction in Washington. The latter view was especially held by the nuclear power plant industry.

The news coverage of the three papers was fairly similar in that sources with neutral or ambiguous attitudes vis-à-vis the President's policy in this area captured more linage than pro and con sources. However, the neutral/ambiguous sources fared far better in the *Times* and the *Tribune* while supporters of the administration's nuclear power positions were most extensively covered in the *Post.* This was the result of the *Post's* tendency to concentrate on NRC officials as news sources who were perceived to articulate the White House line. This was true before and after the accident. In contrast, the *Times* and the *Tribune* concentrated more on local and state sources at the accident site; their attitude toward the administration was mostly ambiguous at this time. The East Coast papers covered critics of NRC decisions and Carter's policy among pro- and antinuclear power forces extensively while the *Tribune* offered a very limited coverage and did not reflect the debate that was going on concerning nuclear power (see table 4.1).

While editorializing differently on specific measures and events, none of the newspapers questioned the underlying policy, and none expressed enthusiastic support. The somewhat supportive, somewhat ambiguous stance of the two East Coast newspapers was compatible with their overall coverage, which paid attention to both proponents and opponents of nuclear power. Of the three newspapers the *Tribune* was the only one to criticize a

TABLE 4.1 Pre-Crisis Coverage: Three Mile Island Accident (Editorials Excluded)

Linage	For/Probably For	Neutral/ Ambiguous	Against/Probably Against	Total Lines
TIMES	13.4%	76.0%	10.6%	1,947
POST	38.7	40.0	21.3	2,191
TRIBUNE	25.8	69.4	4.8	689

NRC order to shut down several nuclear power plants which was in tune with Carter's policy guidelines; in spite of this, the *Tribune's* relevant news coverage was more advantageous from the President's point of view than that of the East Coast newspapers. At first sight this seems to indicate that there was no relationship between editorial position and coverage. However, the *Tribune's* failure to cover the ongoing nuclear power debate in the weeks before the Three Mile Island accident may well have been influenced by its position in support of nuclear power during a period in which antinuclear forces were very active and vocal.

In the three months before the Three Mile Island crisis, the NRC was the dominating source in the coverage of nuclear energy issues. Given the fact that the majority of the commission and its safety director were appointed by Carter, the NRC was perceived as carrying out the President's policy—as being part of the administration. No wonder that administration sources captured the giant share of lines in a comparison with congressional sources (see table 4.2).

In all three newspapers sources supportive of the administration's stand were mentioned more often in front page stories than critical sources.

Journalistic descriptions and news analyses in the overall coverage of relevant topics did not reveal support for or opposition to the Carter administration's policies and actions.

"U.S. AIDES SEE RISK OF MELTDOWN"

After two days of following the experts at the scene who had treated the accident in the Three Mile Island nuclear power plant as an unfortunate but not a national emergency, and beginning with their editions of March 31, newspapers reported that the nation was faced with a major crisis never before experienced here or elsewhere: the danger of a nuclear core meltdown with the release of large amounts of radiation in the area. (The acute

TABLE 4.2   Linage Administration and Congressional Sources: Pre-Crisis

	Administration Sources	Congressional Sources	Total Lines
TIMES	79.8%	20.2%	436
POST	85.7	14.3	463
TRIBUNE	89.4	10.6	236

emergency lasted three days and was reported in newspaper editions of March 31, April 1, and April 2.) Moreover, the moment the experts of the Nuclear Regulatory Commission spoke of the meltdown risk, the possibility of such a catastrophe was driven home to all Americans—especially to those who were residing close to any one of the nuclear plants in the United States.

Of the three newspapers the *New York Times* carried the most alarming front page headline: "U.S. Aides See a Risk of Meltdown at Pennsylvania Nuclear Plant; More Radioactive Gas is Released."[35] In a headline that spread across the whole front page, the *Washington Post* reported, "Mass Evacuation of A-Plant Area Rejected." But in a less prominent second headline, the publication also revealed, "Reactor Heat Raises Danger of Blast or Meltdown."[36] Another front page article, a feature by Ward Sinclair and Warren Brown, captured the dimensions of the acute crisis in its opening sentence: "The day that no one wanted and few believed possible—the day the nuclear power era would drive people from their homes—arrived here today."[37]

The *Chicago Tribune* tried to assure readers that the "Chance of Atomic Reactor Meltdown [is] Called 'Remote'," but the fact that this was reported in a double headline across the front page demonstrated to readers that the accident in Pennsylvania was now a crisis of national proportions. Indeed, the second paragraph in the *Tribune's* lead story explained the risk believed to be present at the Pennsylvania accident site. "In a meltdown," Bill Neikirk and Casey Bukro wrote, "the fuel core of a nuclear reactor becomes super-heated into a molten, radioactive fireball. It is regarded as the ultimate disaster for a nuclear power station. Such a catastrophe has never happened."[38]

Whether the headlines were more alarming or more reassuring, the overall reporting in the three newspapers left no doubt that a nasty accident had become a major crisis. The journalistic descriptions of the situation at the Three Mile Island plant focused on a giant bubble of hydrogen gas that prevented cooling water from reaching the hot uranium fuel rods in the reactor and made for the possibility of a core meltdown.

Although local and state authorities were involved in the management of the emergency situation in Pennsylvania, the nation and the press looked at the President to take a leading role in managing the crisis. By using electronic and print media to communicate with a fearful and nervous population, the White House was successful in telling Americans that the President personally was involved in the crisis management. All three newspapers reported that Harold Denton of the NRC was the President's stand-in crisis manager at the scene of the accident, and all three publications described various White House initiatives in this matter. For example, the *Times* reported that the President had "ordered the chairman of the N.R.C., Joseph Hendrie, to err on the side of safety." In addition, the New York newspaper wrote that the President had established a special task force within the National Security Council "to act as a clearinghouse for information in the case." [39] The *Post* quoted Carter as having said that the events at the Pennsylvania power plant "will probably lead inexorably toward even more stringent design mechanisms and standards [for nuclear plants]." [40] And the *Tribune* detailed a number of steps President Carter had taken to assist local and state officials in the crisis region, for instance, sending specialists of the Food and Drug Administration and federal radiation experts into the area and making Environmental Protection Agency aircraft available to measure radiation levels. [41]

More importantly, Jimmy Carter and the First Lady flew to Pennsylvania and visited the accident site and the community mostly affected by the mishap to demonstrate that the President, a nuclear engineer by profession, was personally involved and interested in the management of the crisis. For this reason, Carter addressed several thousand area residents who had gathered in the Middletown Borough Hall and toured the Three Mile Island plant and control room. Even before the Carters traveled to the site of the nuclear plant, the press had reported that the President was planning to go to the scene of the emergency, and a day later, after the visit had taken place, the newspapers described it in stories and photographs. The President as well as his representative at the accident scene, Harold Denton, received a significant share of media attention during the acute crisis days. And while neither man could or did minimize the potential danger and the possible need for mass evacuation, Carter and others around him made efforts to encourage the people immediately affected to remain calm, to wait for further instructions, and above all to avoid panic.

The media continued to look to Metropolitan Edison officials and to Governor Thornburgh and his staff to be informed about the status of the emergency; the President's stand-in crisis manager Denton began to emerge more and more as the most important and the most trusted source of information as the acute crisis continued. Governor Thornburgh seemed to appreciate this development, after initially complaining about conflicting information he had received, presumably from Met Ed officials and NRC experts trying to sort out the situation at the stricken reactor. After communicating with the President, the Governor, according to a *Times* report, made it known that Harold Denton was going to "dispel some of the multidirectional reports or facts." [42] And in a portrait about Denton, the *Times* revealed that a "hot line" communications link had been established between the White House and crisis-manager Denton at the Pennsylvania crisis-center. [43]

There were reports of initiatives in Congress to reexamine the whole question of nuclear energy and the role of regulators in this area and there were descriptions from the afflicted region about residents leaving their homes, about fear and anger among affected Pennsylvanians, about measures taken and considered by local and state officials. Many of these press accounts reflected a great uncertainty about the extent of what had happened at Three Mile Island and what could take place in the worst case scenario of a core meltdown. [44]

Journalists had difficulties in sorting out the facts concerning the crisis at hand and to follow the often times contradictory experts' descriptions of what was taking place in the stricken reactor and what the consequences were and could be. Mostly, the discrepancy in information was caused by the tendency of Met Ed officials to minimize the risks involved and the willingness of NRC experts to speak about the possibility of the "unthinkable" happening. According to two observers, "[a]t the beginning, at least, the vast majority of reporters had no idea what anybody was talking about. Anchorless on a sea of rads and rems and roentgens, of core vessels and containments and cooling systems, they built their stories around the discrepancies between sources, confident that the news, when they finally came to understand it, would center on the facts in dispute." Observers on the scene pointed out that "[e]ven biased sources were scarce." After one press conference in Harrisburg, "anti-nuclear experts Ernest Sternglass and George Wald. . . took off again. . . [And t]he nuclear industry wasn't afraid of radiation; it was afraid of reporters."[45]

At the height of the Three Mile Island crisis, Energy Secretary James Schlesinger reaffirmed the Carter Administration's support for nuclear power, stating that despite the Pennsylvania accident nuclear energy remained "an essential element" of the nation's energy supply.[46] The few voices expressing antinuclear views and anti-Carter sentiments were on several occasions mentioned in the coverage of one or another of the three newspapers. Thus, it was reported that California Governor Jerry Brown had demanded the closing of a nuclear plant in his state in view of the Three Mile Island accident before he had flown to New Hampshire where he planned to challenge Jimmy Carter in the Democratic primary eleven months later.[47] When activists demonstrated in front of the White House against "Politicians, Profiteers, Nuclear Criminals" and advising those inside the White House that "Nuclear Power Won't Fly," their actions and similar initiatives in other parts of the country were covered.[48]

The uncertainty surrounding the Three Mile Island crisis and the difficulty in assessing its meaning for the nation's nuclear energy policy seemed to have been felt by those in charge of the editorial pages. The *Times* and the *Tribune* did not publish a relevant editorial during the three days of the acute crisis, while the *Post* in its sole relevant editorial piece of the period remained somewhat ambiguous in a first effort to assess the consequences of the accident on policies and politics. The Washington newspaper concluded, "There is one kind of danger, perhaps larger than most Americans previously thought, in continuing with nuclear power. There is another kind of danger, perhaps to other people, in turning to other power sources or to none at all." While criticizing neither Carter's policy in this area nor his handling of the current crisis, the *Post* did point out that ultimately the President would have to address the problems at hand. Criticizing the President's overall management style, the editorial lectured that "[i]t would be helpful to the country to hear President Carter address the choices now emerging. It would be particularly helpful if Mr. Carter were to rise above the technical and administrative quarrels that usually preoccupy him and address the larger principles of policy here—those principles that, taken together, comprise the ethics of risk."[49]

The crisis coverage in three papers was very similar in that each newspaper based more than two thirds of the relevant linage on sources with either neutral or ambiguous attitudes toward the President's's crisis management or his crisis-related policies. In addition, in all three publications sources supportive of the Carter administration's crisis-related actions and policies were used for far more lines than were critical sources. The little opposition to Carter's stand on nuclear energy that was voiced and covered came mostly from antinuclear activists. This kind of coverage fit the expected pattern during the acute phase of a crisis (see table 4.3).

The ambiguous stand taken by the *Washington Post* in the sole editorial it published during this period and the unwillingness of the two other newspapers to make editorial comments during the three days of the acute crisis says much about the prevailing uncertainty concerning the nuclear accident. Given this situation, the reluctance to express opinions about crisis management and, even more so, about related policies during this critical time was understandable. This ambiguous or wait-and-see attitude was certainly com-

TABLE 4.3   Acute Crisis Coverage: Three Miles Island Accident (Editorials Excluded)

Linage	For/Probably For	Neutral/ Ambiguous	Against/Probably Against	Total Lines
TIMES	29.5%	67.1%	3.4%	3,776
POST	17.6	79.7	2.7	2,194
TRIBUNE	16.7	79.4	3.9	1,389

patible with coverage in which sources falling into the neutral-ambiguous category dominated, and pro-administration sources were dominant vis-à-vis critics.

Not surprisingly, sources in the executive branch were used much more often and captured far more lines than congressional sources. Directly involved in the management of the Three Mile Island emergency, the President, members of his administration, as well as officials of the NRC who were in close contact with Carter, were major sources of information (see table 4.4).

Sources supportive of the President's crisis management and related policy were mentioned in front page stories much more often than critical sources.

Except for a very positive portrait of Denton at the Three Mile Island crisis site, a piece that reflected somewhat favorably on the President who had appointed him,[50] all lines attributable to journalistic sources fell into the neutral/ambiguous category in all three publications.

"NUCLEAR PLANT PERIL EASES"

After three days of an intense crisis atmosphere there was a significant change in the status of the Three Mile Island situation. The hydrogen bubble in the crippled reactor had, as crisis manager, Harold Denton told journalists, "all but disappeared."[51] The *Chicago Tribune* summarized the good news in a front page article under the headline "Nuclear Plant Peril Eases." The two East Coast newspapers, too, reported the change for the better on their front pages; all three publications conveyed to the public that the dramatic shrinkage of the gas bubble had relieved "the crisis atmosphere in this still nervous region."[52] The acute crisis with its risk of a nuclear core meltdown had given way to a lingering emergency. (This phase lasted seven days and was reported in the newspapers' editions of April 3, through 9.)

TABLE 4.4   Linage Administration and Congressional Sources: Acute Crisis

	Administration Sources	Congressional Sources	Total Lines
TIMES	80.8%	19.2%	844
POST	82.7	17.3	463
TRIBUNE	100.0	—	232

During this period precautionary measures, for example, the advice to pregnant women and small children to stay away from the stricken area, remained and additional steps were prepared in the event of worsening conditions in the plant. While Denton and other NRC officials were successful in relieving some of the tensions and anxieties, they felt no doubt that the crisis was not over yet. Instead, there was still grave concern about the high radiation levels within the reactor containment building and the need to cool down the stricken reactor.

Given the remaining uncertainties, the newspapers still seemed reluctant to take a strong pro or con stand toward the administration's role in the crisis and its overall nuclear energy position. The Washington newspaper published two editorials, the *Times* and *Tribune* one editorial each during this period. The three papers editorialized in support of a careful and competent investigation of the Three Mile Island problem and a fresh look at the nuclear power. Advising the President to appoint a blue-ribbon commission to ask and answer all necessary questions, the *Times* argued that "whatever the final decision, it cannot be sensibly reached in feverish haste."[53] Since the President had already appointed a task force to investigate the nuclear accident and had not suggested any dramatic measures concerning his nuclear energy policy, it seemed that the editorial was compatible with his stand. The same was true for the editorial in the *Tribune*, which recommended an investigation by an expert panel to be appointed by the President and a prudent look at the issues surrounding nuclear energy. According to the *Tribune* the lesson to be learned from the Pennsylvania crisis was "that while it is naive to believe we can have a risk-free society, it is equally foolish to try to talk about atomic power generation as if it were virtually without risk."[54]

The *Post*, too, asked for "a thorough reconsideration of the safety standards and practices and engineering assumptions that underlie the present and future generations of nuclear reactors." While that was in tune with the President's appointment of a federal investigative task force, the Washington newspaper referred favorably to the handling of the crisis. In one editorial, the newspaper mentioned its "impression that the federal government generally, not just the NRC, rose pretty well to the grisly challenge of dealing with the emergency,"[55] And in a second piece the *Post* commended Denton as the "infinitely more straightforward spokesman [compared with the Metropolitan Edison spokesman] of the Nuclear Regulatory Commission, a kind of one-man Greek chorus."[56] It seemed that the Washington newspaper was somewhat more forthright in expressing support for the President than the *Times* and the *Tribune*. However, in no case was there a direct expression of support for Carter's role during the crisis nor for his related policies.

Although the gravest danger was thought to have passed—at least for

the time being—Denton and other NRC officials remained the most authoritative and most widely used sources when it came to informing the news
media and through them the public about the situation at Three Mile Island.
While continuing to calm the fears, these experts were perceived to be
candid and to give the correct information the President himself had asked
for and promised to the public. The press reported that in order to "head off
a credibility crisis caused by the persistent flurry of conflicting reports, the
Carter administration . . . slapped a gag order on the operators of the Three
Mile Island nuclear plant."[57] The White House made efforts to be perceived
as a driving force in getting to the bottom of the problem, for instance, by
establishing panels and mechanisms to investigate the nuclear mishap and in
the process to find answers to the many questions surrounding the nuclear
accident. As a result, President Carter and other members of his administration remained very much in the news. For example, the newspapers mentioned that the President had arranged the establishment of a federal task
force to begin studying the accident. The papers also reported the President's announcement that an independent commission would be established
"to investigate the causes of the accident at the Three Mile Island reactor
and to recommend safety improvements for all nuclear power plants in the
United States."[58]

Federal departments and agencies were quick to report first findings
about causes and consequences of the Pennsylvania crisis. The media took
note when NRC staffers revealed that, as the *Post* put it in its front page
story, the "extended shutdown of auxiliary cooling pumps, a major violation
of federal regulations, contributed significantly to the events at the Three
Mile Island atomic power plant that led to the nation's worst nuclear accident."[59] It was also reported that the Department of Health, Education and
Welfare had concluded that the levels of radiation in the area surrounding
the Three Mile Island plant had "not endangered the health of area residents
and pose[d] no significant risk for the future."[60] To reassure the population
in the region, HEW Secretary Joseph A. Califano Jr. promised a continued
monitoring of the radiation levels and long-term health studies.

In spite of all of this, the President did not use the Three Mile Island
Crisis to promote his nuclear power policy and his energy concept alto-
gether. When he addressed the nation during the lingering crisis phase to
outline his long-awaited plan to deal with the energy crisis of the time, Jimmy
Carter did not take this golden opportunity to push his ideas in the field.
This unwillingness to exploit a crisis of great concern to the whole nation did
not escape observers. Reporting the presidential address, the *Tribune* noted
that "Carter had little to say about nuclear energy."[61]

While most political actors, namely members of Congress, refrained from
criticizing the President's handling of the crisis and his related policy, anti-

nuclear activists once again began to voice their opposition to both nuclear energy in general and safety measures in the context of Three Mile Island reactor and other nuclear power plants in particular. The headline "Nuclear Critics Plan Political Moves and Mass Protests" over an article in the *Times* exemplified the activity of antinuclear groups and individuals during the lingering crisis period.[62] The Union of Concerned Scientists, for example, expressed its opposition and demanded the resignation of Energy Secretary Schlesinger and NRC chairman Hendrie. Ralph Nader was among those foes of nuclear energy who reentered the public debate on the subject. The *Times* reported that during an antinuclear protest demonstration Nader had accused President Carter and Energy Secretary Schlesinger of having "deceived the American public" by failing to inform them that energy generated from solar, wind, geothermal, and waste wood sources "could easily replace nuclear power."[63] All three newspapers mentioned critics such as Nader, but antinuclear actors had a better chance of making the pages of the *Times* than the *Post,* and by far the hardest time to be mentioned in the *Tribune.*

The papers published numerous descriptions about local and state activities in dealing with the Pennsylvania crisis and about mood and expressed feelings among residents of the areas involved. In addition, there were comprehensive articles and a very lengthy series published in efforts to retrace the events surrounding the nuclear accident.[64]

During the lingering crisis phase the papers based more than half of their relevant coverage on sources that fell into the neutral/ambiguous category, and they used sources supportive of the administration's crisis-related stand for significantly more lineage than critical sources. However, while the two East Coast publications presented their readers with coverage that revealed that antinuclear actors were less reluctant than during the acute crisis to voice their criticism, the Chicago newspaper provided proportionally less space to critical sources than during the previous period (see table 4.5).

The somewhat supportive editorial positions taken by the newspapers were compatible with the news presentations in that their news coverage

TABLE 4.5 Lingering Crisis Coverage: Three Mile Island Accident (Editorials Excluded)

Linage	For/Probably For	Neutral/ Ambiguous	Against/Probably Against	Total Lines
TIMES	34.3%	52.2%	13.5%	3,195
POST	34.3	56.3	9.4	3,223
TRIBUNE	27.1	71.0	1.9	1,656

based significantly more lineage on pro-Carter sources than on opponents of his crisis-related role. The *Times,* with a lukewarm editorial stance toward Carter's relevant policies and actions, provided significantly more space to his critics than the *Post,* which took a somewhat more supportive line. The editorial stance of these two newspapers was compatible with the way they presented their so-called straight news coverage; this was not the case for the *Tribune,* which had an editorial position similar to that of the *Times* but devoted much less space to critical sources than either of the other newspapers. The *Tribune,* too, mentioned the revival of antinuclear initiatives but simply did not provide much space to the groups and individuals involved. Perhaps this kind of coverage had something to do with the *Tribune*'s earlier pronuclear power stand expressed in an editorial during the pre-crisis weeks and thus was indicative of a relationship between editorial position and news coverage.

The President, his representatives at the accident site, and executive departments and agencies were involved in managing the emergency and announced first investigative results as well as longer term mechanisms to examine all aspects of the Three Mile Island events. As a result, administration sources captured more than four times as much space as congressional sources in all three newspapers (see table 4.6). The small amount of disagreement with the administration's crisis-related policies voiced by Democrats and Republicans inside and outside of Congress was more likely to come from the President's partisans than from members of the opposition party. Senator Gary Hart, for example, was critical of safety standards and his colleague George McGovern demanded a stop of all nuclear plant construction and licensing.[65]

In the two East Coast newspapers sources supportive of the Carter administration's crisis-related actions and policies had a front page placement advantage over critical sources. While pro-Carter sources had a clear advantage, critics of the President fared much better here than during the acute crisis period. This was not the case in the *Tribune,* where pro-Carter

TABLE 4.6   Linage Administration and Congressional Sources: Lingering Crisis

	Administration Sources	Congressional Sources	Total Lines
TIMES	88.1%	11.9%	1,059
POST	83.7	16.3	1,366
TRIBUNE	87.5	12.5	504

sources were mentioned in front page stories on several occasions, critical sources not at all.

As far as journalistic descriptions and news analyses were concerned, there was no significant bias for or against the administration's crisis-related measures and policies.

CRISIS AT THREE MILE ISLAND ENDS

Although the tensions surrounding the worst accident in the history of nuclear power plants had eased considerably during the lingering crisis, Harold Denton's declaration, "I consider the crisis is over today with regard to the status of the core,"[66] was understood as the official end of the nuclear emergency in Pennsylvania. (Newspapers reported the ending of the crisis in their editions of April 10, 1979. This marked the beginning of the post-crisis phase; its coverage was examined through May 31.) Almost immediately the lively and at times acrimonious debate over nuclear energy, which had mostly been suspended during the acute and only partially revived during the lingering crisis phase, resumed with much more vigor than in the days and weeks preceding the Three Mile Island accident.

During a press conference one day after the official end of the crisis, President Carter revealed his unchanged attitude toward nuclear power when he said, "There is no way for us to abandon the nuclear supply of energy in this country in the foreseeable future." He also indicated that he would continue to press for a shortening of the long licensing process for nuclear power plants.[67] Still a day later, Carter named the eleven members of the Presidential Commission on the Accident at Three Mile Island, including chairman John G. Kemeny, president of Dartmouth College, and charged the panel with investigating the mishap and with making "recommendations to enable us to prevent any future nuclear accidents."[68] Although his adamant pro-nuclear energy stand made the President the target of angry attacks by antinuclear activists, Carter did not retreat. On the contrary, in late April he sent a letter to congressional leaders reiterating his strong support for nuclear power and further expansion of this energy source.[69]

Whatever the President had to say with respect to nuclear power was of particular interest to the public and the press. The same was true for statements, explanations, first investigative results, and new measures taken or planned in connection with the Three Mile Island case or other nuclear power plants released by the Department of Health, Education and Welfare or by the Nuclear Regulatory Commission and its staff. On several occasions, HEW Secretary Joseph Califano made news, for example, when he revealed that the radiation exposure at the Three Mile Island site had been higher than initially reported and that therefore one additional cancer death had to be expected among those residing within fifty miles of the Pennsylvania power plant.[70] Califano also made headlines when he announced an extensive study project to be undertaken jointly by HEW and the state of Pennsylvania in an effort to monitor the health effects of the Three Mile Island accident on 50,000 people living within five miles of the plant.[71] The Nuclear Regulatory Commission, besides continuing to be involved in the crisis aftermath at the Three Mile Island site, pondered whether or not to close down all those reactors built by the same company as the stricken reactor in Pennsylvania. Eventually, the regulators came to an agreement with the utilities involved to voluntarily shut down four reactors long enough to make improvements on safety equipment. In addition, five plants of the same type that had been shut down before the Three Mile Island crisis were ordered to remain closed and to make safety changes as specified by the NRC.[72]

The press not only reported on what the President, members of his administration, and the NRC wanted publicized in favor of Carter's position on nuclear power but also paid a great deal of attention to the massive opposition against the official administration lines and to embarrassing revelations about the behind-the-scene crisis management during the tense days of the acute emergency. Antinuclear activists such as members of the Union of Concerned Scientists, consumer advocate Ralph Nader, actress Jane Fonda, and California Governor Jerry Brown were most outspoken in their criticism of the administration's stand on this issue. And among these critics, nobody was harsher in attacking the President than Nader. During one news conference Nader charged that Carter had "deceived and lied to the American people" and had "hitched his energy policy to the nuclear power industry."[73] On another occasion the consumer advocate condemned nuclear energy as "our technological Vietnam."[74] In direct opposition to President Carter's position Governor Brown argued that the United States should give up on nuclear energy and certainly not speed up the licensing process for atomic power plants as the President had proposed.[75] Reports about a mass demonstration of 65,000 antinuclear protestors in Washington made the front pages of the three newspapers.[76]

While not participating in the Washington protest demonstration, Senator Edward M. Kennedy argued for a moratorium on the construction of new nuclear power plants, thus opposing President Carter's efforts to in fact speed up the licensing and building of additional reactors. In reporting Kennedy's remarks, which had been made during a meeting with participants in the antinuclear rally in the capital, the *Washington Post* mentioned only the Senator in its front page headline although the same article described a meeting between Carter and antinuclear leaders and the President's rejection of protestors' demands to shut down all nuclear plants.[77] The *New York Times* and the *Chicago Tribune,* however, headlined Carter's stand in his encounter with protestors.[78]

Congress and congressional committees began to investigate the Three Mile Island accident, its handling by the involved parties, and the broader issues of nuclear power and its regulation by the federal government. The most devastating news about the handling of the crisis was the result of Representative Morris Udall's decision to make the transcripts of NRC deliberations during the acute crisis phase available to the media and thus to the public. The NRC records demonstrated that, as the *Tribune* reported in its front page headline, the "U.S. 'operated almost blind' in the nuclear crisis." Forced by the House Interior and Insular Affairs Committee to hand the records over to the committee, the NRC transcripts told, in the words of one news account, "a horrifying story of confusion about the dangers, NRC distrust of plant officials, and hours of concern about public relations and the press."[79]

While ignoring Denton's advice to order a limited evacuation of the area, the chairman of the NRC was repeatedly in touch with the White House and, after conversations with Jody Powell, nudged his colleagues "to come up with a statement that would satisfy the White House press secretary."[80] Critics claimed that "the NRC and the White House was [sic] engaged in news manipulation."[81] The transcripts were embarrassing in another respect: They revealed that Carter had not been fully informed about the extent of the dangers involved in the Three Mile Island accident. Even while the President was on his way to inspect the crippled reactor, the NRC was aware that enough oxygen was present in the hydrogen bubble over the reactor to cause a fire. The Secret Service, charged with protecting the President, had not been aware of this kind of danger.[82] The perception that the President had been left in the dark by experts he had directed was surely a bad reflection on his leadership qualities, which had been criticized even before the Pennsylvania crisis.

While most journalistic sources in news descriptions, background information, and news analyses fit the neutral/ambiguous attitude category, there were a few instances in which news reports and analyses seemed to come down on the side of critics. For instance, in an assessment of Carter's view about nuclear energy, the author portrayed a wishy-washy President. In spite of his refusal to give up on nuclear energy, the article stated, "Carter's statements on the subject have been a throwback to his 1976 campaign-style rhetoric on so many other issues, in which he has appeared to suggest a softening on his position without really doing so."[83] Other journalistic accounts pointed to the deficiencies within the NRC as indications that the agency during the Carter presidency had still not completed the transition from "pro-industry orientation" to "being a genuine public interest body."[84] Such criticism did not speak well of Carter's success in implementing his policy goals that had specifically emphasized better safety measures by the NRC.

Of five relevant editorials in the *New York Times,* one was supportive, two were critical of the President's positions, and two fell into the neutral/ambiguous category. In its only supportive editorial comment, the *Times* applauded Carter's efforts to prevent the construction of the planned Clinch River breeder reactor and his rejection of its "potentially dangerous, unproven and unnecessary" technology. The editorial came down on Carter's side against a Congress that refused "to let the project die."[85] However, the New York newspaper editorialized strongly against the President's view that the United States could not abandon nuclear energy in the foreseeable future. The *Times* argued that "if the plants were deemed an imminent hazard to a vast number of people, they could be closed. It would be very costly, but not impossible."[86] Unlike Carter, the *Times* concluded that no sound decision on the nuclear power issues could be made without the results of various investigations and inquiries. Similarly, the New York newspaper was unhappy with the way the President had instructed the Committee he had appointed, complaining that "Mr. Carter seems to have prejudged matters" by asking the commission "to propose improvements in the use of nuclear power, not to question its continued existence."[87]

In two editorials the *Post* asked Congress to give the Kemeny Commission "sweeping investigative powers" and suggested requiring that nuclear reactor operators be trained and licensed, as airplane pilots were. Each of these opinion pieces was ambivalent in its view of Carter's position.[88] While neutral toward the President's position in these two pieces, the *Post* seemed somewhat critical in discussing the financial consequences for utilities ordered to close down nuclear plants. According to the *Post,* "These considerations should not have been a factor in the thinking of the NRC's members as they struggled with their staff's recommendation [to close the plants temporarily]. But their indecision suggests they were."[89] Given Carter's directions to the NRC to err on the side of safety and to improve safety standards at all plants on the one hand and Ralph Nader's accusation that the President had adopted the nuclear industry's views on the other, this remark could have been understood as an indirect negative reflection on Carter's controversial leadership role in this area.

The *Chicago Tribune* published three relevant editorials, and all of them fell into the neutral/ambiguous category as far as their positions vis-à-vis the Carter administration were concerned. In one editorial the newspaper mentioned the President's announcement of an investigative commission and warned that "important decisions must not be made in the emotional heat of the Three Mile Island accident." Neither endorsing nor rejecting the President's pronuclear stand, the *Tribune* pointed out that the long lead time for the construction of nuclear plants allowed a thorough assessment "before disrupting plans for the future development of energy."[90] While they may have been supportive of Carter's position, the same editorial noted that Carter critic Ralph Nader had raised legitimate questions about NRC decisions concerning reactor safety. Discussing the President's commission to investigate the Three Mile Island crisis, the Chicago newspaper praised the makeup of the panel and remarked that its inquiry ought to "look into broader aspects" than the President's executive order stated.[91] However, the *Tribune* did not suggest that Carter had prejudged the nuclear issue as was charged by the *Times*. All in all, the editorial position of the *Tribune* was neutral or ambiguous.

The newspapers based more lines on neutral or ambiguous sources and supporters of Carter's relevant policies captured more space than did his critics. However, the lively pluralistic debate concerning Carter's crisis management and his stand on nuclear power was reflected in the news coverage as well (see table 4.7).

The *New York Times,* which took a more critical editorial stance, and the *Washington Post* with an ambiguous and somewhat critical position pre-

TABLE 4.7   Post-Crisis Coverage: Three Mile Island Accident (Editorials Excluded)

Linage	For/Probably For	Neutral/ Ambiguous	Against/Probably Against	Total Lines
TIMES	28.3%	48.2%	23.5%	4,659
POST	30.9	46.0	23.1	6,851
TRIBUNE	36.6	47.6	15.8	1,656

TABLE 4.8   Linage Administration and Congressional Sources: Post-Crisis

	Administration Sources	Congressional Sources	Total Lines
TIMES	77.5%	22.5%	2,145
POST	65.8	34.2	3,445
TRIBUNE	63.2	36.8	1,109

sented the news in a very similar fashion; the news coverage in the *Chicago Tribune,* whose editorials fit the neutral/ambiguous category, was more favorable from the President's point of view. While there seemed a relationship between editorial positions and news content, it must be emphasized that the similarities in the news coverage were greater than the differences.

With the crisis declared over, Congress began to investigate and discuss the issues concerning the Three Mile Island accident, nuclear energy policy, and the management of the crisis. This activity on the part of the legislative branch and especially its committees assured congressional sources a great deal of news coverage. As table 4.8 shows, however, significantly more lines were based on administration sources than congressional ones. Democrats inside and outside of Congress were more likely to criticize President Carter in the context of the Three Mile Island accident and related policies and actions or nonactions than were Republicans.

Critics of Carter's relevant positions had a better chance of being mentioned in front page stories than during the previous periods but administration supporters received front page coverage more often than critics in the two East Coast newspapers. The *Tribune* gave pro and con sources equal treatment.

SUMMARY

Measures taken by the Nuclear Regulatory Commission fueled the public debate about benefits and risks of nuclear energy in the months preceding the Three Mile Island accident. While the *Times* and the *Post* covered both sides rather extensively, the *Tribune* restricted its reporting mostly to NRC announcements and actions, at least up to the mishap at the Pennsylvania power plant.

Once it was clear that the nation was faced with its most serious nuclear accident, critics seemed reluctant to publicly voice disagreement with the President or his stand-in crisis manager, Harold Denton of the NRC. This was reflected in the news coverage. It quickly became clear that not even the so-called experts were sure what could be done to prevent a major nuclear catastrophe. In this situation the newspapers either did not editorialize at all on the problem or did so in ambiguous ways.

When the worst had ended at Three Mile Island, antinuclear activists tried to revive the debate that had been cut off by news of the nuclear accident. While the two East Coast newspapers reported this development, it was covered less by the *Tribune.*

The news in the weeks following the crisis reflected an eagerness among antinuclear activists and mainstream politicians inside and outside of Congress to scrutinize both the management of the crisis and the nuclear energy policy of the administration. At the same time, the press reported extensively about what the President and his administration said and did concerning all crisis-related matters.

In one of the four time periods there was a relationship between the editorial positions and the news coverage; during two periods this relationship was weak or inconclusive. The absence of editorials during the short acute crisis period did not permit comparisons between editorials and straight news coverage.

President Carter missed a golden opportunity to dominate the nuclear energy debate and to silence his critics in the wake of the accident. He erred when he declared one day after the Pennsylvania emergency officially ended that the nation had no choice but to continue the use of nuclear power. Instead of leaving such a judgment to the commission he had appointed, the President left himself open to angry attacks by antinuclear activists and to criticism by mainstream politicians, political analysts, and editorial writers. Carter failed to exploit the new doubts about nuclear energy to enlist support for his overall energy program, which he revealed during the Three Mile Island crisis. Had he done so, he might have been able to lead public and elite opinion and to prevent much of the hostility the press reports conveyed in the wake of the nation's first major nuclear accident.

5

THE ATTEMPTED ASSASSINATION OF PRESIDENT REAGAN

CARNAGE ON T STREET

March 30, 1981. Washingtonians and visitors to the capital suffer through a gloomy spring day. Faced with a steady misty rain few of the 3500 union delegates from around the nation who are participating in an AFL/CIO convention at the Hilton have ventured outside to catch some fresh air. The hotel's ballroom is packed when President Ronald Reagan enters to address the meeting. After enjoying the standing ovation that greets him, the 40th President of the United States describes his economic policies and asks his listeners for support. One remark in this eighteen-minute speech seems to get lost in his focus on budget and tax cuts. "Violent crime has surged 10 percent," the President says, "making neighborhood streets unsafe and families fearful in their homes."[1]

A few minutes later, at about 2:25 P.M., that one sentence takes on prophetic dimensions. The President and his entourage leave the hotel through the VIP entrance on T Street. When Reagan steps onto the sidewalk, a group of about one hundred photographers, cameramen, reporters, and a handful of curious onlookers await him. The press is eager to get the President's reaction to the latest developments in the showdown between the Polish government and Lech Walesa's Solidarity union. Michael Putzer of the Associated Press tries to get the President's attention. "Mr. President, Mr. President," he shouts. The man in the blue suit with a white handkerchief in his pocket smiles and waves. To Lou Cannon of the *Washington Post* Ronald Reagan looks this very moment as if "happy to be President,"[2] A second or two later, there is a rapid series of shots. A number of people who look at the President will later describe his facial expression as one of disbelief, shock, and bewilderment.[3] Secret Service agent Jerry Parr pushes the President into the waiting Presidential limousine and onto the floor of the vehicle. Nearby on the sidewalk, White House press secretary James Brady, Secret Service agent Timothy McCarthy and District of Columbia policeman Thomas Delahanty—all hit by bullets—lie in their blood. Agents, policemen, and a union delegate wrestle a gun out of the hands of a resisting John W. Hinckley Jr. Neither the President nor the two Secret Service agents and the driver in the limousine that is speeding away know at this moment that a bullet has punctured Reagan's left lung and rests but three inches away from his heart. In fact, agent Parr radios the Secret Service Command that "Rawhide" (Reagan's code name) is not hurt. Shortly thereafter the President begins to cough up blood. Parr tells the driver to go straight to George Washington University Hospital. There, the President of the United States is brought quickly into Room 5A of the hospital's emergency unit.

Within minutes of the carnage on T Street, the television networks are on the air with specials about the shooting. After some confusion, there is no longer any doubt: The President has been shot. The shocking news spreads like fire throughout the country and the world. At 3:17 P.M. the United States Senate recesses in the middle of a budget debate, when Senator Howard Baker reveals the assassination attempt. At about the same time both the New York and the American Stock Exchange stop trading. Across the continent, the Academy Award ceremonies of the movie industry, scheduled for this evening, are postponed.

The news of the attempt on President Reagan's life dominates the coverage of all daily newspapers in their next day's editions. "Reagan Wounded in Chest By Gunman" and "Reagan Wounded by Assailant's Bullet" read the huge front page headlines in the *New York Times* and in the *Washington Post,* while the *Chicago Tribune* chooses the soothing headline "The President is OK" over its page one report.

The nation is faced with a grave crisis. The President, has been attacked and gunned down. This weighs especially heavy on a nation that is quickly reminded that Reagan is the fifth American President to be shot. The others —Lincoln, Garfield, McKinley, and Kennedy—did not survive.

Thus it is not only this one attempted assassination, however terrifying and crisis-triggering it is, that makes for a national emergency; this particular crisis is magnified by a history of such violent acts in America. A few days later writer Peter Goldman, in an effort to characterize the impact of the crisis, observes, "The most grievous wound of all was struck to the soul of a nation."[4]

AT THE END OF A PRESIDENTIAL HONEYMOON

When the bullet hit him, Ronald Reagan was in the seventieth day of his Presidency and within the honeymoon other political actors traditionally grant incoming chief executives for three months or so. The former Hollywood actor and former Governor of California was still enjoying some of the momentum rooted in his overwhelming election victory over incumbent President Jimmy Carter in November of 1980. Winning 483 electoral votes versus only 41 for Carter and pulling on his coattails enough Republicans into the U.S. Senate to make for a Republican majority in the upper chamber, the crusader for a conservative revolution had shocked the Democrats into political paralysis.

Moments after the new President had finished his upbeat Inaugural Address on January 20, promising an era of national renewal, the nation had learned that the 52 American hostages, held for 444 days in Iran, had been released. Although the outgoing Carter administration had negotiated the freeing of the 52 men and women, many Americans might have unconsciously associated this long-awaited crisis resolution with the advent of this new, patriotic, self-confident President.

About a month after he had taken office, the President had addressed a Joint Session of Congress and a live television audience to detail his declaration of war against waste in the federal government. He had proposed a $41.4 billion budget cut for fiscal 1982 and income tax cuts of 10 percent yearly for three years. His assault on Washington's red tape had begun even earlier—in his first week in office, when he had ordered the review of all federal regulations that in his view did more harm than good. When the President had outlined his prescriptions for the America he envisoned, many Democrats had joined the applause of their Republican colleagues, others— namely the old guard leaders such as Thomas "Tip" O'Neill and Robert Byrd —sat stunned and silent.

However, seventy days into his Presidency, Reagan was no longer without critics. Although aware that as candidate Reagan had pushed his modern-day Anti-Federalism based on his philosophy that Big Government was part of the ills in contemporary America, many Americans had second thoughts about his proposed drastic spending cuts—especially those that affected them personally. Two months after taking office, the President's approval rate among his countrymen was much lower than that of his predecessors at the same time in their term: 59 percent of the public approved Reagan's performance, 24 percent disapproved. In comparison, two months into his presidency, Jimmy Carter's approval rate was 75 percent, the disapproval rate only 9 percent. One presidential adviser was quoted as having worried, "If this President can't sustain a honeymoon beyond 90 days, then we're all in deep trouble."[5]

The Democrats inside and outside of Congress were in the process of regrouping when John Hinckley aimed his gun at Ronald Reagan. They had already chosen Charles T. Manatt as their new National Party Chairman, and they began to talk about a counterbudget of their own.

On the day of the shooting the *Washington Post* and other newspapers carried a column by Rowland Evans and Robert Novak under the headline, "The Honeymoon Is Definitely Over." In it, the pro-Reagan columnists argued that the Democratic opposition was no longer willing to grant the President honeymoon treatment, because Democrats were worried about the overall design of Reagan's program "to steadily reduce the pervasiveness of government."[6]

Ronald Reagan's honeymoon was about over on the seventieth day in office, when the carnage on T Street took place.

THE NEW PRESIDENT AND THE PRESS

Like politicians, the public, and interest groups, the media, too, tend to grant incoming presidents a period during which there is much more restraint on criticizing the chief executive than in the months and years that follow the honeymoon period. The first weeks of the Reagan presidency were no exception in this respect. Indeed, the "Great Communicator" seemed to have charmed not only the electorate but also the media with his relaxed manner and quick wit.

Journalists covering the White House often look at Presidents as having two personas: one belonging to the office-holder, the other to the man. Even those who at the outset found plenty of faults with the new President's agenda, namely his supply-side economic concept, were generally taken by this "friendly, nice man." Also, like other incoming presidential teams before, the leading Reaganites had promised "an open administration,"[7] Perhaps reporters hoped for a welcome change from the tense White House–press relationship during much of the Carter era and were therefore willing to give Reagan the initial grace period.

Jody Powell, President Carter's press secretary, came up with another explanation for "the press not laying a glove on Reagan."[8] As Powell explained it, the predominantly liberal Democrats in the Washington-based media hold a Democratic President such as Carter to much higher standards than a Republican like Reagan, because they do not expect a Republican White House to pursue the policies of their choice. Lamenting this double standard, Powell concluded, "Thus, you have the strange situation of Mr. Reagan catching less hell from this quarter [the press] for chopping away at social programs than did Mr. Carter for cutting the rate of increase in payments."[9]

In spite of the traditional press–president honeymoon during the first weeks of the first Reagan term, there were also early signs that a happy marriage was not in the cards. James Brady, who had been the spokesman for the Reagan team during the transition period, was appointed White

House press secretary. He was well liked and respected by the press corps but he did not belong to Reagan's inner circle and was therefore not perceived to be the ideal person to answer inquiries concerning the President's thinking, plans, and decisions in a credible way.

Soon after Reagan took office, reporters realized that his White House was no more open than under his predecessors, and perhaps even less so. White House correspondent Helen Thomas observed, "Press access to Reagan during his campaign 1980 was extremely limited, more a case of hit-and-run with aides closing in before a reporter could toss a follow-up question. The modus operandi continued at the White House." Reporters learned that the President himself seemed willing to answer questions in his encounters with the press, but that his close aides stepped in and tried to prevent both reporter's ad hoc questions and the President's answers.[10] Journalists felt that Reagan's advisers did not want spontaneous answers and a possible faux-pas by the President: They wanted to control what the media got in the way of information. If one believes David Stockman, who for more than four and a half years was Director of the Office of Management and Budget, Reagan's top advisers, Mike Deaver, Ed Meese, Lyn Nofziger, and Jim Baker, were obsessed with television news and its impact on Presidential policies and politics. According to Stockman, the "public relations men" surrounding the President did not want "a bad time at reality time—every night at 7:00 P.M."[11]

Accordingly, these aides devised an effective news management scheme that centered around their hand-picked "line of the day," Each morning, the White House would decide what topic was to be pushed in order to enhance the President's agenda.[12] One longtime White House reporter observed that the Reagan staff developed news management "to a fine art. . . . It's all on their terms and they calculate what will do them the most good, image-wise."[13]

A CRISIS WITHOUT PRIOR HISTORY

Unlike many, if not most foreign and domestic crises, assassination or attempts to assassinate rarely have a specific pre-crisis history. Assassins or would-be assassins do not seek a public debate about their dark plans. Accordingly, no material directly or indirectly relevant to the attempt on President Reagan's life was published in the days and weeks preceding the shooting on March 30, 1981. However, regardless of the motives behind the attack, once the shots were fired, the crisis seemed to merge Reagan the man, and Reagan the President. This fusion was especially obvious in the post-crisis, when the President was back in the White House and, although still recovering from his injuries, took charge of his political agenda. It would not make any sense to examine only press coverage of directly or indirectly crisis-related topics. Who—with the sole exception of the Ayatollah Khomeini—would not be supportive of a leader felled by an assassin's bullet and yet courageously trying to assure his nation and the world that the government is led as competently as before?

For this reason, the coverage in the *New York Times,* the *Washington Post,* and the *Chicago Tribune* has been examined under two aspects: How did the most important items in Ronald Reagan's presidential program fare (namely budget and tax cuts, attack on government regulation and waste, strong leadership in domestic and foreign affairs)? And how did the crisis, triggered by the shots on T Street, influence the overall coverage of the President's crisis-related and non-crisis agenda?

PRE-CRISIS: CRITICS GAIN MOMENTUM

Two months after becoming President, Ronald Reagan assured his conservative supporters during a speech before the "Conservative Political Action Conference" that the economic package his administration was advocating at this time was "but a first step in reordering the relationship between citizens and government." He described his program as the first phase of his overall effort to return power to the states and to local communities. The *Chicago Tribune* published a detailed account of the Reagan speech in its news section on March 21.[14] In the same edition, the Chicago paper endorsed the President's economic agenda in an editorial by blasting AFL/CIO President Lane Kirkland for criticizing Reagan's proposed budget cuts and tight money policies. "Since between a third and a half of union members voted for Mr. Reagan last fall despite the alarms already being sounded by Mr. Kirkland about budget cuts and tight money," the *Tribune* editorial argued, "we must assume that most of these workers were being more realistic than Mr. Kirkland about the causes and cures of inflation."[15] In another editorial published during the one-and-a-half weeks preceding the assassination attempt, the *Tribune* left no doubt of its support for the Reagan program. When OMB Director David Stockman denied that needy Americans were entitled to government support, the Chicago publication editorialized, "David Stockman's remark on national television Sunday that people have no fundamental right to government assistance has stirred considerable controversy and made him anathema on the left, but he owes no one an apology." In the view of the *Tribune* the so-called entitlements are based on "the belief that some people have, or should have, enforceable claims on the earnings of their fellow men and women."[16]

Three of the four editorials related to the Reagan program published in the *Tribune* during the ten days preceding the assassination attempt were supportive of the President's policies and actions. One was critical of the quarrels between White House aides and Secretary of State Alexander Haig over his and Vice-President George Bush's role in the management of potential crises. The *Tribune* complained that in the third month of Reagan's presidency, "the foreign policy apparatus is still staggering, not running. It is veering wildly under the strains of an increasingly public and ugly quarrel between White House staffers and Secretary of State Alexander Haig." But the editorial supported the outcome of the intragovernmental infight that elevated Bush into the role of crisis manager.[17]

The two East Coast publications were less supportive of the President's program in their editorial evaluations. Commenting on President Reagan's proposed tax reform, the *Washington Post* editorialized, "President Reagan's tax plan provides a point of beginning, but it is much too crude to meet the country's present requirement."[18] In an editorial entitled "Requiem for CETA," the *Post* attacked proposed cutbacks in the funding of jobs under the Comprehensive Employment and Training Act (CETA) arguing that this program was a first target of the administration because "unlike most social programs, it is not protected by an organized group of professional workers who stand to lose their own jobs. The people who hold CETA jobs don't organize letter-writing campaigns. The only way their loss will be detected is in higher welfare and unemployment counts, higher local taxes and fewer community services."[19]

In another editorial the *Post* poked fun at and criticized the prospect of "deregulated sausage," pointing out that the requirement to list the ingredients on the label "is bad for business," because the discovery that sausage contains powdered bone might turn off consumers. The attack on the administration's all-out war against federal regulations closed with the observation, "Perhaps you have concluded that there is a case for at least a few federal regulations, and that one place for them is in the sausage factory."[20] Of the seven relevant editorials the *Post* published during the pre-crisis period six were against or probably against the President's major policies and one fell into the neutral/ambiguous category.

While most of *Post* editorials tended to articulate criticism reluctantly, the anti-President stand in the editorials of the *New York Times* was much more pronounced. In an editorial headlined "Congress and the Reagan Cannonball," the *Times* scolded Congress for letting the Reagan train roar through "like the Wabash Cannonball," complaining, "When the train roared past, it wacked many billions that should be challenged. . . . The Administration is undermining its own desire to reduce the welfare rolls; it has proposed such steep cuts in social programs for the working poor that many might decide that working isn't worth the effort."[21]

The newspaper also attacked President Reagan's plan to force welfare recipients to work along the line of a "Workfare" model he established during his tenure as Governor of California. The *New York Times* editorialized: "Mr. Reagan may not intend to be callous or cruel. But if he wants welfare recipients to do real work, why is he simultaneously chopping back the manpower programs most likely to provide it? The CETA jobs and training program has provided paychecks, dignity, and paths out of poverty for thousands of poor people. Yet it is high on Mr. Reagan's hit list." The editorial concluded, "Jobs are a welcome way to put the poor on the ladder. Ronald Reagan's workfare is a way to put them on display."[22]

Of the seven relevant editorials published in the *Times* during the pre-crisis period, six were critical of the President's policies and one fell into the neutral/ambiguous category.

Thus, while the editorial stance of the *Tribune* was mostly supportive of the President, both *Post* and *Times* were mostly critical of the major points in the presidential agenda.

The opinion of publishers and editorial page editors did not prevent sources with views that differed from those expressed in each paper's editorials from being frequently used in the general news coverage of each paper. However, in all cases there was a correlation between the editorial policy and the overall coverage of the relevant issues: The *Tribune* with its overwhelming editorial support for Ronald Reagan presented an overall coverage in which sources supportive of the President's line captured nearly twice as much space as did critical ones. Also, the coverage was more favorable from the administration's point of view than that in the *Post* and *Times*. The *Post*, with an editorial stance that oscillated between against and probably against the Reagan policies, gave pro-Reagan a somewhat greater lineage advantage over sources critical of the President than the *Times* with its most critical editorial stand against the President's agenda (see table 5.1).

Considering that the traditional political honeymoons granted to incoming Presidents last about three months and that the pre-crisis phase fell well into such a honeymoon period, the sources unfavorable to the administration line got quite a lot of attention in the coverage of all three newspapers. Nevertheless, the favorable sources, namely the President, White House aides, and other leading administration members had no difficulty in getting media attention.

In spite of its criticism on the editorial page, the *Post* accommodated the new President and those who took his side. For example, the newspapers published a lengthy front page article recounting an exclusive interview with President Reagan. Also, in a long story, Republican pollster Richard Wirthlin had the opportunity to explain the President's low standing in public opinion polls after but two months in office. Wirthlin made the best of it contending that more Americans disapproved of the President so quickly because of Reagan's determination to use the political honeymoon period "to translate his budget-cutting campaign promise into practice."[23]

On the other hand, the *Post* did not hesitate to give generous coverage to sources and/or material contradictory to the President's announced goals. For instance, the Washington paper reported in a long article about an analysis by experts at the Center for the Study of Welfare Policy at the University of Chicago which concluded that the President's planned welfare cuts would hit the working poor harder than those who relied on welfare alone. A few days later, the newspaper published an even longer piece under the headline "Reagan's Workfare Program Failed in California, Report Reveals," which was based on a critical evaluation of the workfare program by the California Employment Development Department. Since President Reagan pushed for workfare programs along the line of the model he had enacted during his governorship in California, the conclusion of the publicized report was contrary to Reagan's claims and goals. According to the report, "there was no evidence the program had any success in discouraging people from applying for welfare or in getting those already on the rolls to go off."[24]

The *Times*, too, reported continuously about the initiative and explanations of the administration and the Reagan victories in Congress. For example, when the White House announced that, in an attack on waste and fraud within the government, the administration was preparing criminal and civil actions against those who allegedly misused federal funds, the New York paper reported this in detail. And reporting an administration estimate that proposed budget cuts would eliminate 20 percent of all welfare recipients from receiving public assistance, the *Times* quoted a high administration

TABLE 5.1   Pre-Crisis Coverage: Assassination Attempt
(Editorials Excluded)

Linage	For/Probably For	Neutral/ Ambiguous	Against/Probably Against	Total Lines
TIMES	41.2%	26.5%	32.3%	5,581
POST	45.5	28.4	26.1	3,662
TRIBUNE	54.0	18.4	27.6	1,732

official as having explained that these cuts would not hurt the "needy."[25] On the other hand, the newspaper gave Reagan's opponents on the major issues just as much space. In a front page story, the publication reported about congressional opposition to the President's budget cuts and about efforts by Democrats to "force Mr. Reagan to make significant compromise in his economic package." Representative Stephen Solarz was quoted as saying that "Reagan's priorities are inequitable and regressive, despite his rhetoric about the 'safetynet' to protect the truly needy."[26] Also, the *Times* covered various interest groups who voiced opposition to the Reagan policies, for example, in two successive editions the newspaper reported about the protests of women's groups against the President's budget cuts and his plan to curb federal spending for abortions sought by poor women.[27]

While devoting more lines to pro-Reagan sources than to opponents of the administration's major policies the *Tribune,* too, covered both sides in the debate. For instance, in the edition of March 22, the newspaper reported in an article with a headline spanning four columns that the President was preparing an "assault on waste and fraud in federal programs."[28] In the same edition, however, a lengthy article revealed that congressional Democrats were preparing to attack Ronald Reagan's failure to keep his campaign promise and combat waste and fraud within the government.[29] However, while the pro-Reagan piece was placed on page 3, the critical article was published on page 14.

The Chicago paper placed most articles dealing with the debate of the Reagan program on inside pages. Sources supportive of the administration's stand were used in front page stories on three occasions, and in three instances the publication mentioned sources critical of the President's program in page one articles. Both East Coast newspapers, on the other hand, used sources who supported the President's side more often in page one stories than critical sources.

The battle for media attention between administration and Congress during the pre-crisis period was won by the executive side: however, as table 5.2 shows, congressional sources captured a significant amount of space in all three publications. Still, during this period, leaders of interest groups—not of Congress—took the initiative in responding to the Reagan program.

In the *Tribune*'s journalistic descriptions, background information, and news analyses fell completely into the neutral/ambiguous intent category. More than half of the media-based lines in the news coverage of the *Times* and *Post* were of a neutral or ambiguous nature, over 10 percent were supportive and about a third critical of the President's agenda.

THE PRESIDENT IS SHOT

In its edition of March 31, 1981, the *New York Times* dedicated its complete front page to covering the attempt on President Reagan's life. In addition to extensive continuations of front page stories, the *Times* published a good number of stories related to the event on its inside pages. The other two newspapers, too, played up the shooting big in their editions on the day following the incident. The *Post* reserved most of its front page and additional inside space for stories reporting about the tragic event and related developments, while the *Tribune* followed up its prominent front page lead story by extensive inside page coverage. All three newspapers commented in lead editorials on the assassination attempt and expressed support for the President in a crisis recognized as being difficult for Ronald Reagan personally as well as for the whole nation.

The initial coverage concentrated on descriptions of the shooting, what followed both on the scene of the carnage and in treating the victims in area hospitals, and how America and the world reacted. But revelations of the President's courage, heroism, and quick wit immediately before and after his surgery were reported widely and prominently. "Honey, I forgot to duck," the President was reported to have said to his wife, when she rushed to his side before he was wheeled into the operating room.[30] And he assured concerned friends, "Don't worry about me, I'll make it." Still in the recovery room, Reagan wrote a note to his doctors, jokingly repeating a classic W. C. Fields line, "All in all, I'd rather be in Philadelphia." Such evidence of the President's upbeat human quality was related to the media by White House aide Lyn Nofziger and by hospital spokesman Dr. Dennis O'Leary who shortly after Reagan's surgery was done assured the nation that the President had a "clear head and would be able to make decisions by tomorrow."[31]

Looking at his assembled senior aides, the President reportedly asked before his surgery, "Who's minding the store?"[32] From this moment on and

TABLE 5.2   Linage Administration and Congressional Sources:
Pre-Crisis Assassination Attempt

	Administration Sources	Congressional Sources	Total Lines
TIMES	77.6%	22.4%	3,260
POST	75.1	24.9	2,207
TRIBUNE	69.0	31.0	1,350

all during the acute crisis the administration's crisis managers, clearly supported by hospital spokesman O'Leary, had the overriding objective to
demonstrate that the chief executive's life was not in danger, that he was
able to make necessary decisions, that he was a kind of hero—even while
in pain. Those in close touch with the President immediately pushed the
"business as usual" line by assuring that Vice-President George Bush and
his White House staff were acting as stand-ins for a President fully informed
of the passing domestic and international affairs. Given these crisis-management goals, the non-crisis–related Reagan program had to take a back seat
on the administration's priority list.

During the acute crisis phase (newspaper editions March 31, through
April 4), the papers reported widely and supportively as far as those major
goals were concerned. There was a flood of stories emphasizing the human
side of the President, for example, that "Reagan wept on learning for the
first time that his press secretary James Brady had been shot in the head
and said, "Oh, damn, oh, damn.""[33] The coverage dwelled on the President's
wit, his never-ending ability to crack jokes, and his robust basic health more
common in a man in his 50s than in a 70-year-old.[34] There were also first
reports of an instant jump in Reagan's popularity as measured by public
opinion polls.[35] As far as the crisis-related coverage in the three newspapers
was concerned, there was no criticism.

Editorially, nothing changed in comparison to the pre-crisis days as far as
the *Tribune* was concerned. In its first editorial following the shooting, the
Chicago newspaper stated, "President Reagan, cheerful, optimistic, vigor-
ous in the first flush of his administration must temporarily stop his work to
deal with this crisis that is at once private and public, and so terribly
unnecessary."[36] The two crisis-related editorials the *Tribune* published during this period were clearly in support of the President as was the one that
related to Reagan's non-crisis agenda.

Of three crisis-related editorials in the *Times*, one was supportive of the
President and two fell into the neutral/ambiguous category. However, the
one editorial that related to the President's non-crisis agenda was critical of
his policy goals. While emphasizing the shared values of all Americans of
good will and expressing the hope that the President and the nation may
"soon repair that [glorious American] history" in an editorial entitled "Together," the publication continued to attack the Reagan administration's
budget-cutting approach. Criticizing proposed cuts in federal support for
social science research, the *Times* argued, "Good social science research
helps to protect Government and all society against error, above all the
error being made here: assuming that in facing difficult choices, politicians
really know what they're doing."[37]

The *Post* editorialized in support of the President and his administration in the two-crisis-related pieces the newspaper published during this period. On one occasion, the Washington newspaper wrote, "Thanks in good measure to Mr. Reagan's remarkable recuperative powers—not to speak of his one-liners—his government shifted promptly into a mode of operation for which "business as usual," the White House term, is an exaggerated but acceptable designation."[38] However, the *Post* did not hold back with criticism in the one editorial during the acute crisis that commented on budget and tax cuts and the necessity of balancing the budget. The Washington-based publication scolded the budget-cutting administration for not trying to close tax loopholes, which the editorial called "enormous tax subsidies that only go to some—and hardly to the needy."[39]

Yet, as far as the two East Coast newspapers were concerned the overall editorial stance in this period with respect to crisis-related topics and those relevant to the President's non-crisis agenda was less critical than in the pre-crisis period: the *Tribune* was even more supportive in its editorial columns than during the pre-crisis.

There was a dramatic shift in the news coverage of material either related to the shooting crisis or to the President's non-crisis agenda: In all three papers the lineage advantage of sources that supported the President's line over critical sources was overwhelming (see table 5.3). This pro-President shift was, of course, the result of the outpouring of support for the injured President and a skillful promotion of Reagan as a courageous leader in a time of crisis by his aides. On the other hand, some opponents of Reagan's program who had voiced criticism during the pre-crisis days, were reluctant, if not unwilling, to criticize a President struck by a bullet. As Adam Clymer reported in the *Times*, "Foes were pulling their punches today, cancelling rallies, rewriting speeches and worrying over how to make the distinction clear that they only opposed the President's program, not the President."[40] The combined crisis and non-crisis coverage was similar in the three newspapers. Nevertheless, a relationship between editorial positions and news coverage could be construed in that the editorially more critical East Coast

TABLE 5.3   Acute Crisis Coverage: Assassination Attempt: Crisis- and Non-Crisis–Related Reagan Agenda (Editorials Excluded)

Linage	For/Probably For	Neutral/ Ambiguous	Against/Probably Against	Total Lines
TIMES	66.1%	29.4%	4.5%	5,659
POST	53.4	38.0	8.6	4,709
TRIBUNE	69.0	29.4	1.6	2,111

papers presented a coverage that was not quite as favorable from the President's point of view than that of the editorially very supportive *Tribune*.

The debate of Reagan's non-crisis–related agenda took a back seat to the crisis-related concerns. What was said and discussed in this respect was covered in the *Tribune* and the *Times* more favorably for the Reagan side in that both newspapers provided more column lines for sources favorable to the Reagan agenda than for critical ones. In the *Post*, sources critical of the administration's program captured more lines than those in support of the Reagan agenda, namely because the Washington newspaper paid much more attention to Democrats in Congress who spoke out against the President's non-crisis agenda (see table 5.4).

Sources in favor of the crisis managing goals of the Reagan administration and/or its program dominated front page stories during this period. In the *Times*, sources supportive of the President in crisis and non-crisis–related matters were used in front page stories in 38 cases, critical sources on 6 occasion only. In the *Post* the front page story placement was 33–2 in favor of pro-Presidential sources: in the *Tribune* the sources who supported the President were used in page one stories in 16 instances, critical sources were not mentioned at all in front page stories.

During the acute crisis days the executive branch was preoccupied with managing the crisis, namely assuring the nation and the world that—as Vice-President George Bush put it during a visit on the Senate floor—"the Reagan Administration was functioning normally."[41] In the overall news coverage of the crisis and the non-crisis–related activities, the administration captured much more space than congressional sources in all three papers (see table 5.5). This was not surprising, given the fact that much of the news in the aftermath of the shooting was provided by President Reagan's White House staff. However, as far as the non-crisis–related coverage of the Reagan agenda was concerned, there was a complete turnaround in the space distribution for administration and congressional sources during the acute crisis period in comparison to the pre-crisis days: In the coverage

TABLE 5.4 Acute Crisis Coverage, Assassination Attempt: Non-Crisis–Related Reagan Agenda (Editorials Excluded)

Linage	For/Probably For	Neutral/ Ambiguous	Against/Probably Against	Total Lines
TIMES	37.4%	49.5%	13.1%	1,582
POST	15.7	42.4	41.9	856
TRIBUNE	70.8	16.8	12.4	274

of all three newspapers congressional sources captured more column lines than administration sources. This was an indication that the administration was preoccupied with putting on a convincing "business as usual" façade and that the President himself was unable to push the Reagan program. Instead, congressional actors were able to dominate the non-crisis–related debate and news coverage.

In the *Times,* 38.6 percent of crisis- and non-crisis–related relevant lines based on journalistic descriptions, background information, and news analyses revealed sympathy for the President's agenda (mostly crisis-related), 60.1 percent fell into the neutral/ambiguous category while 1.3 percent were critical of the President's (non-crisis) agenda. Of these types of lines in the *Post,* 18.7 percent were supportive of the President's (crisis) agenda while 81.3 percent fell into the neutral/ambiguous category. In the *Tribune,* 86.9 percent of the media-based lines revealed neutral or ambiguous and 13.1 percent supportive attitudes toward the President's's crisis- and non-crisis agenda.

PRESIDENT: ON THE MEND

Even after the nation had seen the first photograph of the recuperating President, taken in the hospital and perceived as visible proof that Ronald Reagan was indeed recovering from his injuries, the crisis lingered on. (The lingering phase was examined in newspaper editions starting April 5, through April 11.) The media carried day-in day-out reports about the President's health status based on briefings by deputy press secretary Larry Speakes, hospital spokesman Dr. Dennis O'Leary, and descriptions by others closely in touch with the President. The daily status update gave White House aides plenty of opportunity to praise the President's good attitude even under adverse circumstances, describing him, for example, as "very alert, telling stories, and laughing."[42] Also, Reagan's aides did not miss any opportunity

TABLE 5.5   Linage Administration and Congressional Sources, Acute Crisis: Crisis- and Non-Crisis–Related Reagan Agenda

	Administration Sources	Congressional Sources	Total Lines
TIMES	71.2%	28.8%	2,101
POST	64.8	35.2	1,550
TRIBUNE	75.2	24.8	765

to assure the nation that the still suffering President was taking care of the most urgent affairs of state. On one occasion, the State department revealed that from his sick-bed Reagan had sent a letter with "strong language" to Leonid Brezhnev that expressed the President's concern for the situation in Poland.[43] Repeatedly, White House aides emphasized that the President was briefed regularly on the Polish developments.[44]

Although Democratic opponents of the President's economic package and other major non-crisis agenda points were well aware that the attempt on Reagan's life had brought about a surge in his popularity and talked about this development to reporters, they nevertheless renewed their drive against Reagan's budget and tax cut plans.[45] All three newspapers, especially the Washington-based *Post,* reported frequently and in detail on efforts by Democrats in Congress to alter the administration's proposed cuts. Many headlines that appeared during this period pointed to the opposition to the President's economic package: "Democrats Offer Own Cut List," "Reagan Budget-Cut Plan Jolted as Panel Democrats Hold Firm," "Hill Panel Defies Reagan on Regulatory Fund Cuts" were among such headlines in the *Post.* "Reagan Cuts Called Harmful to Elderly," "2 Leading Democrats Join Drive Against Reagan Economic Plan," "Democrats in House Press Attacks on President's Economic Proposals," were examples of headlines in the *Times* over articles using sources critical of the President's non-crisis program. The *Tribune* also took notice of the growing opposition to Reaganomics, publishing stories under headlines like "Senate Unit Hits Reagan on Budget," "Reagan Cuts Will Hurt Aged, Experts Report," and "Rostenkowski Will Press Fight on Reagan Tax Program."

Efforts by the administration to counter the oppositional moves assured coverage by the three publications. When Budget Director David Stockman and others defended the President's program, they were, of course, covered. On one occasion, for example, the *Times* reported that Stockman had defended the Reagan budget against charges that it constituted "a blueprint for disaster" for millions of low-income elderly Americans.[46] Understandably, the *Chicago Tribune* gave generous coverage to Illinois Governor Thompson, when he said he backed President Reagan's federal spending and was prepared to ask for tax increases in his state in order to offset federal cuts.[47]

The President and his aides were aware that his absence from the White House had played—after a period of mostly suspended politics on Capitol Hill—into the hands of those who opposed the program he put forward before the assassination attempt. The *Post* quoted a White House aide commenting on Reagan's budget setbacks in Congress as saying, "It's hard for me to believe that a phone call from the president wouldn't have made the difference."[48] And, according to his top aides, the President began to speak about his intention to soon address the nation via television to push his tax cut proposals and his budget plan. [49]

Editorially, the two East Coast papers seemed to return to the overwhelming critical stance of the pre-crisis because, with the exception of one piece in the *Times*, they no longer commented editorially on the assassination attempt. It was this topic that had shifted both of these newspapers during the height of the crisis into a benign, if not supportive mode vis-à-vis the combined crisis and non-crisis Reagan agenda.

The New York newspaper published one crisis-related editorial that reflected on the various reactions to the shooting and advocated gun control. Without criticizing the President directly, the *Times* stated, "Think what a breakthrough it would be if President Reagan, as he leaves the hospital this week, were to endorse reasonable handgun controls."[50] The other six editorials the *Times* published during this period, all of them non-crisis–related and commenting on Reagan's other major agenda points, expressed opinions critical of the President's policies, decisions, and/or actions. For example, the *Times* attacked Reagan's Interior Secretary James Watt for planning "dramatic and disturbing changes in the way national parks are run." Another editorial blamed Reagan for not offering "leadership" to the ailing auto industry, lamenting, "Mr. Reagan clings to the notion that Government has no right to interfere in private business. Why?" In still another critical editorial, the *Times* chided the President for joining the conservative attack on the Congressional Budget Office, stating, "When the agency predicted last month that Mr. Reagan's program would not balance the budget by 1984, as promised, the President himself joined the assault [on the CBO and especially on its director Alice Rivlin]."[51]

The *Washington Post* published three editorials in this period relevant to the President's major non-crisis agenda points; one was supportive, two were critical of the President's stand. While applauding the administration for "relaxing some of the automobile regulations" and thus "offering the right kind of help to an industry in trouble," the newspaper editorialized against Reagan's plan to abruptly get rid of the Social Security minimum and against proposed welfare cuts, charging that the proposed measures would make "some very poor people poorer."[52]

The *Chicago Tribune* remained supportive of the President's's non-crisis program; its two relevant editorials published during this period continued to express support for the non-crisis–related Reagan agenda. On one occasion, the newspaper applauded Reagan's farm program, commenting that it was a "generally sound one." In another editorial the newspaper took positive note of the administration's willingness to alter its initial welfare cut plan so that recipients of public assistance were not robbed of the incentive to work.[53]

The news coverage of topics either related to the shooting crisis or to the President's leading non-crisis policies reflected the renewed activity of political actors who were critical of the President's non-crisis agenda. In fact, in the *Post* sources critical of Reagan's program captured nearly as many lines as did sources supportive of the President's while pro-Reagan sources held a better than 2–1 space advantage over critical sources in the *Times* and in the *Tribune* (see table 5.6). Clearly, sources who were in favor of Reagan's crisis and non-crisis positions lost the dominance they had captured during the acute crisis. The editorially most critical *Times* and the *Tribune* with a pro-Reagan editorial stance covered the relevant news very similarly. The *Post,* on the other hand, presented coverage least favorable to the President even though the paper was editorially less critical than the *Times*. In this period, there was no relationship between editorial positions and news coverage.

Efforts on the part of the President's opponents to revive the discussion of non-crisis issues were successful; accordingly, in all three newspapers, the coverage of the non-crisis issues provided more space to sources critical of the President's positions than supportive ones (see table 5.7).

Sources supportive of the presidential agenda were used far more in front page stories than critical ones. This was especially the case in the two East

TABLE 5.6   Lingering Crisis Coverage, Assassination Attempt:
Crisis- and Non-Crisis–Related Reagan Agenda (Editorials Excluded)

Linage	For/Probably For	Neutral/ Ambiguous	Against/Probably Against	Total Lines
TIMES	45.3%	32.2%	22.5%	4,053
POST	34.7	33.5	31.8	2,868
TRIBUNE	54.9	18.3	26.8	1,533

TABLE 5.7   Lingering Crisis Coverage, Assassination Attempt:
Non-Crisis–Related Reagan Agenda (Editorials Excluded)

Linage	For/Probably For	Neutral/ Ambiguous	Against/Probably Against	Total Lines
TIMES	26.9%	42.5%	30.6%	2,925
POST	22.3	33.7	44.0	2,071
TRIBUNE	39.6	14.4	46.0	894

Coast papers where the reports about Reagan's health continued to make the front pages frequently. Also, these two publications covered the developments surrounding the President's's non-crisis agenda quite often in page one stories. The *Tribune,* on the other hand, placed these types of stories mostly on inside pages.

Because Congress dominated the non-crisis–related debate, while the administration was still preoccupied with managing the lingering crisis caused by the attempt on Reagan's life, congressional sources captured a great amount of space. In the combined coverage of crisis-related issues and of the non-crisis Reagan agenda congressional sources were used for more lines than administration sources in the *Post* and in the *Tribune* while the *Times* used administration sources for more lines than congressional ones (see table 5.8). While Republicans were mostly supportive of the President's overall positions, Democrats led the renewed attack on the President's economic program and other important policy proposals.

Journalistic descriptions, background information, and news analyses were mostly neutral or ambiguous and did not reveal support for or opposition to the President's combined crisis and non-crisis agenda.

CHIEF EXECUTIVE LOBBIES FOR HIS PROGRAM

With the announcement that the physicians who treated the President had okayed their patient's release from the hospital, the crisis was over. (The post-crisis coverage was examined for a 15-day period starting with the editions of April 12.) Although the recuperating President was only slowly eased into a seminormal work schedule, his presence in the White House and his determination to once again lead the fight for his agenda countered the efforts of actors inside and outside of Congress to defuse his program, namely in the area of budget and tax matters. What played into Ronald Reagan's hand was the continued lumping together of non-crisis–

TABLE 5.8 Linage for Administration and Congressional Sources, Lingering Crisis: Crisis- and Non-Crisis–Related Reagan Agenda

	Administration Sources	Congressional Sources	Total Lines
TIMES	56.6%	43.4%	2,205
POST	37.0	63.0	1,993
TRIBUNE	46.3	53.7	1,049

related issues and of reminders of and references to the shooting ordeal and its aftermath. The President and his aides seemed to promote this kind of mixture, and the media seemed just as willing to refer to the presidential convalescence in articles otherwise dedicated to non-crisis issues; at the same time there were references to Reagan's non-crisis policy priorities in stories about his health.

Reporting on Ronald Reagan's release from the hospital and his return to the White House, the *Times* mentioned in the same article that "White House officials are eager for Mr. Reagan to try to restore some momentum to the [economic] program by speaking on it."[54] Another *Times* article about the President's denial that he was willing to compromise on tax cuts quoted White House aides as saying that Reagan in a meeting "was concerned and agitated—he was irritated" about those compromise reports. A reference to the assassination attempt followed: "It was the group's first business meeting in the Executive Mansion since Mr. Reagan returned there on Saturday after 12 days of hospitalization for treatment of the gunshot wound he suffered on March 30."[55] In the same edition, another front page story in the *Times* began with the following lead: "The Reagan Administration, buffeted by a surprising congressional setback last week while the President was recuperating from a gunshot wound, is gearing up now to try to recapture its political momentum."[56]

The other two newspapers also mixed references to the crisis and its aftermath into the coverage of Reagan's non-crisis priorities. Reporting on the White House meeting concerning the budget, the *Tribune* closed the same article with a description of a phone call President Reagan made to his press secretary, James Brady, the victim of the assassination attempt with the most serious injuries. And in an article about Reagan's campaign for budget and tax cuts, the Chicago publication referred to the crisis when it mentioned, "The President, still secluded in the White House family quarters, worked to make up for the time and momentum lost during his recovery from a wound suffered in an assassination attempt three weeks ago."[57] Describing White House concerns over opposition in Congress to Reagan's economic package, an article in the *Post* began, "President Reagan, slowly working up to a half-day schedule, yesterday received a gloomy assessment of the legislative prospects for his economic program."[58] The newspapers published "now-it-can-be-told" accounts of the attempt on the President's life and how his doctor's assessed the seriousness of his injuries shortly after the incident. Those reports made clear that, as a headline in the *Tribune* put it, "Doctor Feared 'We might lose' Reagan."[59] An interview about the shooting and its aftermath, given by the President to wire service reporters, was carried by all three papers on the front pages of their editions of April 23, 1981. The results of a Washington Post/ABC opinion poll, analyzed by the Washington publication on April 25, demonstrated that the assassination attempt had resulted in increased admiration for Ronald Reagan and that many Americans extended their positive feelings for the President to his program. According to the *Post*'s Barry Sussman, "The public opposition that began to emerge in March, before Reagan was shot in an assassination attempt, appears to have been blunted, at least for the time being, by a burst of admiration for the president's courage and good humor." The poll revealed that Reagan seemed to have "overwhelming public support" for his far-reaching economic package.[60]

Those who had led an offensive against the Reagan agenda before the shooting and during the lingering crisis were overshadowed by a White House campaign that seemed to exploit the sympathies for the stricken President to enlist support for his program rather successfully. There was an Easter recess in Congress, but representatives and senators still had plenty of opportunity to speak out. The few who did could count on media coverage. For example, the *Times* covered Senator Edward Kennedy, when he denounced the President's economic package claiming that Reagan's cut would hurt "real human beings."[61] The *Post* took notice when several members of Congress filed a suit against the administration to counter a hiring freeze on health-care jobs that allegedly hurt programs for Vietnam Veterans.[62]

While the overall coverage of the President's agenda with its very frequent references to his recent ordeal was clearly dominated by sources supportive of the chief executive, the editorials of all three newspapers seemed to make efforts to leave the crisis behind, which indeed had ended. The *Tribune*'s editorial writers who had supported the President very much before and during the crisis periods, took a relatively harder line. Of the four editorials the Chicago-based newspaper published in the two-and-a-half weeks after Reagan's return to the White House, two were supportive and two were critical. While not in favor of an alternative budget proposals by the Democrats, the Chicago newspaper editorialized harshly against an administration plan that threatened to eliminate funds for the Legal Services Corporation and for a program providing legal services to the poor in civil cases. Doing away with this service, the *Tribune* concluded, would prove the administration to be "insensitive both to the poor and to the ideal that just as no man is above the law's obligation, no man is so poor to be beneath the law's attention and protection."[63]

During this period, the *Times* expressed on two occasions editorial support for the President's policies, in six instances the newspaper's editorials were critical of the Reagan program, while one editorial fell into the neutral/ ambiguous category. An editorial headlined "100 days" and reviewing the first hundred days of the Reagan presidency seemed to sum up the editorial stance of the New York–based publication in this period. "Mr. Reagan's program may be dangerously wrong," the *Times* stated, "but he is, indisputably, President and doing what he said he would do. Not bad for three months, but not yet confidence winning." While acknowledging that liberals were "dancing to Mr. Reagan's tune," and that he did command "the public's support," the newspaper concluded: "If these first hundred days are any guide, Mr. Reagan's ambitions may well be defeated by his self-imposed inhibitions. For his Administration seems to deny the need to manage the inevitable change, everywhere."[64] While critical of Reagan's economic package and of some aspects of the Reagan leadership in foreign policy, the *Times* seemed very much aware of the President's appeal to the nation at large and his influence on politicians.

Of the six editorials the *Post* published during this period, two were neutral or ambiguous and four fell into the critical category. Assessing the tax-cut proposals of President Reagan and House Ways and Means Committee chairman Dan Rostenkowski, the *Post* came to the conclusion that "the Rostenkowski alternative is far safer and surer than the Reagan supply-side plan."[65] Applauding the Congressional Budget Office, which had been criticized by the President, for an analysis of the effects that the President's budget cuts would have on the poor, the *Post* made the point that "what we are talking about is not just adjusting numbers on a balance sheet, but changing the circumstances in which people actually live."[66]

The overall coverage of the post-crisis period reflected in all three newspapers the renewed push by the President to get his policy preferences, namely in the economic area, legislated by Congress. The mixture of non-crisis issues with references to the assassination attempt, the health status of the chief executive, and so forth, proved beneficial to the presidential side as far as the overall news coverage was concerned. As table 5.9 demonstrates, the newspapers covered the crisis- and non-crisis–related news fairly similarly. Nevertheless, there was somewhat of a relationship between editorial positions and the so-called straight news in that the *Tribune*, which

TABLE 5.9   Post-Crisis Coverage Assassination Attempt:
Crisis and Non-Crisis–Related Reagan Agenda (Editorials Excluded)

Linage	For/Probably For	Neutral/ Ambiguous	Against/Probably Against	Total Lines
TIMES	62.6%	23.8%	13.6%	2,882
POST	58.6	20.8	20.6	3,466
TRIBUNE	68.5	17.8	13.7	1,883

was the least critical of the three papers, presented its readers with a coverage most favorable to the President while the very critical *Post* had the most negative coverage of the three publications.

In the coverage of non-crisis–related issues pro-Reagan sources recaptured their space advantage over critical sources that they had lost during the lingering crisis (see table 5.10).

The placement advantage for pro-Reagan sources was overwhelming— in large part the result of stories using the President himself, his close aides, or his physicians as sources. Very often, these sources captured front page placement.

Given the new activism of the President and his administration, administration sources recaptured their space advantage over congressional sources in all three newspapers. In the overall coverage of crisis and non-crisis policies and actions, the linage advantage for sources in the executive branch was impressive (see table 5.11).

Journalistic descriptions and news analyses fell mostly into the neutral/ ambiguous intent category. In the *Post*, 63.7 percent of these lines were neutral or ambiguous while 36.3 percent revealed critical attitudes toward the Reagan agenda. In the *Times*, 97.9 percent of the media-based lines appeared neutral or ambiguous and 2.1 percent conveyed a critical attitude vis-à-vis the President's non-crisis policies. In the *Tribune*, of all the lines

TABLE 5.10   Post-Crisis Coverage Assassination Attempt: Non-Crisis–Related Reagan Agenda (Editorials Excluded)

Linage	For/Probably For	Neutral/ Ambiguous	Against/Probably Against	Total Lines
TIMES	55.5%	27.7%	16.8%	2,329
POST	44.1	27.6	28.3	2,523
TRIBUNE	59.0	20.6	20.4	1,272

TABLE 5.11   Linage Administration and Congressional Sources, Post-Crisis: Crisis and Non-Crisis-Related Reagan Agenda

	Administration Sources	Congressional Sources	Total Lines
TIMES	80.7%	19.3%	1,956
POST	73.0	27.0	1,198
TRIBUNE	76.1	23.9	1,271

attributable to media sources, 24.4 percent seemed to reveal support for and 12.2 percent opposition to the Reagan agenda, 63.4 percent fell into the neutral/ambiguous category.

SUMMARY

In the days preceding the assassination attempt the news reflected significant opposition to President Reagan's major policy goals, namely to cut taxes and social programs. This fits the normal state of affairs in American pluralist politics and it is surprising only because it happened near the end of the political honeymoon that is traditionally granted to incoming presidents.

As soon as the management of the assassination crisis became the number-one priority of the administration, the President's supporters dominated the news. There was virtually no opposition concerning crisis-related goals of the White House. Additionally, the debate over Reagan's policies took a back seat to the attention paid to the shooting incident.

During lingering crisis phases press coverage is expected to reflect the efforts by presidential opponents to return to political normality, but it is also anticipated that such efforts will have limited success. In this case, however, critics of the "Reagan revolution" were able to mount a formidable attack and get much media attention while the still hospitalized President and his aides were preoccupied with handling the consequences of the shooting incident. Although the administration continued to dominate the news in directly crisis-related matters, it lost out to its opponents with respect to the coverage of Reagan's larger policy goals.

When the President returned to the White House and personally pushed his political agenda again, his remarkable demeanor during the crisis became inseparable from "Reaganomics" and his other goals. The ability of the President and his aides to keep the memories of his ordeal alive and to profit from frequent references to his health status while he mounted his lobbying effort on behalf of his programs assured favorable news coverage.

There was a relationship between editorial positions and news reporting in three periods examined; there was no relationship in one period, the lingering crisis phase.

In the aftermath of the crisis, the President was able to enlist the support of the American public as well as political elites. His budget and tax cuts were adopted by both houses of Congress. In a sense, the crisis triggered by the shots on T Street resulted in a renewed honeymoon for the President and his policy priorities.

6

THE GRENADA INVASION

OPERATION URGENT FURY

Pre-Dawn on Tuesday October 25, 1983. U.S. Marines and Army Rangers backed by a dozen warships off-shore begin a landing operation on Grenada, a Caribbean island state about twice the size of the District of Columbia and with about 110,000 inhabitants. First, 400 Marines are flown by helicopters from the USS *Guam* off the Grenadian coast to Pearls Airport. The invaders fight members of Grenada's Revolutionary Army, the militia, and some Cubans, but within two hours the airfield and its surroundings are secured. While the first stage of the invasion, aimed at gaining control of the northern part of the island, unfolds according to plan, the 500 Army Rangers who parachute off transport planes onto the Point Salinas area to gain control over the southern half are greeted by a barrage of machine-gun and antiaircraft fire. Still a few hours later, 750 additional paratroopers are able to touch down at Point Salinas as reinforcements. Some time later, 250 Marines make an amphibious landing north of St. George's to aid a group of SEALS, members of a special Navy force, in fighting their way into Governor's House, where British-Appointed Governor-General Sir Paul Scoon has been held under a kind of house arrest by the Revolutionary Military Council since the death of Prime Minister Maurice Bishop earlier this month. Eventually, the initial invasion force, which also includes 300 soldiers from six Caribbean neighbors of Grenada, is strengthened by several thousand additional U.S. troops. The military action, which carries the code name "Operation Urgent Fury," is well on its way.

At about 8:50 A.M., the True Blue campus of St. George's Medical College, where most of the 800 or so Americans who are students there reside, is under the control of Army Rangers. Seventeen minutes later, President Reagan steps into the White House briefing room to tell waiting reporters and the public what has taken place and is still unfolding.[1] "Early this morning, forces from six Caribbean democracies and the United States began a landing or landings on the island of Grenada in the Eastern Caribbean," he reveals, offering three reasons for his invasion decision: first, to protect up to one thousand Americans on the island, most of them the medical students; second, "to forestall further chaos"; and finally, "to assist in the restoration of law and order and of governmental institutions to the island of Grenada." Standing next to Ronald Reagan during this briefing is Eugenia Charles, Prime Minister of Dominica and chairperson of the Organization of Eastern Caribbean States (OECS), who clearly agrees with the President's claim that the U.S. acceded to "an urgent, formal request" from several members of the OECS as well as nonmembers Barbados and Jamaica "to assist in a joint effort to restore order and democracy" on Grenada.[2]

The news of the invasion comes on the heels of a tragic event some 48 hours earlier, when Americans learned that a terrorist attack on U.S. Marine headquarters in Beirut had killed more than 100 Marines, who had been part of a multinational peacekeeping contingent. The final death toll will eventually climb to 241. Not surprisingly, the coverage of the Grenada invasion replaces follow-up reports of the Beirut massacre as the number-one news item in the electronic and print media. The *New York Times,* the *Washington Post,* and the *Chicago Tribune* are in this respect representative of the press. "U.S. Invades Grenada, Fights Cubans; Reagan Cites Protection of Americans" reads the headline in the *Post*'s editions of October 26. The *Times* chooses a triple headline spread over the full six column width of the newspaper's page one: "1,900 U.S. Troops, with Caribbean Allies, Invade Grenada and Fight Leftist Units; Moscow Protests; British are Critical." The *Tribune* presents its first page invasion coverage under the short headline "GIs Battle in Grenada."

When the fighting is over, Ed Magnuson of *Time* magazine will point out in one meaningful sentence the very essence of the Grenada crisis, when he writes, "For the first time since the end of the Vietnam War, the U.S. had committed its troops to a combat attack."[3]

REAGAN AT THE 1000-DAY MARK

When the Marines landed on the Grenadian shores, Ronald Reagan had just passed the 1000-day mark of his presidency. As far as the Democratic contenders for the 1984 presidential election were concerned, the campaign had already begun. At this time, former Vice-President Walter Mondale and Senator John Glenn were considered the front-runners in the Democratic contest. And while Ronald Reagan claimed that he had not yet decided whether to run for reelection, there was little doubt that he wanted a second term even before he signed a letter of intent to the Federal Election Commission sometime in October.

The President's political fortunes were not quite as bright as they had been during the first years of his presidency, when he was able to push the most important aspects of his agenda through Congress. By now liberals, stunned by the dimension of the 1980 Reagan victory, had firmly regrouped; union leaders, women's rights activists, and the black minority in particular massively opposed the Reagan administration's policies. They kept the so-called "fairness issue" alive, charging that the President's far-reaching tax and budgetary policies were beneficial to the haves and harmful to the have-nots.

Even the right wing of the Republican party was somewhat disillusioned with Reagan, who had refrained so far from pushing the social agenda that was high on the priority list of traditional conservatives. Also, in the days and weeks before the Grenada invasion, there had been a number of personnel changes within the Reagan administration that, in the eyes of right-wingers, had weakened their cause: While the President had accepted the resignation of Interior Secretary James Watt, a favorite of the right, he had also okayed William Clark's switch from National Security Adviser to Secretary of the Interior. With that move, the traditional right wing of the Republican party as well as neoconservatives felt they had lost their voice in foreign and national security policies. They were even more annoyed when Reagan appointed Robert McFarlane to succeed William Clark as National Security Adviser instead of their choice—U.N. Ambassador Jeane Kirkpatrick. Once Reagan's most enthusiastic supporters, some conservatives now felt that the President was not tough enough in his dealings with the Soviet Union and its client states.

The President's approval ratings had dropped. A Gallup poll released at the beginning of September and based on interviews conducted in mid-August revealed that more Americans (45 percent) disapproved of the way the President handled his job than approved of it (43 percent). However, in the wake of the uproar over the shooting down of a South Korean airliner by the Soviet Union on September 1, Reagan's ratings had improved: In the first half of October, 46 percent of the public approved, 37 percent disapproved of the President's job performance.[4]

What seemed to work in favor of the President was the economic recovery that had occurred during 1983. Still, in trial presidential heats against possible Democratic rivals, Reagan failed to demonstrate overwhelming strength. For example, in a poll conducted by the President's own pollster, Richard Wirthlin, Reagan led John Glenn by three and Walter Mondale by five percent—not too impressive a margin for the incumbent.[5]

Finally, when the U.S. forces invaded Grenada, it was not yet known how the American public was going to react to the Marine massacre two days earlier. Hours after he had received the bad news from Beirut, the

President reportedly told his advisers that the terrorist attack should not affect the decision to launch what Reagan preferred to call a "rescue mission" on Grenada. When during a White House meeting the question was raised whether it was advisable to go ahead with the Grenada plan, the President was said to have answered, "If this [Grenada] was right yesterday, it's right today, and we shouldn't let the act of a couple of terrorists dissuade us from going ahead."[6] Ever since, it has been suspected, however, that the invasion was a welcome move to refocus the attention of the American public from the massacre in Beirut to the Grenadian intervention.

THE PRESIDENT AND THE PRESS

White House Press Secretary Larry Speakes displayed a sign on his desk that proclaimed: You don't tell us how to stage the news, and we don't tell you how to cover it. Thus, President Reagan's press office did not make any secret of the fact that the White House "staged" the news. It was exactly this successful effort in staging and, in the view of many reporters, in manipulating the news that led to growing frustration on the part of the White House press corps. By controlling what information was given to the media and what was withheld, the White House—regardless of what Larry Speakes' sign proclaimed—also influenced how reporters could cover the news.

The news management under Reagan was based on two principles that became more obvious in the months and years that followed the prolonged honeymoon period granted the 40th President by the fourth estate. First, the White House media experts relied on a nearly daily basis on photo opportunities that typically showed the President greeting a foreign visitor, opening a White House meeting, or descending from his helicopter on a return to the Presidential mansion; on "ad hoc" mini–press conferences in the Oval Office that left reporters little time to ask uncomfortable questions; and on carefully prepared speeches before all kinds of supportive groups. Second, the President and his closest aides made great efforts to plug leaks that provided reporters with information that the highest level of the White House did not want released. While not all leakers were silenced, it became more difficult for journalists to get information not authorized by Reagan's inner circle.

The press–president relationship reached a low point when the news media were barred from witnessing a major military action of U.S. forces and from reporting about it—the invasion of Grenada. For three days, the military prevented eyewitness accounts by reporters. White House aides claimed that not the President but the military had decided to exclude the press because they did not want to jeopardize the lives of journalists. Most in the media did not buy this explanation but charged that the administration had followed the example of Prime Minister Margaret Thatcher who had barred the press from covering the decisive phase of the British landing on the Falkland Islands. The prevention of first-hand press accounts of the actions and conditions on the Caribbean island was perceived by many in the media as the ultimate news manipulation by the U.S. administration. Yet, large segments of the public seemed to side with the President in the debate over press freedom and the right of the public to be informed versus the government's right and duty to protect national security interests. Responding to a story about this debate in *Time* magazine, one reader argued, "There comes a time when Americans must choose between freedom of the press and national security. National security was more at stake than freedom of the press in Grenada."[7]

TINY ISLAND—HUGE THREAT

In his so-called "Star Wars" speech on March 23, 1983, which described for the first time his concept of a new space-based Strategic Defense Initiative, President Reagan spoke of the growing Soviet threat in the American hemisphere. As one example of Communist expansionism in the region, he mentioned "the Soviet-Cuban militarization of Grenada." Showing a satellite photograph of the island, Reagan charged that the Cubans, backed by the Soviet Union, were building an airfield with a 10,000 foot runway even though "Grenada doesn't even have an Air Force."[8]

While satellite pictures were published, Reagan's reference to the Communist connection in Grenada and its threat to American strategic interests almost got lost in the press coverage of the address, which, understandably, concentrated on the President's revelation of his "Star Wars" defense plans, his overall national security concept, and his demands for hefty defense spending.

Also, the charge that Grenada was being transformed into a Cuban-Soviet military base was not new. Speaking before members of the National Association of Manufacturers in early March, the President had complained that Grenada "is building now or is having built for it . . . a naval base, a superior air base, storage bases and facilities for the storage of munitions, barracks and training grounds for the military."[9] In both instances, the press seemed to take notice of the Grenada references in Presidential speeches only, when representatives of the island's leftist government denied Reagan's militarization charges. On March 11, for example, the *Chicago Tribune* used an AP dispatch which reported that the Grenadian Ambassador in Washington,

Dessima Williams, had denied the President's charge of military bases on the island and had invited Reagan to visit Grenada and see for himself. The article then recounted what the President had said about the Grenadian threat before the Association of Manufacturers. [10]

Similarly, in its editions of March 26, the *New York Times* referred to the Grenada remarks made during the President's "Star Wars" speech—two days after reporting extensively on the major points of his speech. Placed on the "Washington Talk" page as the lead-off item in the "Briefing" column, the *Times* revealed that a Miami-based company, "working with Cuban engineers, recently completed a $2.9 million dredging contract at the airport site, and another American concern designed the facility's fuel storage tanks." The item also quoted a Grenadian official who had pointed out that "the airport is open to the public and it was not necessary for the President to use aerial photographs."[11] A few days later, the *Times* seemed to belittle Reagan's Grenada remarks in a kind of mini-editorial placed under the regular editorials. "Conceivably, Grenadans are lying when they say the runway is strictly for tourism," the *New York Times* commented, "but having melodramatically waved his photograph, Mr. Reagan will have a harder time convincing Americans that the sky is really falling in Grenada."[12]

Even before the President's public charges and the denials by Grenadian officials, the *Washington Post* had published a front page story about the Reagan administration's preoccupation with the Caribbean island and its leftist government led by Prime Minister Maurice Bishop. According to the *Post* account, "The Reagan administration, concerned that Cuba is developing better ways to extend its military influence in Central America, considered a covert intelligence operation against the leftist government of Grenada in 1981 and is now closely monitoring new Cuban activities on the tiny eastern Caribbean island." The article quoted a "senior Republican" member of the Senate Intelligence Committee who had revealed that, upon learning of a possible CIA operation, the committee members had come to the conclusion, "it [Grenada] was just a small island and so the Cubans or Communists control it, so what?"[13]

Neither the revelation of those earlier CIA plans, which were never carried out, nor the President's efforts to portray Grenada as a threat received much attention. Just as the Senate Intelligence Committee was reported to have thought in 1981, the reaction of American politicians and of the American media seemed to indicate a "so what?" attitude.

Most of what was published in the three newspapers about the Caribbean island, its officials, and its condition during the weeks and months following the Reagan references was relegated to small news items and articles on inside pages. This was the case, for example, when Grenadian officials charged in early April that the United States was preparing an invasion of their island and when Prime Minister Maurice Bishop visited Washington and New York.

Even the news of an attempted coup in Grenada in mid-October did not make the front pages. However, both the *Times* and the *Post* reported later in page one stories that Maurice Bishop had been killed and that, according to Radio Free Grenada, a "revolutionary and military council" had taken control of the island and enacted a 24-hour shoot-on-sight curfew.[14] From this point on, the press reported increasingly about the developments in Grenada. There were reports of a meeting by eastern Caribbean leaders considering a concerted response to an even more radical regime in Grenada, of a possible danger to about 1000 Americans on the island, and of American war ships, headed for duty off the Lebanese coast but being sent instead toward Grenada to be available for the evacuation of American nationals from the island. It was reported that the new rulers on the island had assured American officials of the safety of U.S. citizens on Grenada and that they had warned Grenadians of an invasion by American or Caribbean forces. But there was no indication that the papers gave much credence to the Grenadian invasion charges. On October 24, one day before U.S. Marines invaded Grenada, the *Post* referred to sources who believed that the "news of the bombing against U.S. Marines in Beirut made any U.S. intervention a less immediate possibility.[15]

In the only editorial published in one of the three papers in the days following the Grenadian coup and the death of Bishop, the *Post* criticized the Reagan administration for its failure to establish a relationship with Bishop and thus strengthen his hand against rivals "thought to be even more on the left." The editorial wondered "whether the administration created some of its current embarrassment by taking a confrontational attitude to the prickly Mr. Bishop rather than trying to measure his possible disenchantment with Cuba and give him a bit more room on his right."[16]

Much of the published material concerning Grenada fell into the neutral/ ambiguous category because most of this coverage occurred during the few days preceding the invasion when reports were mostly based on observers and sources in Barbados or elsewhere in the Caribbean who tried to sort out what was going on in Grenada. Before the coup, Bishop and representatives of his government had been the leading foreign sources in the news concerned with Grenada and these sources had been very critical of the Washington administration. In the combined domestic and foreign coverage critical sources had a space advantage over pro-Reagan sources in the *Times,* which had published some critical editorial remarks on the subject. The *Post,* which had also expressed reservations about the President's Grenada approach, provided pro-administration sources with somewhat more lineage than critics. In the *Tribune,* which did not publish a relevant editorial prior to the invasion, the space advantage of pro-Reagan sources over critics of the President was significantly greater than in the *Post* (see table 6.1).

In the domestic coverage as well sources fitting the neutral/ambiguous category dominated, and pro-administration sources captured by far more lineage than critics of the President's Grenada view. This was so because prior to the violent domestic changes on the island, the relevant debate was dominated by charges and countercharges between Ronald Reagan and his administration on one hand and Maurice Bishop and his government on the other. Accordingly, among domestic sources those supportive of the President, namely members of his administration, had the stage for themselves. Indeed, there simply was no domestic debate concerning the White House stand on Grenada before the invasion occurred (see table 6.2).

Given the lack of interest among domestic political actors and only sporadic press coverage of the Grenadian issue before the coup, articles relating to the Grenadian issue seldom made the front pages during the pre-crisis months. There were no front page stories in the Chicago newspaper. In the *Times*, sources favorable to the administration's Grenada view made front page stories on seven occasions, critical sources in two instances. In the *Post*, pro-Reagan sources had a 6–4 placement advantage as far as page one stories were concerned.

The domestic Grenada news was dominated by what the President and

TABLE 6.1   Overall Pre-Crisis Coverage, Grenada Invasion: Domestic and Foreign Sources, Directly Relevant (Editorials Excluded)

Linage	For/Probably For	Neutral/ Ambiguous	Against/Probably Against	Total Lines
TIMES	17.9%	60.2%	21.9%	1,519
POST	18.6	67.8	13.6	1,977
TRIBUNE	31.0	50.2	18.8	606

TABLE 6.2   Pre-Crisis Coverage, Grenada Invasion: Domestic Sources, Directly Relevant (Editorials Excluded)

Linage	For/Probably For	Neutral/ Ambiguous	Against/Probably Against	Total Lines
TIMES	20.2%	77.5%	2.3%	858
POST	27.9	70.6	1.5	1,062
TRIBUNE	43.1	55.9	1.0	388

his administration had to say. With the exception of revelations that the Senate Intelligence Committee had refused to approve a covert CIA operation against the Bishop regime in 1981, congressional sources were simply nonexistent in the newspaper coverage.

AMERICAN TROOPS INVADE GRENADA

In their first editions following the invasion news the *New York Times* and the *Washington Post* gave an extraordinary amount of front page and inside page space to stories, news analyses, editorials, photographs, and maps describing, explaining, and commenting on the events surrounding the military operation. Both East Coast publications dedicated most of their front pages to the Grenada developments, providing limited prime space to the only other front page topic—the Beirut Marine massacre. The *Chicago Tribune*, too, made the invasion its lead stories on its front page and provided additional, extensive coverage on its inside pages.

Like the rest of the media, none of the three newspapers could rely on firsthand reports from the scene by their own reporters. Western correspondents had been ordered off the island after the coup by the new revolutionary and military council that had ousted Maurice Bishop. No press representatives had been allowed to accompany the invasion troops, and a few journalists (among them a correspondent of the *Washington Post*) who had tried and succeeded in reaching Grenada by boat, had been picked up by American invaders and transported off-shore aboard the USS *Guam*.[17] Thus, in their coverage of the acute Grenada crisis, the media were unable to rely on firsthand, journalistic accounts in efforts to answer the basic "who-what-when-where-why?" questions of the fourth estate.

That was, of course, as unidentified administration sources revealed within hours after the invasion, the purpose behind the decision to bar the press from covering "Operation Urgent Fury." The military leadership, it was reported, had been impressed with the way the British had managed to curb their press during the Falkland Island operation.[18] Ultimately, the reaction in the media over this kind of censorship may have had a negative impact on the coverage—from the administration's point of view.

Nevertheless, those who opted for barring press coverage of the invasion had calculated correctly that without firsthand reporting from the scene, the press would have to depend mostly on information provided by the White House and the Departments of State and Defense. The coverage in all three newspapers reveals that they indeed relied heavily on the administration's answers to the "who-what-when-where-why?" questions. On October 26, in their editions that broke the invasion news to readers, the front pages of all three newspapers illustrated the information monopoly of the administration.

Of the five front page stories the *Times* published the day following the invasion, three originated in Washington, one in Bridgetown, Barbados, and one in London. The three articles with the dateline Washington were mostly based on named and unnamed administration sources. The report from Barbados referred at one point to the Reagan administration and repeatedly to eastern Caribbean officials sympathetic to the invasion. Finally, the sole front page article without input from administration officials or sources in the region involved in the military operation described the unsuccessful effort of Prime Minister Margaret Thatcher to convince President Reagan to reconsider his invasion plans.[19]

Of the four front page articles the *Post* dedicated to the Grenada crisis on October 26, three originated in Washington, while one had the dateline Bridgetown. With the exception of the piece originating in Barbados, all these articles relied heavily on official statements by the President, by the Secretary of State, by other officials in the White House, and Departments of Defense and State. Even the article from Bridgetown referred repeatedly to administration sources.[20]

Although the *Tribune* made references to Prime Minister Thatcher's failure to prevent the invasion and to the condemnation of the move by the Soviet news agency Tass on the day following the invasion, its front page story datelined Washington was mostly based on President Reagan's and Secretary of State Shultz's justifications for the intervention. Another front page story in the *Tribune*'s edition of October 26 relied in part, and especially in the lead paragraphs, on Pentagon and other administration officials.[21]

In the editions of the following day, the lead front page stories in all three newspapers relied fully or partially on administration sources.[22] There is no doubt that the lack of independent press reports from Grenada assured the administration ample space on front pages and elsewhere on inside pages.

On the other hand, the widespread media dissatisfaction with the ban of reporters from the invasion scene may have whetted the appetite of editors and reporters to search for all kinds of sources in efforts to piece together a complete and true picture of the Grenadian events. Thus, during the acute crisis, the newspapers—the two East Coast papers more than the Chicago paper—made much use of domestic and foreign sources who knew or claimed to know what was going on in Grenada. For example, reports on the status of the combat on the island was in part based on what ham radio operaters transmitted from Grenada to the United States. Other accounts were based on telephone conversations with Americans on the island. Still other descriptions were taken from communiqués of the Cuban government, Radio Havana and the official Cuban government news agency Prensa Latina, all claiming that the Castro government was in touch with the Cuban Embassy in Grenada.

Many of these sources did not support the official line of the Reagan administration. For instance, describing conversations between ham operators in and outside of Grenada, one *Post* story quoted an American living on the island who claimed that "there had been no threats whatsoever to any Americans."[23] He thus denied the President's claim that the primary motive for the invasion was to protect the lives of American citizens, including medical students. In one dispatch from Bridgetown, *Tribune* correspondent George de Lama wrote of "a stonewall of silence" around Grenada that had given Cuba a great propaganda opportunity, because "Radio Havana has been almost the only alternative to official U.S. accounts of the Cuban resistance to American forces."[24]

The search for sources outside the U.S. administration to inform journalists might have resulted in more attention to anti-administration sources than would have been the case, had the media been allowed to see for themselves. Critical foreign sources captured more space than foreigners supportive of the American move. This was hardly surprising because not only foes such as the Soviet Union, Cuba, and Nicaragua, but also friends in Europe and Latin America just condemned the American intervention. On the other hand, significant lineage, especially in the *Times,* was based on eastern Caribbean officials who strongly supported the U.S. involvement in the region.

Still, in the overall coverage of the two acute crisis days (newspaper editions of October 26 and 27) sources supportive of the President's invasion decision captured more space in the three papers than sources critical of Reagan's Grenada stand. While pro-administration sources dominated the combined domestic and foreign coverage of the *Tribune,* their linage advantage over critical sources was much smaller in the other two newspapers (see table 6.3).

TABLE 6.3   Overall Acute Crisis Coverage, Grenada Invasion: Domestic and Foreign Sources, Directly Relevant (Editorials Excluded)

Linage	For/Probably For	Neutral/ Ambiguous	Against/Probably Against	Total Lines
TIMES	38.5%	37.0%	24.5%	4,794
POST	38.2	32.5	29.3	4,887
TRIBUNE	55.3	22.8	21.9	1,481

As far as the domestic crisis coverage was concerned, all three newspapers devoted significantly more space to sources supportive of the crisis-managing President. In the *Tribune,* sources who favored the administration's Grenada stand captured about nine times as much lineage as critical sources. This was by far the most favorable pro-Reagan coverage among the three newspapers. The *Post* published four lines based on domestic supporters of the President for each line attributable to domestic critics of the President in this matter. In the coverage of the *Times* the space advantage of domestic pro-Reagan sources over domestic critics of his Grenada policy was better than 2–1 (see table 6.4).

How did the newspapers react editorially to the news of the invasion and to the President's initially given reasons for the military operation? On the day following the invasion, all three newspapers articulated their views. The *Times* rejected the reasons the Reagan administration had given for its military move and spoke of a mere "hypothetical threat" to the lives of Americans. Also, according to the editorial, order and authority had not collapsed on the island. "The deed is political. It promises to rid the Caribbean of a pro-Soviet gnat." In its conclusion, the editorial modified its criticism just a bit, remarking that the President might deserve the benefit of the doubt, if Cuba and the Soviet Union had indeed moved to establish a puppet regime as a basis for other operations in the region. "But if that were clear," the *Times* remarked, "why was it not proved, or even asserted?"[25]

Examining some "good" and some "bad" reasons to invade Grenada and expressing doubt about the ones given by the President, the *Tribune* reserved its editorial judgment by observing, "The only vindication of this action will be success, it must be shown—soon—that the Grenadians welcome the invasion and are able to take control of their affairs without further U.S. involvement."[26]

Pointing out that "[t]he burden of proof is still on the Reagan administration to justify the immensely grave act of invading a sovereign state," the *Post* editorial on the day after the invasion did not exclude the possibility

TABLE 6.4   Acute Crisis Coverage, Grenada Invasion: Domestic Sources, Directly Relevant (Editorials Excluded)

Linage	For/Probably For	Neutral/ Ambiguous	Against/Probably Against	Total Lines
TIMES	42.9%	38.8%	18.3%	3,391
POST	47.1	42.0	10.9	3,392
TRIBUNE	66.1	26.8	7.1	1,158

that the lives of Americans were indeed endangered. Also, the *Post* pointed out that "the appeal of six democratic nations asserts a claim."[27] The Washington newspaper was the only one among the three who followed up with a relevant editorial the following day. With 24 more hours to ponder the crisis, the *Post* editorialized that on several points "our misgivings about the invasion has deepened." But again, the door was left open for agreeing with the President. "From the evacuated Americans we will be learning more about the merits of the operation as a rescue mission. If the danger was really great, then the purpose was worthy."[28]

While all three newspapers expressed reservations about the President's justification for the invasion, the *Times* editorial gave an overall critical impression, because it did not leave much room for the possibility that Reagan had good reasons for the invasion. The editorials in the other newspapers did not discount the possibility that, as the *Post* put it, the "purpose was worthy."[29] This gave the editorials in *Tribune* and *Post* an ambiguous mentality. The difference between the editorial in the New York newspaper on one side and the editorial pieces in the Washington and Chicago publications on the other was one of nuances. Yet it is interesting to note that, among domestic sources, the space advantage of pro-administration sources versus anti-administration sources was considerably smaller in the *Times* than in *Post* or *Tribune*.

Pro-administration, domestic sources made front page stories much more often than domestic critics of the President's Grenada move while critical foreign sources had a page one placement advantage over foreigners supportive of the U.S. invasion.

While administration officials who were very supportive of the invasion decision dominated the domestic Grenada debate, there were other supporters of the President's move, namely conservative members of Congress and Grenadian exiles living in the United States. The *Tribune*, for instance, quoted Republican Senator Malcolm Wallop as one of those who applauded the Grenada move. Wallop, according to the Chicago newspaper, said, "We are seeing an increasing level of Soviet adventuring all over the world. It's time we responded."[30] And Senator Steve Symms praised the invasion as "signaling a welcome change in foreign policy."[31] On the other hand, a number of liberal members of Congress voiced opposition almost immediately after learning about the invasion. Democratic Senator Daniel Patrick Moynihan reportedly characterized the invasion as "an act of war" that the United States did not have a right to.[32] There was some outright criticism among the declared Democratic candidates for the Presidential nomination in 1984 (Former Senator George McGovern called the invasion "utterly irresponsible") and some possible support, if, as Senator John Glenn pointed out, the American citizens on Grenada had indeed been in danger.[33]

Finally, demonstrations against the Grenada action took place during this period. All three newspapers reported on the different reactions among politicians inside and outside of Congress, all three described the reactions of the first evacuees from the island. Yet, the two East Coast publications paid more attention to protest demonstrations and other critical expressions than did the *Tribune,* and the New York newspaper gave more space to sources critical of the President's Grenada stand than the Washington newspaper.

The greatest resentment against the Reagan administration's Grenada policies manifested itself in the news coverage of issues indirectly related to the invasion, namely the ban of the media from the island. In this category, anti-administration sources, many of them drawn from media circles, were dominant vis-à-vis administration supporters in this matter (see table 6.5).

Although a number of representatives and senators reacted immediately to the intervention in Grenada and made the news, administration officials captured about ten times as much space as did legislative sources (see table 6.6). This was not surprising considering that journalists were not allowed to witness the military actions on the island and that members of Congress as well as the public had no choice but to rely mostly on information provided by administration officials.

Most journalistic descriptions, background information, and news anal-

TABLE 6.5   Acute Crisis Coverage, Grenada Invasion: Domestic Sources, Indirectly Relevant

Linage	For/Probably For	Neutral/ Ambiguous	Against/Probably Against	Total Lines
TIMES	18.2%	40.3%	41.5%	318
POST	—	33.1	66.9	393
TRIBUNE	—	—	100.0	143

TABLE 6.6   Linage Administration and Congressional Sources, Grenada Invasion: Acute Crisis

	Administration Sources	Congressional Sources	Total Lines
TIMES	90.5%	9.5%	1,417
POST	91.9	8.1	1,600
TRIBUNE	91.6	8.4	704

yses did not reveal a position for or against the administration's Grenada actions and policies. However, about 20 percent of media-based lines in the straight news section of the *Times* and about 12 percent in the *Post* revealed critical attitudes toward one or another aspect of the intervention move.

"WE GOT THERE JUST IN TIME"

In his prime time television address to the nation on October 27, the President described the military status of the Grenada operation as the "mopping-up phase." He also revealed that American forces had discovered three large warehouses with military equipment on the island as proof that "a Soviet-Cuban colony [was] being readied." However, Reagan said, "We got there just in time."[34] With American students safe and the threat of a Communist military base on Grenada removed, the acute crisis had ended. During the six days of the lingering crisis (newspaper editions October 28 through November 2), there were still sporadic fire exchanges between GIs and some Grenadian and Cuban resisters, but once it was confirmed by the President that 600 Cuban soldiers had been captured by the multinational force it was clear that the invaders were in control of the island state.

The three newspapers covered the Reagan speech extensively in front page stories that extended onto inside pages. The *Washington Post* reported in another front page piece that many Republicans and Democrats on Capitol Hill believed that the address had helped the President to buttress support for his Grenada move.[35]

The President, other officials in the White House, the State and Defense departments, and military spokespersons remained the dominant sources. Even after reporters were able to visit the island and give firsthand accounts —initially the American military allowed only certain kinds of guided tours for journalists—military and administration officials both in Grenada and Washington remained the major sources for news about the developments surrounding the Grenadian operation.

Moreover, many medical students returning aboard military transport planes to the United States spoke out in support of the President's claim that he had okayed the invasion in order to rescue Americans and prevent another hostage crisis. The press published articles containing students' assessment of the invasion. A front page story in the *Times,* for example, reported in its lead paragraph that students evacuated from Grenada "praised the Reagan Administration and United States invasion forces for bringing them safely away."[36] The *Post* reported at length about two returning students who like other evacuees "agreed that President Reagan's decision to invade most likely had saved them from future harm."[37] In another article in the Washington newspaper, a group of American students claimed that they had been held for a few hours by Grenadian militia members and that the Cubans on the island were "out to get us."[38] The *Tribune* reported about two Chicago area students who "expressed deep gratitude to the U.S. government for their rescue."[39] In another *Tribune* story, students from various parts of the country were quoted with praise for the rangers who had rescued them. Medical student Jeff Geller said, according to the *Tribune*, "I have been a dove all my life, but I was glad to see them [the rangers]."[40] Stories like these in addition to the many articles based on administration sources were likely to have an impact on public opinion favorable to the President. Exactly that was suggested by members of Congress who, as the *Times* reported, had said that they "hesitated to speak out because of the comments of returning students."[41]

On the other hand, with the acute crisis over, there was less constraint on others who disagreed with the President to voice their misgivings. A good example was House Speaker Thomas "Tip" O'Neill. As the *Times* reported in a front page story, the Massachusetts Democrat, who "had been holding his fire in recent days," ended his self-restraint calling the administration's foreign policy in Grenada and Lebanon "frightening."[42] Also, most of the declared Democratic candidates for their party's presidential nomination voiced their disagreement with the President's Grenada move more openly.[43]

As far as the foreign coverage was concerned, Cuban and Soviet officials were reported to be continuing their criticism of the American operation on Grenada. While there were still reports about misgivings among friendly countries and governments, these were far fewer than during the acute crisis phase. A new and attractive source, the Queen of England, expressing unhappiness over the American Grenada invasion, assured that even the *Tribune*, with less foreign coverage than the two East Coast papers, would take notice.[44] Finally, there were more articles reporting about support for the invasion among Grenadians and their neighbors.[45]

In the combined domestic and foreign news coverage pro-Reagan sources captured significantly more column lines than critics of the President's Grenada action (see table 6.7). The Grenada news was most favorable from the administration's point of view in the *Tribune* and least so in the *Post*. The Washington paper, unlike *Times* and *Tribune* devoted more space to foreign critics than to foreign supporters of the invasion.

Among domestic sources, those supportive of the President's Grenada stand fared best compared with critical sources in the *Tribune*, where pro-Reagan sources captured nearly thirteen times as much space as did anti-administration sources. The *New York Times* devoted nearly five times and the *Post* three-and-a-half times as much space to domestic Reagan supporters as to his critics (see table 6.8).

During the lingering crisis, the *Times* published two editorials directly relevant to the Grenada crisis; in both the newspaper was critical of the administration's Grenada actions. Questioning whether the invasion was needed to rescue students and whether the leftist regime and Cubans had to be removed by force, the *Times* argued that "the real inspiration and justification for the Grenada invasion lies in those false feelings of impotence— fanned by years of deceptive politicking about American retreats."[46] A few days earlier, the newspaper had editorialized that "[t]o liberate Grenada from some local henchmen, and perhaps from Cubans, America has defined its duty and security in ways that make it look like a paranoid bully."[47]

While calling it "disturbing" that the Reagan administration used findings after the intervention in Grenada to justify its action, the *Post* admitted that "the news from Grenada may be running the president's way." The editorial mentioned reports by students that supported the rescue argument and the presence of Cuban personnel and weapons on the island as perhaps backing Reagan's claim that a Soviet-Cuban base was being built on the Caribbean island.[48] The *Post* was less ambiguous in a second editorial commenting on Grenada that was critical of the administration because "the uniformed

TABLE 6.7 Overall Lingering Crisis Coverage, Grenada Invasion: Domestic and Foreign Sources, Directly Relevant (Editorials Excluded)

Linage	For/Probably For	Neutral/ Ambiguous	Against/Probably Against	Total Lines
TIMES	51.4%	32.2%	16.4%	8,207
POST	39.4	41.5	19.1	10,212
TRIBUNE	59.1	30.8	10.1	3,258

TABLE 6.8 Lingering Crisis Coverage, Grenada Invasion: Domestic Sources, Directly Relevant (Editorials Excluded)

Linage	For/Probably For	Neutral/ Ambiguous	Against/Probably Against	Total Lines
TIMES	54.4%	34.3%	11.3%	6,405
POST	42.3	45.8	11.9	7,769
TRIBUNE	59.8	35.5	4.7	2,650

military seems to have had an unusually large degree of control over this [Grenada] operation, notwithstanding its political essence."[49]

In the one editorial directly relevant to the Grenadian crisis, the *Chicago Tribune* pointed out that "[t]he case supporting the U.S. invasion of Grenada grows stronger with evidence of a major Soviet-backed Cuban military buildup there." The editorial concluded that this demonstrated "that Grenada was an appropriate place for the U.S. to demonstrate its willingness to use force to resist Soviet designs in our part of the world."[50] Having made this point, the *Tribune* lamented that the Reagan administration had not balanced its show of strength with efforts to establish good relations with the Soviet Union. Nevertheless, as far as the Grenada action was concerned, the editorial was supportive of the President.

Was there a relationship between the editorial stand and the news coverage of directly crisis-related matters? It seems that such a relationship can be construed: The *Tribune,* which in spite of its reservations about the overall foreign policy approach of the administration seemed to subscribe to the President's justification for the invasion, was more accommodating to sources supportive of Reagan than the other two publications. This was the case in the overall Grenada coverage (domestic and foreign sources), and even more so when it came to the domestic coverage. In the East Coast papers, which took a more critical editorial stance, the news coverage was not quite as favorable to the President as was that of the *Tribune.*

Regardless of their editorial views, the three newspapers used domestic sources in favor of the President's handling of the Grenada situation in front page stories much more often than domestic critics. There was a placement turnaround as far as foreign sources were concerned. While critical foreign sources had been used more often on page one than those in favor of the American move on Grenada during the acute crisis phase, foreigners in favor of the Grenada stand made front page stories more often than critical ones in the lingering phase.

While Reagan's opponents of the invasion seemed to hesitate to speak their mind, they did not when it came to matters only indirectly relevant to the Caribbean crisis. The media kept alive the debate surrounding the barring of journalists from witnessing the Grenadian intervention. All three newspapers editorialized sharply against the exclusion of the press. The *Times* recalled the refusal of the Soviet government in September to let reporters near the scene where Korean Flight 007 had been shot down. That, the editorial noted, had not been terribly surprising, but "there is plenty of reason for surprise now, in Grenada, for this time it's the United States Government that has been trying to keep the public in the dark."[51] The *Post* called it "inexcusable" that the administration did "not permit firsthand American media coverage of Grenada invasion" during the first and the intense combat phase of the operation.[52] And the *Tribune* criticized the administration's news ban and its disregard for a long-standing American tradition, warning that "freedom was badly served by banning journalists from Grenada during the crucial early days."[53] While giving the administration the opportunity to present its view on this issue, the newspapers covered the critics of the press ban, namely media representatives, repeatedly. And there was another issue of indirect relevance to the crisis that was covered during this period: the debate between Congress and administration about the War Powers Act and its application to the Grenadian operation. While many in Congress insisted that provisions of the act applied, the administration had a different view.

The *Post* and the *Tribune* devoted significantly more space to sources critical of Reagan's position in indirectly crisis-related matters than to his supporters. The *Times,* which covered the secondary issues much more extensively than did the other two newspapers, covered critics of the President in these issues extensively but provided somewhat more space to Reagan supporters (see table 6.9).

Although administration sources captured much more space than congressional sources, the gap was not as huge as during the acute crisis phase. Lawmakers, many of whom had not said much either way during the acute crisis days, were more willing to express either support for or opposi-

TABLE 6.9   Lingering Crisis Coverage, Grenada Invasion: Domestic Sources, Indirectly Relevant

Linage	For/Probably For	Neutral/ Ambiguous	Against/Probably Against	Total Lines
TIMES	35.6%	34.1%	30.3%	1,071
POST	14.0	17.9	68.1	342
TRIBUNE	4.4	16.7	78.9	473

TABLE 6.10   Linage Administration and Congressional Sources, Grenada Invasion: Lingering Crisis

	Administration Sources	Congressional Sources	Total Lines
TIMES	82.8%	17.2%	3,892
POST	81.5	18.5	3,228
TRIBUNE	84.2	15.8	1,591

tion to the intervention once the fierce combat phase on Grenada had ended (see table 6.10).

Journalistic descriptions, background information, and news analyses during this period fell overwhelmingly, in the *Tribune* completely, into the neutral/ambiguous category. About 18 percent of these types of lines in the *Times* and about 7 percent in the *Post* seemed to reveal critical attitudes vis-à-vis the relevant policies of the administration.

"ALL HOSTILITIES HAVE CEASED"

On November 2, 1983 Secretary of Defense Caspar Weinberger informed President Reagan and the public that the fighting on Grenada had ended. In their editions of the following day, the two East Coast newspapers and the Chicago publication published front page stories that quoted Weinberger as having said that "all hostilities have ceased."[54] The same stories reported that the withdrawal of American troops from the Caribbean island, initially about half of them, would begin shortly. This made it official: Merely eight days after "Operation Urgent Fury" had begun, the crisis was over.

This did not mean that the President paid less attention to questions surrounding the Grenadian operation. Especially until his departure for a trip to the Far East on November 8, Reagan led the administration campaign to justify the intervention and to enlist public and elite support. Considering the press coverage, it was a very successful undertaking. For example, when Reagan explained during a White House briefing for reporters that the Grenada move was "a rescue mission, not an invasion" and strongly objected to comparisons with the Soviet invasion of Afghanistan four years earlier, this was reported in the three newspapers.[55] When the President greeted in the White House thankful American medical students who had been airlifted by military transport planes from the island, the event was covered as was a Presidential speech thanking wounded GIs and eulogizing those who had been killed in Grenada and Lebanon.[56]

The President was not the only high official active in the weeks following the Grenadian crisis. (For the coverage of the post-crisis phase, newspaper editions of November 3 through November 25 were examined.) When Deputy Secretary of State Kenneth W. Dam revealed during his testimony before a House Foreign Affairs subcommittee that documents seized by American troops on the island showed "a Soviet, Cuban, and North Korean relationship with Grenada resulting in signed agreements to donate $37.8 million in military equipment," it was carried by the newspapers as was the content of the documents, once the administration made those arms pacts available.[57]

After the President had left Washington for the Far East, Vice-President George Bush seemed to take over the Grenada crusade. The *Washington Post* published a lengthy front page article, illustrated with photographs, that described how Bush inspected a public display of weapons captured in Grenada and flown to and exhibited at Andrews Air Force Base. In addition, the *Post* carried an article describing how the general public viewed the exhibited military arsenal.[58] This kind of reporting seemed to support the administration's charges of a "Communist threat," and resulted in a growing public sentiment favoring Reagan's invasion decision. Among the first to realize this were members of Congress. Accordingly, as the *New York Times* summed up in one headline, "Capitol Hill Outcry Softens as Public's Support Swells." While acknowledging that opposition to the invasion still existed in Congress, Hedrick Smith reported that "many lawmakers seem to sense a public wave of patriotism over the Grenada operation, and have responded to it."[59] The biggest boost for the Reagan administration came when the Speaker of the House, Thomas O'Neill, who had criticized Reagan's Grenada intervention harshly, reversed himself and called the invasion "justified." All three newspapers reported this turnaround in front page stories.[60]

Still, with all the widely reported support for the pro-Reagan side, there was also opposition. The most drastic move took place in Congress, when seven Democratic Representatives asked the House to impeach the President for having ordered the invasion of Grenada. All three newspapers reported this, but not very prominently. The *Times* and the *Post* published small one-column items on inside pages while the *Tribune* mentioned the impeachment request at the conclusion of the inside page continuation of a lengthy front page story.[61] There were a few dissenters to the pro-Reagan conclusion drawn by a congressional delegation during its visit to Grenada, and this was mentioned in the East Coast papers.[62] Also, the *Times* took note of protesters demonstrating against the Grenada intervention, and the *Post* described Senator Alan Cranston's charge that the President was "trigger-happy."[63]

While critical foreign voices received frequent coverage—namely Fidel Castro and other Cuban sources, there were also more reports from Grenada quoting sources who favored the invasion. Bernard Weinraub, for example, observed in an article published in the *Times*, "what startles Americans here is that Grenadians seem to adore the American invaders." He quoted a 61-year-old woman who said, "Darling, if it wasn't for the Almighty and Mr. Reagan, we would not be here."[64] The *Tribune* reported that the Governor General of the island, Sir Paul Scoon, wanted American troops to stay "as long as possible."[65] And the *Post* wrote about an opinion poll revealing that most Grenadians applauded the United States for having invaded their country.[66]

The *Washington Post,* which had taken a somewhat critical to ambiguous Grenada stand during the crisis periods, came out with an editorial endorsement of Reagan's invasion decision, pointing out, "As Grenada drifts off the front page, it is time for those of us who adopted a question-asking attitude during the intervention to move toward a more settled view." Characterizing its previous position as "skeptical," the *Post* now concluded, "All things considered, we think that President Reagan made the right decision in Grenada.[67] In another editorial, the newspaper advised the President to reduce American involvement in Grenada, "and to get out quickly." The editorial asked, "Is the president paying too much attention to his press notices to see the swamp he could yet fall into by overplaying his hand?"[68] In spite of this ambiguous piece, there was no doubt that on its editorial page the *Post* had switched to a firm pro-Reagan stand as far as the Grenada intervention was concerned. The *Chicago Tribune* did not publish editorials directly related to the pro versus con discussion surrounding the invasion and, presumably, retained its supportive position expressed editorially during the lingering crisis.

The *New York Times,* unlike the other two newspapers, continued to criticize the intervention in its editorials. Under the headline "The Mouse That Grinned," the paper commented sarcastically on the massive American economic aid showered on Grenada in the invasion aftermath, suggesting Grenadians "must have decided that the only remedy for its poverty was to become the enemy of the United States, in the expectation of being quickly defeated and then rehabilitated by American aid."[69] In another editorial the *Times* criticized those who, under the influence of public support for the invasion, had switched into the pro-Reagan camp. Reviewing the administration's justifications for the military operation, the *Times* concluded that "people around the world who do not automatically assume American virtue are left to conclude that the United States is either a bully or a paranoid— quick to attack where it can do so safely or when it feels compelled to demonstrate muscle."[70]

Table 6.11 demonstrates that pro-Reagan sources fared better in comparison to the President's critics in the overall (combined foreign and domestic) coverage. In terms of numbers there was no significant difference in the way domestic and foreign sources combined were covered. However, as far as the foreign coverage was concerned, the *Times* and *Tribune* gave more lines to sources supportive of Reagan's Grenada policy than to his critics. The *Post,* on the other hand, devoted more space to foreign critics than supporters of the President because the Washington paper tended to pay more attention to oftentimes critical foreign diplomats at the UN and the OAS and to foreign leaders, for example Castro, than the other two newspapers.

In the domestic Grenada coverage (see table 6.12), the *Washington Post,* which had thrown its editorial support behind Reagan's Grenada move, published about ten lines based on his domestic supporters for each line attributed to his critics. In the *Tribune,* for each line based on critical sources nearly four lines were attributed to supportive ones. The *Times* published about three-and-a-half lines based on domestic supporters for each line devoted to domestic critics. While pro-Reagan sources captured significantly more space than critical ones in all three papers, the gap between pro and con was considerably larger in the *Post* than in *Times* and *Tribune.*

The placement of sources was similar in the three papers: Domestic sources in favor of the President's Grenada stand and critical foreign sources made the front pages more often than critical domestic and supportive foreign sources.

While pro-Reagan sources dominated the domestic coverage, which thereby seemed to reflect the domestic wave of support for the President's Grenada stand, in matters indirectly related to the Grenada crisis the administration's critics captured more space than its supporters (see table 6.13). The *Times*

TABLE 6.11 Overall Post-Crisis Coverage, Grenada Invasion: Domestic and Foreign Sources, Directly Relevant (Editorials Excluded)

Linage	For/Probably For	Neutral/ Ambiguous	Against/Probably Against	Total Lines
TIMES	50.4%	31.8%	17.8%	8,393
POST	44.2	42.1	13.7	8,161
TRIBUNE	48.8	36.2	15.0	2,202

TABLE 6.12 Post-Crisis Coverage, Grenada Invasion: Domestic Sources, Directly Relevant (Editorials Excluded)

Linage	For/Probably For	Neutral/ Ambiguous	Against/Probably Against	Total Lines
TIMES	49.8%	36.0%	14.2%	6,393
POST	50.3	45.0	4.7	6,476
TRIBUNE	51.3	35.5	13.2	1,733

covered secondary issues—namely the ongoing debate about the press curbs and charges of military blunders during the invasion—much more extensively than did the *Post* and the *Tribune*. The *Tribune* addressed both of those issues, charging that "foulups and stupid decisions were legion and legendary" during the invasion of the island. The editorial criticized the Pentagon harshly for barring press coverage of the early invasion phase, writing, "The authorities apparently thought they could do a better job of reporting the facts than professional reporters. They were wrong."[71] The *Times*, which criticized the ban of the press from Grenada during the invasion, editorialized nevertheless in support of the American kind of press freedom and attacked Fidel Castro for trying to exploit the controversy surrounding the barring of the media during the Grenada invasion. The paper pointed out, "at least the Pentagon draws its power from the same Madisonian Constitution that guarantees America's press freedom. When Fidel Castro governs under similar constraints he may qualify as a lecturer on the subject."[72]

Administration sources captured much more space in the Grenada coverage than congressional sources (see table 6.14). However, in the East Coast newspapers the linage advantage of the administration was not quite as huge as during the two crisis periods. In the *Tribune*, on the other hand, adminis-

TABLE 6.13   Post-Crisis Coverage, Grenada Invasion: Domestic Sources, Indirectly Relevant (Editorials Excluded)

Linage	For/Probably For	Neutral/ Ambiguous	Against/Probably Against	Total Lines
TIMES	17.8%	43.5%	38.7%	1,391
POST	14.2	54.2	31.6	120
TRIBUNE	—	67.6	32.4	71

TABLE 6.14   Linage Administration and Congressional Sources, Grenada Invasion: Post-Crisis

	Administration Sources	Congressional Sources	Total Lines
TIMES	79.5%	20.5%	3,782
POST	79.7	20.3	3,071
TRIBUNE	85.9	14.1	902

tration sources captured more space vis-à-vis congressional sources than during the lingering crisis.

Journalistic descriptions, background reporting, and news analyses revealed reservations against the administration's Grenada policies. While most of the lines based on media sources fell into the neutral/ambiguous category, 29 percent of that type of line in the *Times,* 8 percent in the *Post* and 22 percent in the *Tribune* seemed to reveal critical attitudes.

SUMMARY

In the absence of a public debate about the island state of Grenada, the President and members of his administration were the dominant domestic news sources concerning Grenada, and what they had to say was part of an exchange of accusations with the leftist rulers of the island.

During the short acute phase of the invasion presidential supporters managed to be in the news much more than domestic critics of the military action. However, instant opposition was voiced and reported by a number of domestic politicians and groups. These critical expressions spoiled the pro-presidential rally effect expected during such crises. One condition for support and/or suspension of criticism was simply not present: There was no agreement among Americans that the United States was faced with a threat to the lives of citizens and to its sphere-of-interest.

But the praise for the President's action by students evacuated from Grenada, the discovery of warehouses with military equipment on the island, and an administration forcefully justifying the intervention took the wind out of many critics' sails. This turnaround was reflected in the news.

In the aftermath of the crisis, domestic news coverage was dominated by Reagan and his supporters. Whereas the *Times* and the *Tribune* reflected the rise in domestic dissent toward Reagan's Grenada policy, this was not the case in the *Post* presentation of the news.

Excluding the pre-crisis phase, which did not involve much domestic debate about Grenada, a comparison of editorial positions and the content of news reports shows that there was a relationship between the two in the remaining three time periods.

Beginning with the invasion and continuing through the post-crisis weeks, Reagan's domestic opponents captured more news space than his supporters dealing with issues indirectly related to the invasion decision. Perhaps criticizing the President in the secondary Grenada debate—especially over the issue of news management itself—was a substitute for not doing so on the primary issue of having ordered the invasion.

7

CONCLUSIONS

RALLY-'ROUND-THE-FLAG PHENOMENON CONFIRMED

Referring to foreign crises and other major events in American foreign relations, Richard Brody has pointed out that media coverage "will be unusually full of bipartisan support for the president's actions." However, according to Brody, "[w]hen opinion leadership does not rally or run for cover, the media must and do report this fact."[1] This was confirmed by the three foreign and three domestic crises of varying severity presented in the preceding chapters. Indeed, the expected patterns of press coverage in pre-, acute, lingering, and post-crisis phases were confirmed to a significant extent, especially with regard to the acute crisis periods. In five of six acute crisis phases (three domestic and two foreign) the news coverage reflected a rally-'round-the-president reaction by domestic political actors and/or an unwillingness to criticize a president's crisis-related policies. The Cuban Missile Crisis, the Dominican Republic Invasion, the Detroit Riot, the Three Mile Island Accident, and the Attempted Assassination of President Reagan were such emergencies, and during the acute phase of each one the crisis-related news coverage was indicative of the rally phenomenon.

In its acute stage the Grenada Invasion did not have the expected media coverage. This is not surprising, considering that there was no agreement among domestic political elites, not even among members of Congress, that the intervention was justified. The *Times* more than the *Post* and both of these much more than the *Tribune* reflected the debate over Reagan's decision to invade the Caribbean island. Still, the dominance of pro-Reagan sources over critical ones in the *Tribune* was so great that this coverage fit the acute crisis phase pattern. This was not so obvious in the East Coast papers, especially if one takes into account the coverage of the issues indirectly related to Reagan's Grenada move, namely the decision to prevent the media from witnessing and reporting firsthand about the invasion.

The coverage of Grenada during the lingering phase of the crisis was an exception as well. Contrary to the expected pattern that is thought to reflect efforts by political actors to revive a pluralist debate, the coverage of the

Times and the *Tribune* (not of the *Post*) was more favorable to the President than during the acute crisis days. In a way, a delayed rally occurred and was reflected in the coverage. In the five other cases, the expected coverage occurred during the lingering phase with the following exceptions: The *Chicago Tribune*'s coverage of the Detroit Riot and the Three Mile Island Accident did not quite fit the anticipated pattern but chapters 4 and 5 of this text show that in both instances the editorial positions of the paper explained these deviations.

In those instances in which presidential policies related to an upcoming crisis were articulated, the coverage of pre-crisis periods revealed the conflicting views one would expect in American politics. An exception was the *Tribune*'s coverage of issues related to the safety of nuclear power plants in the months preceding the Three Mile Island Accident: The paper reported on major decisions and findings of the Nuclear Regulatory Commission but ignored the debate between friends and foes of nuclear power mostly.

During the post-crisis periods, the news coverage confirmed the expected pattern in that it reflected debates over issues related to the preceding crises. Presidential opponents sometimes captured a greater amount of space than supporters; in other cases, supporters of the President's crisis-related policies captured significantly more space than his critics.

In explaining media coverage of the Vietnam War Daniel C. Hallin observed that "the administration's problems with the 'fourth branch of government' resulted in large part from political divisions at home."[2] Here as well, the relationship between mixed domestic reactions and press coverage explains the findings for the acute phase of Grenada and for most pre-, lingering and post-crisis periods.

PRESIDENTS AND CRISIS COVERAGE

Even without the benefit of content analyses, it is obvious that not all crises that see presidents in central roles result in domestic rallies and in patterns observed in the six cases. What about the Watergate Scandal, the Iranian Hostage Crisis, or the Iran-Contra Affair? These three incidents were all serious crises. Watergate during Richard Nixon's and Iran-Contra during Ronald Reagan's presidency represented threats to the peace of mind of many Americans. The Iranian Hostage Crisis during the Carter years threatened both the lives of American citizens and the nation's peace of mind. However, in the Watergate and the Iran-Contra cases the threats were caused by secret and, at the very least, questionable decisions and activities of the chief executives and their closest aides. Surely, if a crisis is clearly caused by a president or his staff, one can't expect a rally-'round-the-flag reaction with glowing news coverage. In the days and even weeks following the hostage-taking in Teheran, the nation rallied behind President Carter. However, with the crisis dragging on and Jimmy Carter unable and unwilling to take much action, critics voiced their dissatisfaction with the man in the White House. As it became apparent that the President was unable to solve the crisis, he looked to many Americans as having contributed to the hostage situation in the first place. Rightly or wrongly, the perception grew that the Iranians had dared the United States because of its weakness under President Carter.

The domestic reaction and coverage during the acute phase of the Grenada Invasion was not as favorable toward the President as during the other five crises. The reason was obvious almost immediately after the news of the intervention was revealed: There were serious doubts that the lives of Americans on Grenada were in jeopardy and that a Communist threat existed. Accordingly, at least some critics—among them members of Congress—regarded the invasion as the result of an unwise presidential move, as a self-inflicted crisis. The Cuban Missile Crisis and the Dominican Invasion, too, began with distinct moves by presidents: Kennedy's blockade decision and Johnson's "green light" for the landing of U.S. Marines. However, in the acute phases of these two episodes not even domestic opposition politicians expressed doubts about the justification for the presidential moves. These differences explain why the news coverage and the editorial positions during the acute phases of two very similar crises (the Dominican and the Grenada Invasion) differed significantly.

The manner in which a president and his administration handle a particular crisis situation also influences domestic reaction and media coverage. For example, during the lingering phase of the Dominican Republic Invasion, President Johnson's zig-zag policy concerning U.S. support for the various factions in the Dominican situation alternately angered political moderates and conservatives. During the lingering phase of the crisis triggered by the attempt to assassinate President Reagan, the injured chief executive could not and his close aides did not pay attention to the President's agenda unrelated to the crisis; this allowed opponents of the "Reagan Revolution" to dominate the debate.

Domestic reaction and press coverage during acute crisis periods are apparently independent of a president's esteem among political elites and the general public and of his relations with the news media. Presidents Johnson and Carter experienced political difficulties and were not on good terms with the press when they had to deal with the Detroit Riot and Three Mile Island. Yet, in both instances, the news coverage followed the expected favorable pattern. However, there may well be a connection between presidents' political prestige and their relations with other political actors and the way they fare in post-crisis periods. Chief executives who are held in fairly high esteem by elites and by the public and who are skillful in handling the media seem to fare much better in post-crisis periods than presidents in politically troubled waters and with poor press relations. Kennedy and Reagan, both known as great communicators and both enjoying a great deal of political support, fared well in the press in the aftermath of the Cuban Missile Crisis, the Attempt to Assassinate President Reagan, and the Grenada Invasion. (Reagan's relationship with the news media was not the best by the latter part of 1983 but his White House staff was successful in staging the news so that it was beneficial to the President.) Johnson did quite well in the wake of the Dominican Invasion, when he had a good deal of political support and a normal relationship with the press. Two years later, however, in the weeks following the Detroit Riot Johnson and his supporters were unable to dominate the crisis-related debate. At this point, LBJ's political fortune had declined dramatically and his relationship with the press had become hostile. The situation was similar for Jimmy Carter after Three Mile Island: At a time, when he had little political support and poor relations with the press, the President was unable to dominate the relevant post-crisis debate and coverage.[3]

Of course, one could also speculate that another factor influences the domestic reaction and the news coverage during post-crisis times—the distinction between domestic and foreign crises. While no evidence for such a distinction was seen in the other phases, there may be a difference in the after-crisis periods: In the three foreign incidents, the post-crisis coverage was much more favorable to the president's side than to his critics. (The only exception was the *Tribune*'s post-crisis coverage of developments and issues related to the Dominican Republic Invasion.) In two out of three domestic crises, opponents of the president's crisis-related policies captured substantial and at times more space than presidential supporters. The third domestic case, the Attempt to Assassinate President Reagan, was exceptional in several respects and was dominated by pro-Reagan sources in the post-crisis days.

THE 1968–1974 WATERSHED AND CRISIS COVERAGE

In early 1985, President Reagan's then science adviser Dr. George Keyworth complained, "We're trying to build up America and the press is trying to tear down America."[4] This statement was in line with other attacks on the news media in the 1980s. The six crises did not reveal dramatic changes in the way the press covered emergencies of different severity before and after the widely assumed 1968–1974 turning point in press– president and press–government relations. During the acute days of the three examined crises that occurred after the 1968–1974 period, only the Grenada Invasion resulted in one-sided critical editorials in one of the three newspapers. The other newspapers were supportive or mixed in their editorial positions. The critical editorial position of the *New York Times* was shared and expressed by a number of politicians inside and outside of Congress. During the acute phase of the Three Mile Island Accident there was a widely felt uncertainty about the nuclear emergency. Two of the papers did not comment editorially, the third newspaper was ambiguous toward President Carter's nuclear power policy. In the acute phase of the crisis triggered by the attempt on President Reagan's life, the two newspa- pers (*Times* and *Post*) that had previously criticized the President's agenda very harshly muted their editorial positions considerably while the *Tribune* continued its editorial support for Reagan. This suggests that when the chips are down, when the nation is faced with an emergency, the press—regard- less of its previous editorial positions—tends to react like the political elite in that it either rallies behind the chief executive or mutes its criticism.

The editorial positions during acute crisis periods before 1968 were not fundamentally different; there were cases of full and reluctant support, of opposition, and of ambiguous wait-and-see positions before and after the 1968–1974 period. In fact, the harsh criticism of Presidents Kennedy (in editorials and by journalistic sources in the so-called straight news of the *Chicago Tribune* especially during the pre-crisis period of the Cuban Missile Crisis of 1962) and Johnson (in editorials and by journalistic sources of the three newspapers in some periods of the Dominican Republic Invasion of 1965 and the Detroit Riot in 1967) was seldom matched by the editorials and the news coverage concerning the three crises occurring after 1968–1974.

This finding should not be taken as an indication that nothing changed in the way the press covers presidents and governments on a day-in day-out basis. The focus here has been on serious and medium-level crises. In one respect, a change did take place: In the 1960s the newspapers seemed to identify more closely with either side of the political spectrum than in the late 1970s and early 1980s. In the earlier period, the *Tribune* tended to support the conservative Republican line while the *Times* and the *Post* preferred liberal Democratic positions. There were hardly surprises in the way editorial stands were taken and expressed in those years. This changed in the years following the turbulent 1968–1974 period. Certainly, the East Coast newspapers continued to express more liberal views and the Chicago paper more conservative preferences, but their editorials no longer fit quite as consistently the positions of any one particular party or ideological camp as in the earlier period. This was especially obvious in the case of the *Tribune*.

EDITORIAL POSITIONS AND NEWS COVERAGE

In the weeks and months preceding the Cuban Missile Crisis, the *Times* and the *Post* editorials supported President Kennedy's Cuba policy, while the *Tribune* sided with his conservative critics. In the East coast papers, domestic news sources supportive of Kennedy were used for significantly more column lines than were critical ones; the *Tribune,* however, devoted slightly more space to Kennedy's critics than his supporters. This is a more dramatic case of a relationship between editorial positions and so-called straight news coverage.

Such relationships were not exceptions during the time periods studied here. Rather, in most of the twenty-four phases of the six case studies, a relationship was found between editorials and news reporting. This tendency did not prevent journalists and editors from using news sources that did not agree with their particular views and it did not necessarily mean that sources that shared the opinion of editorial page editors were used for more space than sources with opposite views. In many cases, however, it meant that sources compatible with the editorial policy of a newspaper had a better chance of being mentioned in a story of this publication than in one with the opposite or with a neutral/ambiguous stance.

During two of the 24 time periods no strong editorial opinions were published and in these instances editorial positions and news coverage could not be compared. In 16 of the remaining 22 periods a relationship between editorial positions and news content was easily recognizable. Two more periods fit this pattern, when certain peculiarities of the editorial positions and the treatment of sources were examined (i.e., the pre- and the lingering crisis periods of the Detroit Riot of 1967). There was only one case in which the news coverage was contrary to the editorial positions (i.e., the lingering crisis phase of the attempt to assassinate President Reagan). In addition, there were three inconclusive cases.

Considering that a relationship between editorial positions and domestic coverage was recognizable in 18 of 24 periods, one conclusion is obvious: The political views expressed in newspapers' editorials influence their news coverage. Although my research did not reveal reasons for the relationship between editorials and news coverage, my guess is that it might be the result of what would seem a logical tendency: editors and reporters might flock to and be hired by press organizations compatible with their own attitudes, political and otherwise. My research does not answer the question whether or not the relationships between news coverage and editorials were the result of deliberate bias in the selection of sources and in space consideration. I do not exclude the possibility that certain decisions in this area of judgment were made consciously, but I suspect that they were more likely the results of a natural or unconscious bias brought about by the shared attitudes among the people working in each media organization.

It seems that the six case studies support a combination of the mirror/messenger and the biased press view: The news coverage was in most instances reflective of what went on in the political realm; however, the coverage in various newspapers was different and seemed influenced by the editorial positions of each paper.

WHY ARE PRESIDENTS UNHAPPY WITH THE PRESS?

Of the 72 examined pre-, acute, lingering, and post-crisis periods (four in each of the six crises covered by three newspapers) the relevant domestic news coverage was favorable to presidents in 66 instances in that sources supportive of the particular presidential policies were used for more lines than were critics of the president. In only 6 periods was more space attributed to presidential critics than to supportive sources.

Given such a pro-president and pro-administration coverage before, during, and after crises—why are presidents, their staffs, their administrations, and their supporters unhappy with the way the media cover the news? Why is the press accused of being unpatriotic, irresponsible, and "always against us," especially in the context of crises?[5] One can only speculate about the reasons. However, the findings drawn from the case studies may offer some clues or at least good guesses.

One reason for presidents' dissatisfaction with the press may have to do with the importance presidents and their supporters place on editorials, especially in the *Washington Post* and the *New York Times*, which are believed to influence the rest of the press and political elite in the United States and the rest of the world. Contrary to domestic news coverage, editorials tend to be more critical of presidential actions and policies in the examined time periods.

Or perhaps there is a simpler explanation for chronic presidential unhappiness with the press: Presidents may be unrealistic in their expectations of how the news media should cover them and their policies. Perhaps they are thin-skinned and resentful when critics receive significant news coverage—even when sources supportive of a president are more extensively covered than his critics.

Another possible reason: The foreign news and therefore the overall coverage, i.e., the combined foreign and domestic coverage alone. In the 36 pre-, acute, lingering, and post-phases of the three foreign crises examined in this study, foreign news sources critical of the relevant presidential policies captured more space than supportive ones in 30 instances. In only 6 periods were more lines based on foreign supporters than on foreign critics of a president's crisis-related policies. Perhaps occupants of the White House do not like it when foreign critics among foes and allies get the attention of the American press and affect the overall news coverage negatively from the point of view of presidents and their administrations.

Actions by administrations to curb the news as the Kennedy and the Reagan White House tried during the Cuban Missile Crisis and the Grenada Invasion do not influence the news coverage in favor of presidents. Instead, as the two examples demonstrated, news curbs created a secondary and additional news coverage in which presidential critics had a better chance of dominating the news than did presidential supporters.

The six case studies overall revealed the following: a crisis coverage pattern, especially during the acute phases of emergencies. In the most crucial times of both foreign and domestic crises the news reflected a domestic rally-'round-the-president reaction—if it occurred. No evidence was found that the press covered crises in a fundamentally different way before and after the 1968–74 "watershed" in press–president relations. Evidence was found, however, of a relationship between the editorial positions of newspapers and the way they reported the so-called straight news.

NOTES

INTRODUCTION

1. Harrison Rainie, "Media 'always against us,' " *Daily News* (New York), p. 25.
2. "President's News conference on Foreign and Domestic Issues," *New York Times,* December 21, 1983, p. A22.
3. President Reagan made this assessment in an interview with *Time* magazine. See "An Interview with the Presient," *Time,* December 8, 1986, p. 18.
4. Many government officials and media observers have made the point that the attitude of the press toward government and presidents has grown much more hostile since the Vietnam and Watergate experiences. See, for example, Hamilton Jordan, *Crisis;* Henry Grunwald, "Trying to Censor Reality," p. 102.
5. Pierre Salinger made this observation during the "Good Morning America" broadcast over the ABC network on November 22, 1983.
6. Daniel P. Moynihan, "The Presidency and the Press," p. 187.
7. Samuel P. Huntington, *American Politics: The Promise of Disharmony* (Cambridge, Mass.: Belknap Press of Harvard University Press, 1981), p. 102.
8. Martin Linsky, *Impact,* p. 45.
9. Huntington, pp. 101, 102.
10. See Daniel C. Hallin, *The "Uncensored War": The Media and Vietnam.*
11. Herbert J. Gans, *Deciding What's News,* pp. 63, 64.
12. Richard M. Pious, *The American Presidency,* p. 12.
13. Thomas E. Cronin, *The State of the Presidency,* p. 54.
14. Robert Entman, "The Imperial Media"; Doris Graber, *Mass Media and American Politics,* Theodore White, *The Making of the President 1972,* pp. 327–359.
15. Richard E. Neustadt, *Presidential Power.*
16. Michael Baruch Grossman and Martha Joynt Kumar, *Portraying the President,* p. 308.
17. Rowland Evans is quoted in Linsky.
18. Benjamin I. Page and Robert Y. Shapiro, "Effects of Public Opinion on Policy," pp. 175–190.
19. Richard A. Brody and Benjamin I. Page, "The Impact of Events on Presidential Popularity."
20. Paul Lazarsfeld, Bernard Berelson, and Hazel Gaudet, *The People's Choice;* Joseph T. Klapper, *The Effects of Mass Communication.*
21. Donald Shaw and Maxwell E. McCombs, *The Emergence of Political Issues: The Agenda-Setting Function of the Press;* Shanto Iyengar, Mark D. Peters, and Donald Kinder, "Experimental Demonstrations of the 'Not-so-minimal' Consequences of Television News Programs," pp. 848–858.
22. Bernhard C. Cohen, *The Press and Foreign Policy,* p. 13.

23. Benjamin I. Page, Robert Y. Shapiro and Glenn R. Dempsey, "The Mass Media Do Affect Policy Preferences"; Page, Shapiro and Dempsey, "What Moves Public Opinion?" pp. 23–43.

24. Gans, p. 292.

25. Linsky, Graber.

26. Linsky, p. 70.

27. Richard A. Viguerie, *The New Right: We're Ready to Lead*, p. 91.

28. Charles Mohr, "The Press: How to Use It or Lose It," p. A24.

29. Robert Cirino, *Don't Blame the People*, pp. 31, 179.

30. William Small, *To Kill a Messenger*, p. 10.

31. Edward Jay Epstein, *News From Nowhere*, pp. 13–25.

32. Quoted in Edith Efron, *The News Twisters*, p. 3.

33. Ben H. Bagdikian, *The Media Monopoly*, p. 182.

34. Gladys Engel Lang and Kurt Lang, *The Battle For Public Opinion*, p. 28.

35. Michael Schudson, *Discovering the News*, p. 3.

36. Walter Lippmann, *Public Opinion* (New York: The Free Press, 1949), p. 226.

37. Hallin, pp. 5, 6.

38. Peter Braestrup, *Big Story*, p. 515.

39. See Tom Wicker, *On Press*, pp. 15, 16; Samuel Kernell, *Going Public*, p. 215.

40. Leon V. Sigal, *Reporters and Officials*, p. 5; see also Epstein, *News From Nowhere*, and Todd Gitlin, *The Whole World is Watching*.

41. Kurt Lang and Gladys Engel Lang, *Politics and Television*.

42. Epstein, *News From Nowhere*, p. xii.

43. Charles V. Hamilton, "America in Search of Itself," pp. 487–493.

44. Gans, p. 44.

45. Graber, p. 239.

46. Grossman, Kumar, p. 308.

47. John E. Mueller, *War, Presidents and Public Opinion*, p. 209.

48. Graber, p. 329.

49. *Ibid.*, p. 225.

50. *Ibid.*, pp. 229–232.

51. Examples of this type of literature: For the characterization of the news media's place in the governmental system Douglass Cater, *The Fourth Branch of Government;* for press coverage of specific policy areas Bernhard C. Cohen, *The Press and Foreign Policy;* for the Washington press corps Stephen Hess, *The Washington Reporters;* for the relationship between journalists and governmental officials Leon V. Sigal, *Reporters and Officials;* for the influence of the press on policymakers Martin Linsky, *Impact.*

52. An example of a journalistic account is Hedley Donovan, *Roosevelt to Reagan. A Reporter's Encounter with Nine Presidents;* of a former White House insider's account Jody Powell, *The Other Side of the Story;* of a scholarly analysis Grossman and Kumar, *Portraying the President.*

53. See Hallin, *The "Uncensored War": The Media and Vietnam;* Peter Breastrup, *Big Story;* and Gladys Engel Lang and Kurt Lang, *The Battle for Public Opinion.*

54. Dan Nimmo and James E. Combs, *Nightly Horrors*, pp. 179–185.

55. Montague Kern, Patricia W. Levering, and Ralph B. Levering, *The Kennedy Crises;* p. 196.

56. Graber, p. 225.

57. See Grossman and Kumar; Bagdikian. Also, Stephen Hess, *The Washington Reporters.*

58. See Bagdakian; Gans.

59. I coded all news items relevant to each of the six crises that appeared in the daily political sections of the three newspapers, in the *Times* mostly sections A and B, in the *Post* section A, in the *Tribune* mostly section 1 but also following sections that contained current political news. I also coded all relevant editorials. Not coded were articles appearing in the Sunday news of the week and magazine sections nor other parts of the newspapers such as the business, travel, or book sections. Also excluded from coding were letters-to-the editor, columns on the op-ed pages, photo captions, and transcripts of speeches.

The length of pre- and post-crisis coding periods was determined by considering the manageability of the relevant published material. For example, the pre-crisis period of the Grenada Invasion began on January 1, 1983 and lasted through October 25, when the landing of U.S. troops on the island took place. The reason for this long pre-crisis coding: Not much relevant material was published. On the other hand, the pre-crisis coding for the Cuban Missile Crisis started on August 22, 1962—two months before the acute crisis began, because the press coverage reflected the very lively domestic and international Cuba debate. Beginning and end of each acute and lingering crisis period are explained in each case study. The overall time periods studied were the following:

Cuban Missile Crisis: August 22, 1962 through January 31, 1963.

Dominican Republic Invasion: January 1 through May 31, 1965.

Detroit Riots: July 1 through August 31, 1967.

Three Mile Island Accident: January 1 through May 31, 1979.

Assassination Attempt President Reagan: March 21 through April 26, 1981.

Grenada Invasion: January 1 through November 25, 1983.

60. Benjamin I. Page and Robert Y. Shapiro, "The Mass Media and Changes in Americans' Policy Preferences: A Preliminary analysis."

61. Raymond Coffey and Storer Rawley, "Why U.S. Acts," *Chicago Tribune*, pp. 1,10. (Quoted from p. 10.)

62. Dan Balz and Thomas E. Edsall, "GOP Rallies around Reagan; Democrats Divided on Grenada," *The Washington Post*, p. A8.

63. *Ibid.*

64. Leo Bogart, "The Public's Use and Perception of Newspapers," pp. 716–717.

1. THE CUBAN MISSILE CRISIS

1. Hugh Sidey, *John F. Kennedy, President*, p. 340; David Detzer, *The Brink*, pp. 177, 118. Both books used for descriptions of October 22, 1962.

2. Theodore C. Sorensen, *Kennedy*, p. 703.

3. Pierre Salinger, *With Kennedy*, p. 254.

4. Robert F. Kennedy, *Thirteen Days*, pp. 131–139.

5. Arthur M. Schlesinger, Jr., *The Imperial Presidency*, pp. 323, 324.

6. Anatolii Andreievich Gromyko, *Through Russian Eyes: President Kennedy's 1036 Days*, p. 168.

7. Schlesinger, *A Thousand Days*, pp. 274, 287; Sorensen, *Kennedy*, pp. 294, 295, 308.

8. Sorensen, p. 669.

9. Schlesinger, *A Thousand Days*, p. 794.

10. Sorensen, p. 670.

11. Dr. George H. Gallup, *The Gallup Poll Public Opinion 1935–1971*, p. 1780.

12. Kenneth W. Thompson, ed., *Three Press Secretaries on the Presidency and the Press*, p. 95.

13. Richard E. Neustadt, *Presidential Power.*
14. Sorensen, p. 310.
15. Kenneth W. Thompson, ed., *The White House Press on the Presidency*, p. 11.
16. Kenneth W. Thompson, ed., *Ten Presidents and the Press*, p. 73.
17. *Ibid.*
18. *Ibid.*
19. Thompson, ed., *Ten Presidents and the Press*, p. 75.
20. John Tebbel and Sarah Miles Watts, *The Press and the Presidency*, p. 481.
21. Transcript of Kennedy's press conference appeared in *New York Times*, September 14, 1962, p. 12.
22. "Kennedy's Patience," *Chicago Tribune*, September 15, 1962, p. 10, part 1; "Kennedy, Cuba and the USSR," *New York Times*, September 14, 1962, p. 30; "Soviet-Cuban Crisis," *Washington Post*, September 14, 1962, p. A14.
23. "Third Choice," *Washington Post*, September 29, 1962, p. A8.
24. "Running Against Castro," *Washington Post*, October 19, 1962, p. A16.
25. "Cuba and the Doctrine," *New York Times*, September 1, 1962, p. 18.
26. "Mr. Kennedy Again Calls for Reserves," *Chicago Tribune*, September 8, 1962, p. 12, part 1; "Krushchev's Threat," *Chicago Tribune*, September 12, 1962, p. 16, part 1; "Our Baby," *Chicago Tribune*, September 26, 1962, p. 12, part 1; "Padded Shoulders," *Chicago Tribune*, October 22, 1962, p. 20, part 1.
27. Arthur J. Olson, "Boats Off Cuba Fire at U.S. Navy Plane, Havana Cautioned," *New York Times*, September 1, 1962, pp. 1, 2; Norman Runnion, "Navy Training Plane Fired on Near Cuba," *Washington Post*, September 1, 1962, pp. 1, A7; Joseph Hearst, "Cuba Gets U.S. Warning," *Chicago Tribune*, p. 1; Tad Szulc, "Modernized Army Called Cuba's Aim," *New York Times*, September 3, 1962, pp. 1, 2; "2 More Senators Urge Intervention to Defeat Castro," *Washington Post*, September 3, 1962, p. A16; "Ask Military Intervention," *Chicago Tribune*, September 3, 1962, p. 1.
28. Jack Raymond, "Goldwater Calls Cuba Policy Weak," *New York Times*, September 15, 1962, p. 1; Bill Becker, "Cuba Quarantine is Urged by Nixon," *New York Times*, September 19, 1962, p. 1.
29. William L. Ryan, "Writer Tells How Russians Control Cuba," *Chicago Tribune*, September 16, 1962, p. 3, part 1; Anthony Burton, "Closeup of Russ in Cuba," *Chicago Tribune*, September 17, 1962, p. 1; Jules Dubois, "Report Russ Shear Power from Castro," *Chicago Tribune*, September 25, 1962, p. 1.
30. Tad Szulc, "Reprisals for Cuba Trade Tougher than Expected," *New York Times*, October 5, 1962, p. 1; Dan Kurzman, "U.S. Sets Up Port Bars to Cuba Armers," *Washington Post*, October 5, 1962, p. 1; Murray Marder, "Berlin-Cuba Deal Report," *Washington Post*, October 16, 1962, p. 1.
31. Sorensen, p. 698.
32. Salinger, p. 261.
33. *Ibid.*
34. "Capital's Discussions on Crisis Kept a Tight Secret for a Week," *New York Times*, October 23, 1962, p. 19.
35. Salinger, p. 269.
36. "Our Course is Set," *Chicago Tribune*, October 23, 1962, p. 14, part 1.
37. "The Choice," *Chicago Tribune*, October 28, 1962, p. 20, part 1.
38. "The New Adlai," *Chicago Tribune*, October 27, 1962, p. 11, part 1.
39. "Quarantine on Cuba," *New York Times*, October 23, 1962, p. 36.
40. "An Inning For Diplomacy," *New York Times*, October 27, 1962, p. 24.
41. "Meeting the Cuban Crisis," *Washington Post*, October 23, 1962, p. A16.

42. "Looking Beyond Cuba," *Washington Post,* October 27, 1962, p. A12.

43. Kern, Levering, and Levering, *The Kennedy Crises,* p. 140.

44. John H. Fenton, "Campuses Voice Some Opposition," *New York Times,* October 24, 1962, p. 25.

45. "District Police Prepare to Control Peace Rally," *Washington Post,* October 25, 1962, p. A7.

46. "Cuba Pickets Get Bum's Rush at Indiana U.," *Chicago Tribune,* October 25, 1962, p. 7, sect. 1.

47. "Cuba Protest Parade Set by Students," *Chicago Tribune,* October 25, 1962, p. 1.

48. "President Calm Despite Tension Throughout Day in White House," *New York Times,* October 23, 1962, p. 19; Edward T. Folliard, "President Appears Calm, Competent During Crisis," *Washington Post,* October 25, 1962, p. A6; "Kennedy Held Calmest Man in White House," *Chicago Tribune,* October 23, 1962, p. 9, sect. 1.

49. "White House Appeal for Caution in Presentation of News," *Washington Post,* October 25, 1962, p. A6; "U.S. Urges Editors to Use Care on Information Vital to Security," *New York Times,* October 25, 1962, p. 21.

50. Salinger, pp. 272, 273.

51. Warren Unna, "U.S. Stands Fast on Goal in Cuba," *Washington Post,* October 26, 1962, p. 1; William McGaffin, "Crisis is Born" September 14–October 22; Suspicion to Certainty on Cuba," *Washington Post,* October 26, 1962, p. A19; Max Frankel, "Soviet Stressed Frankness to U.S.," *New York Times,* October 27, 1962, p. 1.

52. Salinger, pp. 269, 270.

53. Salinger, p. 285.

54. "The New Shaft of Sunlight," *Washington Post,* October 29, 1962, p. A14.

55. "A Triumph of Reason," *New York Times,* October 29, 1962, p. 28.

56. James Reston, "The President's View," *New York Times,* October 29, 1962, p. 1.

57. "Russia Now Favors Inspection," *Chicago Tribune,* October 29, 1962, p. 16, part 1.

58. "Venture in Statesmanship," *Washington Post,* November 2, 1962, p. A16.

59. "Ten Days That Shook the World," *New York Times,* November 4, 1962, p. 8E.

60. "Cuba: Plus and Minus," *New York Times,* November 10, 1962, p. 24.

61. "Unanswered Questions," *Chicago Tribune,* November 14, 1962, p. 20, part 1.

62. "News as a Weapon," *Chicago Tribune,* November 2, 1962, p. 16, part 1.

63. "Capehart Warns Against 'Deeding Cuba' to Reds," *Chicago Tribune,* October 30, 1962, p. 4, part 1; William Moore, "Goldwater Hits Invasion Pledge by U.S.," *Chicago Tribune,* October 30, 1962, p. 5, part 1; "Exiles Assert Caves in Cuba Hide Missiles," *Chicago Tribune,* November 3, 1962, p. 4, part 1; William Anderson, "Withdraw No Cuba Invasion Pledge: G.O.P.," *Chicago Tribune,* November 6, 1962, p. 7, part 1.

64. "New National Group Opposes No-Invasion Assurance to Cuba," *New York Times,* October 31, 1962, p. 19.

65. "Scott Challenges Kennedy on Bases," *New York Times,* October 31, 1962, p. 19; "Exiles Say Cuba is Hiding Missiles," *New York Times,* November 3, 1962, p. 8; Leonard Ingalls, "Goldwater Demands Stevenson's Ouster," *New York Times,* November 13, 1962, p. 1.

66. "Venture in Statesmanship," *supra* note 58.

67. "Goldwater Talk Scored by Adlai," *Washington Post,* November 14, 1962, p. A14.

68. Murrey Marder, "Uncertainty Clouds Communists' Next Steps in Cold War," *Washington Post,* October 29, 1962, pp. 1, A5.

69. David Binder, "U.S. Forces Keep Watch on Cuba," *New York Times,* November 5, 1962, p. 1.

70. Carroll Kilpatrick, "Kennedy Makes Visit to Middleburg Estate," *Washington Post,* October 29, 1962, p. A4.

71. "Press Revolt Over News Gag," *Chicago Tribune,* November 1, 1962, pp. 1,2.

72. "Pentagon Policy Decried," *New York Times,* November 1, 1962, p. 17.

73. "Reporter Criticizes Kennedy on News Curbs," *Washington Post,* November 17, 1962, p. A7.

74. Robert F. Kennedy, *Thirteen Days,* pp. 184–186.

75. "In the Caribbean," *New York Times,* November 21, 1962, p. 32.

76. "Krushchev on Cuba," *New York Times,* December 14, 1962, p. 6.

77. "The Cuban Prisoners," *New York Times,* December 14, 1962, p. 6.

78. "Progress in Cuba," *Washington Post,* November 22, 1962, p. A26.

79. "The President and the Press," *Washington Post,* November 22, 1962, p. A26.

80. "A Deal With Russis?" *Chicago Tribune,* December 10, 1962, p. 24, part 1.

81. "Cubans to Honor Kennedy," *Chicago Tribune,* October 29, 1962, p. 12, part 1.

82. Gallup, pp. 1786, 1793, 1800.

83. E. W. Kenworthy, "President Calls Advisers on Cuba to Parley Today," *New York Times,* November 23, 1962, p. 1; Kenworthy, "President Sees Advisers on Cuba," *New York Times,* November 24, 1962, p. 1; Kenworthy, "President to Thank Cuba-Alert Forces in Visit Tomorrow," *New York Times,* November 25, 1962, p. 1; Kenworthy, "President Honors Units on Tour of Alerted Bases," *New York Times,* November 27, 1962, p. 1; Tad Szulc, "President to See Mikoyan on Cuba and Other Issues," *New York Times,* November 28, 1962, p. 1; Szulc, "President Meets Mikoyan 3 Hours; U.S. Sees No Gain," *New York Times,* November 30, 1962, p. 1.

84. Laurence Burd, "President Cites Flyers Who Bared Peril," *Chicago Tribune,* November 27, p. 1; Robert Young, "Kennedy, Mikoyan Will Discuss Cuba," *Chicago Tribune,* November 28, 1962, p. 1; Young, "No Breakthrough with Mikoyan," *Chicago Tribune,* December 1, 1962, p. 1; "Kennedy Cites Radio Outlets in Cuba Crisis," *Chicago Tribune,* December 5, 1962, p. 14, part 1; Willard Edwards, "Kennedy Takes Steps to Bar Red Missiles," *Chicago Tribune,* December 13, 1962, p. 1; "Warn Allies on Ship Use in Cuba Trade," *Chicago Tribune,* January 12, 1963, p. 1.

85. Chalmer M. Roberts, "Official Washington Shows Rare Buoyancy," *Washington Post,* December 14, 1962, p. 1.

86. "Kennedy's Cuba and Congo Policies Severely Criticized by Goldwater," *Washington Post,* January 1, 1963, p. A2; "Plane Brings 100 U.S. Citizens Back From Cuba," *New York Times,* January 14, 1963, p. 3; "U.S. Loses Initiative in Cuba: Keating," *Chicago Tribune,* January 14, 1963, p. 9, part 1; Jules Dubois, "3 Red Rocket Bases in Cuba, Exiles Report," *Chicago Tribune,* December 28, 1962, p. 3, part 1; "Cuba Said to Hide Arms At 21 Sites," *New York Times,* November 28, 1962, p. 5.

87. "GOP Senator Will Conduct Own Bay of Pigs Investigation," *Washington Post,* January 23, 1963, p. A5; Robert Barkdoll, "Partisan Bay of Pigs Inquiries Decried By Javits, Humphrey," *Washington Post,* January 28, 1963, p. A6; William Moore, "GOP Backs Bay of Pigs Probe," *Chicago Tribune,* January 23, 1963, p. 1; Moore, "Bay of Pigs Quiz Demanded by Goldwater," *Chicago Tribune,* January 24, 1963, p. 1; Kenworthy, "Goldwater Asks Senate Inquiry Into U.S. Role in Cuba Invasion," *New York Times,* January 24, 1963, p. 1.

88. Kern, Levering, and Levering, *supra* note. 43, p. 196.

2. THE DOMINICAN REPUBLIC INVASION

1. "Power—and the Ticking of the Clock," *Newsweek*, May 10, 1965, p. 38; Merle Miller, *Lyndon: An Oral Biography*, p. 425.
2. "Presidential Text," *New York Times*, April 29, 1965, p. 14.
3. "Text of Johnson's Talk," *New York Times*, May 1, 1965, p. 6.
4. Miller, p. 425.
5. Max Frankel, "Johnson Charges Red Plotters Took Over Dominican Uprising; Increases U.S. Forces to 14,000," *New York Times*, May 3, 1965, p. 1.
6. Dr. George H. Gallup, *The Gallup Poll Public Opinion 1935–1971*, p. 1936.
7. "A Path for Reasonable Men," *Newsweek*, April 19, 1965, p. 25.
8. Miller, pp. 375, 376.
9. "Hundred-Day Mark," *Newsweek*, April 19, 1965, p. 26.
10. John Tebbel and Sarah Miles Watts, *The Press and the Presidency*, p. 491.
11. Kenneth W. Thompson, ed., *Ten Presidents and the Press*, 1983, p. 79.
12. Thompson ed., *Three Press Secretaries on the Presidency and the Press*, p. 55.
13. Tebbel and Watts, p. 490.
14. *Ibid.*, p. 491.
15. Thompson, ed., *The White House Press on the Presidency*, p. 64.
16. Thompson, *Three Press Secretaries on the Presidency and the Press*, p. 55.
17. Tebbel and Watts, p. 498; Arthur Schlesinger Jr. *The Imperial Presidency*, p. 215.
18. Ben H. Bagdikian, *The Effete Conspiracy*, p. 133.
19. *Ibid.*, p. 131.
20. Miller, p. 424.
21. Explanation in "Dominican Forces Split on Bosch," *Washington Post*, April 26, 1965, pp. 1, 15.
22. Miller, pp. 424, 425.
23. Tad Szulc, "U.S. to Evacuate Nationals Today in Dominican Crisis," *New York Times*, April 27, 1965, pp. 1, 2; "Dominican Revolt Fails After a Day of Savage Battle," *New York Times*, April 28, 1965, pp. 1, 3; Dan Kurzman, "Bosch Appeals to U.S. for Support in War," *Washington Post*, April 28, 1965, p. 19.
24. Jules Dubois, "Coup Frustrated," *Chicago Tribune*, April 26, 1965, p. 4.
25. Dubois, "Fights 'Second Cuba'," *Chicago Tribune*, April 27, 1965, p. 2.
26. Dubois, "Loyal Forces Tell Winning Domingo Fight," *Chicago Tribune*, April 28, 1965, p. 2.
27. "Johnson Voiced Concern," *New York Times*, April 28, 1965, p. 3.
28. "Shock in Washington," *New York Times*, April 26, 1965, p. 6.
29. "Boxer Was in Caribbean," *New York Times*, April 27, 1965, p. 2.
30. See for example, Szulc, "U.S. to Evacuate Nationals Today in Dominican Crisis," *New York Times*, April 27, 1965, pp. 1, 2.
31. See, for example, Dubois, "Fights 'Second Cuba' " and "Loyal Forces Tell Winning Domingo Fight," *supra* notes 25, 26.
32. "Cuba Charges U.S. Forces Plan a Dominican Landing," *New York Times*, April 28, 1965, p. 9.
33. Miller, p. 425.
34. "Revolt in Santo Domingo," *New York Times*, April 26, 1965, p. 30.
35. Charles Mohr, "405 Marines Land to Aid Evacuation," *New York Times*, April 29, 1965, pp. 1, 14.
36. "Evacuees Arrive, Tell of Terror," *New York Times*, April 29, p. 14.
37. "Envoy Sees Red Plot," *New York Times*, April 29, 1965, p. 14.

38. Mohr, "405 Marines Land to Aid Evacuation," *New York Times,* April 29, 1965, p. 1.

39. Dubois, "Rebel Troops Fire on Tribune Writer," *Chicago Tribune,* May 1, 1965, p. 1.

40. Dubois, "Report From Latin America," *Chicago Tribune,* May 2, 1965, p. 2.

41. See, for example, Frankel, "U.S. Steps Mainly Inspired by Fear of 'Another Cuba'," *New York Times,* May 2, 1965, pp. 1, 5.

42. "Marines in Santo Domingo," *New York Times,* April 30, 1965, p. 34.

43. "Confusion in Santo Domingo," *New York Times,* May 2, 1965, p. 10E.

44. Frankel, "Johnson Charges Red Plotters Took Over Dominican Uprising," *supra* note 5.

45. "Dominican Troop Build-Up," *New York Times,* May 3, 1965, p. 32.

46. "Dominican Sequel," *New York Times,* May 4, 1965, p. 14.

47. "Unhappy Republic," *Washington Post,* April 29, 1965, p. A20.

48. "Back to 1916?" *Washington Post,* April 30, 1965, p. A24.

49. "Dominican Outlook," *Washington Post,* May 2, 1965, p. E6.

50. "The Marines Land," *Chicago Tribune,* April 30, 1965, p. 20.

51. Frankel, "Johnson Charges Red Plotters Took Over Dominican Uprising," *New York Times,* May 3, 1965, p. 1.

52. William Moore, "Senators Praise Johnson's Fast Action in Crisis," *Chicago Tribune,* May 1, 1965, p. 2, sect. 1.

53. "Congressional Leaders Support Johnson," *New York Times,* May 4, 1965, p. 21.

54. John M. Goshko, "U.S. Troops Withdrawal Awaits OAS Peace Plan," *Washington Post,* May 4, 1965, pp. 1, 12.

55. Chalmer M. Roberts, "Johnson Plunge Into Latin Crisis Shows There Will Be No 2nd Cuba," *Washington Post,* May 1, 1965, p. A15; Dan Kurzman, " 'We Don't Want More Coups,' Rebel Citizen-Soldier Says," *Washington Post,* May 5, 1965, p. A20.

56. "The Drag on Our Arm," *Chicago Tribune,* May 6, 1965, p. 16, sect. 1.

57. "Where Are We Going in the Caribbean?" *Chicago Tribune,* May 13, 1965, p. 24, sect. 1.

58. "Appeasement?" *Chicago Tribune,* May 19, 1965, p. 16, sect. 1.

59. "By Our Own Words," *Chicago Tribune,* May 21, 1965, p. 18, sect. 1.

60. "The O.A.S. Peace Force," *New York Times,* May 7, 1965, p. 40.

61. "Reversing the Gears," *New York Times,* May 18, 1965, p. 38.

62. "The Shattered Truce," *New York Times,* May 17, 1965, p. 34.

63. "On the Right Track," *Washington Post,* May 7, 1965, p. A24.

64. "Dominican Truce," *Washington Post,* May 6, 1965, p. A24.

65. "Bundy in Santo Domingo," *Washington Post,* May 17, 1965, p. A20.

66. "Dominican Crisis," *Washington Post,* May 21, 1965, p. A24.

67. "Eisenhower Says U.S. Acted in Crisis as He Would Have," *New York Times,* May 10, 1965, p. 8; "Johnson's Dominican Move Was Right as Day is Long, Barry Says," *Chicago Tribune,* May 9, 1965, p. 1.

68. John D. Morris, "Kennedy Critical of Johnson Move," *New York Times,* May 8, 1965, p. 1; John M. Goshko, "OAS Votes to Postpone May 20 Rio Conference," *Washington Post,* May 13, 1965, p. 1.

69. Dubois, "High G.I. Spirit in Dominican Fighting," *Chicago Tribune,* May 9, 1965, p. 3, sect. 1.

70. Dubois, "Domingo General, Foe of Reds, Forced Out," *Chicago Tribune,* May 11, 1965, p. 1.

71. "How to Make Life Safe For the Reds," *Chicago Tribune*, May 30, 1965, p. 16, sect. 1.

72. "New Realities and Newer Realities," *Chicago Tribune*, June 5, 1965, p. 10, sect. 1.

73. "Unrest in Latin America," *New York Times*, May 23, 1965, p. 10E.

74. "The Role of the O.A.S.," *New York Times*, May 30, 1965, p. 10E.

75. "L.B.J. and the Intervention," *New York Times*, June 3, 1965, p. 34.

76. "The Dominican Truce," *New York Times*, May 25, 1965, p. 40.

77. "Dominican Stalemate," *New York Times*, May 27, 1965, p. 36.

78. "Dominican Independence," *New York Times*, June 1, 1965, p. 38.

79. "Opportunity for the OAS," *Washington Post*, May 25, 1965, p. A18.

80. "Caribbean Climate," *Washington Post*, May 29, 1965, p. 8A.

81. "The OAS Peace Mission," *Washington Post*, June 4, 1965, p. A24.

82. "Dr. Mora's Rough Road," *Washington Post*, June 1, 1965, p. A16.

83. Semple, "President Urges Machinery to End Latin Subversion," *New York Times*, May 29, 1965, p. 1; Lawrence Stern, "President Urges Forceful OAS to Meet Subversion," *Washington Post*, May 29, 1965, p. 1; "1,700 More GIs Ordered Home From Domingo," *Chicago Tribune*, May 29, 1965, p. 8, sect. 1.

84. Goshko, "Rusk Sees Moderation Developing on Island," *Washington Post*, May 31, 1965, p. 1; Edwin L. Dale Jr., "Rusk Supports Plebescite on Dominican Constitution," *New York Times*, May 31, 1965, p. 1; "Rusk Rules Out U.S. 'License' to Intervene," *Chicago Tribune*, May 31, 1965, p. 3, sect. 1.

85. Richard F. Shepard, "Robert Lowell Rebuffs Johnson as Protest Over Foreign Policy," *New York Times*, June 3, 1965, p. 1; Laurence Stern, "Poet Shuns Johnsons' Culture Season, Says U.S. Policy Lacks Rhyme, Reason," *Washington Post*, June 4, 1965, p. 1.

86. Douglas Robinson, "Betancourt in City, Scores U.S. For its Dominican Intervention," *New York Times*, June 4, 1965, p. 9.

87. "Collins Criticizes Use of Force as Only Answer to Communism," *New York Times*, May 26, 1965, p. 16.

88. Dubois, "Dump Imbert Moves by U.S. Disclosed," *Chicago Tribune*, May 23, 1965, p. 6, sect. 1.

89. Dubois, "Fidel Foiled in Domingo, Reds Remain," *Chicago Tribune*, May 26, 1965, p. 3, sect. 1.

90. Tom Wicker, "The U.S. and the Junta," *New York Times*, May 28, 1965, p. 10.

91. Goshko, "Attempts to Reach Dominican Solution are U.S. Managed," *Washington Post*, June 6, 1965, p. A25.

92. "Lippmann Lauds Press for Dominican Coverage," *Washington Post*, May 28, 1965, p. A13.

3. THE DETROIT RIOTS OF 1967

1. "An American Tragedy 1967—Detroit," *Newsweek*, August 7, 1967, p. 18.

2. *U.S. Riot Commission Report*, p. 88.

3. Gene Roberts, "U.S. Troops Sent Into Detroit," *New York Times*, July 25, 1967, p. 1.

4. Max Frankel, "President Calls on Nation to Combat Lawlessness," *New York Times*, July 25, 1967, pp. 1, 20.

5. Descriptions are found in: Richard Hofstadter and Michael Wallace, *American*

Violence; U.S. Riot Commission Report; Newsweek, August 7, 1967; *New York Times,* July 25, 1967.

6. "The GOP: It's Spring," *Newsweek,* April 17, 1967, p. 31; "Wing and a Prayer," *Newsweek,* May 22, 1967, p. 26.

7. "Brief Interlude," *Newsweek,* July 17, 1967, pp. 22, 23.

8. George E. Reedy, "The President and the Press," in *Three Press Secretaries on the Presidency and the Press,* p. 106.

9. John Tebbel and Sarah Miles Watts, *The Press and the Presidency,* p. 497.

10. David Halberstam, *The Best and the Brightest,* p. 640.

11. *Ibid.,* p. 623.

12. Tebbel and Watts, p. 489.

13. William Chapman, "Alert-Room at Justice Keeps Tab on Rioting," *Washington Post,* July 4, 1967, p. 1.

14. Louise Hutchinson, "Airs Plea to Shriver Before Riot," *Chicago Tribune,* July 19, 1967, p. 2, sect. 1.

15. "Subsidized Riots," *Chicago Tribune,* July 20, 1967, p. 14, sect. 1.

16. "This Law Won't Stop Riots . . . But This One Will Help," *New York Times,* July 19, 1967, p. 38.

17. "Black Racism," *New York Times,* July 24, 1967, p. 26; "Newark—and Beyond," *New York Times,* July 15, 1967, p. 24.

18. "The Gravest Responsibility," *New York Times,* July 16, 1967, p. 12E.

19. "Agitation," "Scapegoat Bill," "Fever Pitch," *Washington Post,* July 1, 1967, p. A 12; July 13, 1967, p. A18; July 20, 1967, p. A16.

20. "Housing for the Cities," *Washington Post,* July 22, 1967, p. A12.

21. Fred P. Graham, "Restraint Urged in Race Riot News, *New York Times,* July 8, 1967, p. 10.

22. George Lardner Jr., "McNamara Deplores Lack of Firearms Control Law," *Washington Post,* July 2, 1967, p. A3.

23. James Yuenger, "Percy, Weaver Clash on U.S. Housing Aid for Poor," *Chicago Tribune,* July 18, 1967, p. 11, sect. 1.

24. M. S. Handler, "Wilkin's Assails Riot Bill Backers," *New York Times,* July 11, 1967, p. 15.

25. "Kennedy Prepares Bill for Slum Housing," *Washington Post,* July 6, 1967, p. 8.

26. "Kennedy Puts in Bill to Produce Jobs in the Slums," *New York Times,* July 13, 1967, p. 24.

27. Louise Hutchinson, "Airs Plea to Shriver Before Riot," *Chicago Tribune,* July 19, 1967, p. 2, sect. 1.

28. Donald Janson, "New Left Convention Next Month Will Seek Strategy to Defeat Johnson," *New York Times,* July 9, 1967, p. 38.

29. Martin Arnold, "Newark Meeting on Black Power Attended by 400," *New York Times,* July 21, 1967, pp. 1, 34.

30. "Johnson TV Talk on Troop Order," *New York Times,* July 25, 1967, p. 20.

31. "Rule of Law," *New York Times,* July 25, 1967, p. 34.

32. "The Agony of Detroit," *New York Times,* July 27, 1967, p. 34.

33. "The Voice of Negro Leadership," *New York Times,* July 27, 1967, p. 34.

34. "While Cities Burn," *New York Times,* July 26, 1967, p. 38.

35. "Johnsons TV Talk on Troop Order," *supra,* note 30.

36. "While Cities Burn," *supra,* note 36.

37. "And in the Capital," *Washington Post,* July 26, 1967, p. A20.

38. "The Greatest Tragedy of All," *Washington Post,* July 25, 1967, p. A12.

39. "A Question of Priorities," *Washington Post,* July 27, 1967, p. A16.

40. "Contagion in the Streets," *Chicago Tribune,* July 26, 1967, p. 10, sect. 1.

41. "The Federal Poultice," *Chicago Tribune,* July 27, 1967, p. 14, sect. 1.

42. Roy Reed, "President Labors to Ease Disorder," *New York Times,* July 27, 1967, p. 19.

43. See, for example: "Johnson is Said to Lose Sleep in Detroit Crisis," *New York Times,* July 26, 1967, p. 22. Also: Roy Reed, "President Labors to Ease Disorder," *New York Times,* July 27, 1967, p. 19; "Troop Chief A Veteran of Three Wars," *Washington Post,* July 26, 1967, p. A22.

44. Gene Roberts, "U.S. Troops Sent Into Detroit," *New York Times,* July 25, 1967, p. 1.

45. Philip Warden, "Congress Seeks Riot Solution," *Chicago Tribune,* July 26, 1967, p. 6, sect. 1.

46. M. S. Handler, "4 Negro Leaders Call for Order," *New York Times,* July 27, 1967, p. 1; Stuart Auerbach, "Top Negro Leaders Call For an End to Rioting," *Washington Post,* July 27, 1967, p. 1. "4 Negro Civil Rights Assail Riots," *Chicago Tribune,* July 27, 1967, p. 1.

47. Jerry M. Flint, "Detroit Riots Seem at End," *New York Times,* July 28, 1967, p. 1.

48. "Snipers Open Fire Anew in Torn Detroit," *Chicago Tribune,* July 28, 1967, p. 1.

49. "Sickness of the Cities," *New York Times,* July 28, 1967, p. 30.

50. "Crisis in the Cities," *New York Times,* July 29, 1967, p. 24.

51. "After the Riots," *Washington Post,* July 31, 1967, p. A14.

52. "Johnson's Message," *Chicago Tribune,* July 29, 1967, p. 6, sect. 1.

53. Richard L. Lyons, "House GOP Assails Johnson on Riots," *Washington Post,* July 29, 1967, A8; Aldo Beckman. "G.O.P. Blasts LBJ as 'Weak' in Riots," *Chicago Tribune,* July 29, 1967, p. 5, sect. 1.

54. John Herbers, "Morton Rebukes G.O.P. on Johnson," *New York Times,* July 28, 1967, p. 1.

55. "Brown Blasts Johnson and Rights Chiefs," *Washington Post,* July 28, 1967, p. 1; Ben A. Franklin, "S.N.C.C. Head Advises Negroes in Washington to Get Guns," *New York Times,* July 28, 1967, p. 14; Louis Dombrowski, "Negro Leader Hails Rioters as Patriots," *Chicago Tribune,* July 28, 1967, p. 7, sect. 1.

56. "Carmichael Urges a 'Vietnam' in U.S.," *New York Times,* July 28, 1967, p. 10.

57. Henry Raymont, "New Book on Urban Problems Urges Major Federal Program," *New York Times,* July 28, 1967, p. 12.

58. Gerald Grant, "Cardinal Calls for Race "Reparations," *Washington Post,* July 30, 1967, p. 1.

59. Andrew J. Glass and Jesse W. Lewis Jr., "Segment of America in Open Insurection," *Washington Post,* July 30, 1967, pp. 1, A4; Wayne Thomis, "Detroit Holocaust . . . An Analysis," *Chicago Tribune,* July 30, 1967, pp. 4, 5; Max Frankel and Gene Roberts, "Army's Entry Into Detroit: How Decision Was Made," *New York Times,* July 30, 1967, pp. 1, 50.

60. Jerry M. Flint, "Romney Accuses Johnson on Riots," *New York Times,* August 1, 1967, p. 1.

61. *Ibid.* Also: "Romney Says LBJ Played Politics in Detroit Riot," *Chicago Tribune,* August 1, 1967, p. 15, sect. 1; "Romney Says LBJ Played Riot Politics," *Washington Post,* August 1, 1967, p. 1.

62. Examples of use of Republican sources critical of LBJ: Robert H. Phelps, "Rockefeller Hails Romney Role," *New York Times,* August 2, 1967, p. 1; George Lardner Jr.,

"Dirksen Sees Senate Drive for Strong Antiriot Action," *Washington Post,* August 10, 1967, p. 1; "LBJ Fiddled as Detroit Burned: Barry," *Chicago Tribune,* August 30, 1967, p. 26, sect. 1.

63. Examples of use of Democrats critical of the President as sources: Fred B. Graham, "Fulbright Links Vietnam to Riots," *New York Times,* August 9, 1967, p. 23; David Hoffman, "RFK Urges War Freeze, Billions to Ease Slums," *Washington Post,* August 7, 1967, p. 1.

64. Homer Bigart, "Rap Brown Calls Riots 'Rehearsal for Revolution,'" *New York Times,* August 7, 1967, p. 1.

65. Robert B. Semple Jr., "Johnson Calls on Senate to Pass Full Urban Aid," *New York Times,* August 17, 1967, p. 1.

66. Carroll Kirkpatrick, "Panel on Rioting Urges Increase of Negroes in Guard," *Washington Post,* August 11, 1967, p. 1.

67. Jerry M. Flint, "Humphrey Urges New Aid to Poor," *New York Times,* August 3, 1967, p. 1.

68. "Humphrey Urges End of City Slum Conditions," *Washington Post,* August 22, 1967, p. A6.

69. George Lardner Jr., "States Voted Riot Role by House," *Washington Post,* August 9, 1967, p. 1.

70. Robert B. Semple Jr., "$40-Million Voted for Rent Subsidy by Senate Panel," *New York Times,* August 29, 1967, pp. 1, 23. (Quote taken from p. 23.)

71. "Coalition for Better Cities," *New York Times,* August 2, 1967, p. 36.

72. "The Governors Speak Up," *New York Times,* August 11, 1967, p. 30.

73. "Leaderless Consensus,' *New York Times,* August 25, 1967, p. 34.

74. "Slogans Run Riot," *New York Times,* August 9, 1967, p. 38.

75. "A Vote for Jobs," *New York Times,* August 31, 1967, p. 32.

76. "Disarm Snipers," *New York Times,* August 2, 1967, p. 36.

77. "The Anti-Crime Bill," *New York Times,* August 10, 1967, p. 10.

78. "White National Guard," "Trigger Happy Guard," *New York Times,* August 14, 1967, p. 30, and August 24, 1967, p. 36.

79. "Negroes in the Guards," "Controlling Riots," "Trigger-Happy Guard," "Interstate National Guard?" *Washington Post,,* August 9, 1967, p. A20, August 22, 1967, p. A16, August 24, 1967, p. A20, August 31, 1967, p. 20.

80. "The Victims," *Washington Post,* August 7, 1967, p. A14.

81. "Urban Coalition," *Washington Post,* August 27, 1967, p. B6.

82. "Training Troops For Riot Control," "Don't Weaken the Guard," "Subsidized Riots?" *Chicago Tribune,* August 14, 1967, p. 18, sect. 1, August 29, 1967, p. 12, sect. 1, August 10, 1967, p. 18, sect. 1.

83. "The Harvest," *Chicago Tribune,* August 2, 1967, p. 10, sect. 1.

84. "Who Stands to Profit From Riots?" *Chicago Tribune,* August 3, 1967, p. 18, sect. 1.

4. THE THREE MILE ISLAND ACCIDENT

1. B. Drummond Ayres Jr., "Three Mile Island: Notes From a Nightmare," *New York Times,* April 16, 1979, pp. 1, B10. (Quote taken from p. B10.)

2. *Ibid.*

3. Richard D. Lyons, "Atom Plant is Still Emitting Radioactivity," *New York Times,* April 29, 1979, pp. 1, A20. (Quoted from p. A20.)

4. David Burnham, "U.S. Aides See a Risk of Meltdown at Pennsylvania Nuclear

Plant; More Radioactive Gas is Released," *New York Times,* April 31, 1979, pp. 1, A8. (Quoted from p. A8.)

5. Dan Nimmo and James E. Combs, *Nightly Horrors* p. 65.

6. Other sources used for description of the Three Mile Island accident: "A Nuclear Nightmare," *Time,* April 9, 1979, pp. 8–19; Tom Mathew, "Nuclear Accident," *Newsweek,* April 9, 1979, pp. 24–33; Peter M. Sandman and Mary Paden, "At Three Mile Island" in Doris Graber, ed., *Media Power In Politics,* pp. 267–273.

7. "Carter: Black and Blue," *Time,* March 5, 1979, p. 11.

8. "Small-Stick Diplomacy," *Newsweek,* March 5, 1979, p. 37.

9. "Carter: Black and Blue," *supra,* note 7. p. 11.

10. "Next: Challenges at Home," *Time,* April 2, 1979, p. 12.

11. See the cover of the *New York Times* Sunday Magazine, May 15, 1977.

12. John Tebbel and Sarah Miles Watts, *The Press and the Presidency,* p. 525.

13. Jody Powell, *The Other Side of the Story,* pp. 38–39.

14. Michael Baruch Grossman and Martha Joynt Kumar, *Portraying The President,* p. 11.

15. Hedley Donovan, *Roosevelt To Reagan,* p. 226.

16. Jimmy Carter, *Keeping Faith,* p. 127.

17. Donovan, p. 224.

18. Carter, p. 127.

19. Kenneth W. Thompson, ed., *Ten Presidents and the Press,* p. 93.

20. Executive Office of the President, Energy and Policy Planning, *The National Energy Plan,* p. V.

21. Richard Halloran, "Nuclear Energy Confusion," *New York Times,* January 28, 1979, p. F17.

22. "A Nuclear Nightmare," *Time,* April 19, 1979, p. 8.

23. David Burnham, "Nuclear Agency Revokes Support for Safety Study," *New York Times,* January 20, 1979, p. 1; J. P. Smith, " '75 Report on Reactor Safety is Called Unreliable by NRC," *Washington Post,* January 20, 1979, p. 1; "U.S. Debunks its Report on Atom Energy Safety," *Chicago Tribune,* January 20, 1979, p. 5, sect. 1.

24. Burnham, "Nuclear Agency Revokes Support for Safety Study," *op. cit.*

25. "A-plant Shutdown Rapped," *Chicago Tribune,* March 17, 1979, p. 11, sect. 1.

26. Casey Bukro, "Nuclear Plant Gets OK to Dump Radioactive Water Into Susquehanna," *Chicago Tribune,* March 30, 1979, pp. 1, 18, sect. 1. (Quote taken from p. 18.)

22. David Burnham, "Nuclear Accident is Laid to Failure of Overall Safety System at Plant," *New York Times,* March 30, 1979, p. 1.

28. J. P. Smith, "Future of Nuclear Power is Clouded," *Washington Post,* March 30, 1979, pp. 1, A2. (Quote taken from p. A2.)

29. "How Safe are Nuclear Reactors?" *New York Times,* January 24, 1979, p. A22.

30. "Subtracting from Reactor Safety," *New York Times,* March 15, 1979, p. A22.

31. "The Credibility Meltdown," *New York Times,* March 30, 1979, p. A24.

32. "On Risks, Nuclear and Other," *Washington Post,* March 18, 1979, p. D6.

33. "A Nuclear Accident," *Washington Post,* March 30, 1979, p. A22.

34. "Overkill in Nuclear Safety?" *Chicago Tribune,* March 18, 1979, p. 4, sect. 2.

35. Burnham, "U.S. Aides See a Risk of Meltdown at Pennsylvania Nuclear Plant; More Radioactive Gas is Released," *New York Times,* March 31, 1979, p. 1.

36. Thomas O'Toole and Bill Richards, "Mass Evacuation of A-Plant Rejected," *Washington Post,* March 31, 1979, p. 1.

37. Ward Sinclair and Warren Brown, "The Day Few Believed Possible Arrives in the Atomic Age," *Washington Post,* March 31, 1979, p. 1.

38. Bill Neikirk and Casey Bukro," Chance of Atomic Reactor Meltdown Called "Remote'," *Chicago Tribune*, March 31, 1979, p. 1.

39. Burnham, "U.S. Aides See a Risk of Meltdown at Pennsylvania Nuclear Plant; More Radioactive Gas is Released," *New York Times*, March 31, 1979, pp. 1, 8. (Quoted from p. A8.)

40. O'Toole and Richards, "Mass Evacuation of A-Plant Area Rejected," *Washington Post*, March 31, 1979, pp. 1, A8. (Quoted from p. A8.)

41. Neikirk and Bukro, "Chance of Atomic Release Meltdown Called "Remote'," *Chicago Tribune*, March 31, 1979, pp. 1, 5, sect. 1.

42. Ben A. Franklin, "Conflicting Reports Add to Tension," *New York Times*, March 31, 1979, pp. 1, A8. (Quoted from p. A8.)

43. B. Drummond Ayres Jr., "Regulator of a Nation's Reactor," *New York Times*, April 2, 1979, p. 15.

44. Richard D. Lyons, "Carter Visits Nuclear Plant, Urges Cooperation in Crisis, Some Experts Voice Optimism," *New York Times*, April 2, 1979, p. 1; Thomas O'Toole and Edward Walsh, "A-Reactor Core Is Cooling, Gas Bubble Still a Hazard," *Washington Post*, April 2, 1979, p. 1; Casey Bukro and Bill Neikirk, "Carter Tours Reactor Plant," *Chicago Tribune*, April 2, 1979, p. 1.

45. Peter M. Sandman and Mary Paden, "At Three Mile Island," in Doris Graber, ed., *Media Power In Politics*, p. 269.

46. Richard Halloran, "Schlesinger Praises Atomic Power Role, *New York Times*, March 31, 1979, p. A7.

47. Wallace Turner, "Brown Asks Plant Closing on Coast," *New York Times*, April 2, 1979, p. 1; "Protests by Atom Foes Grow as Nuclear Reaction Spreads," *Chicago Tribune*, April 2, 1979, p. 8.

48. Patrick Tyler and Jean S. Fugate Jr., "No Fallout is Detected in Md. Sampling," *Washington Post*, April 1, 1979, p. A6.

49. "Three Mile Island," *Washington Post*, April 1, 1979, p. B6.

50. Ayres Jr., "Regulator of a Nation's Reactor," *supra*, note 43.

51. Richard D. Lyons, "Nuclear Plant Peril Abates, but Level of Radiation Inside is Worrying Safety Officials," *New York Times*, April 3, 1979, p. 1.

52. Casey Bukro and Bill Neikirk, "Nuclear Plant Peril Eases," *Chicago Tribune*, April 3, 1979, p. 1.

53. "Breaking the Nuclear Fever," *New York Times*, April 4, 1979, p. A26.

54. "Reflection on A-Power," *Chicago Tribune*, April 3, 1979, p. 2, sect. 3.

55. "Harrisburg: The Vietnam Syndrome," *Washington Post*, April 4, 1979, p. A22.

56. "Let 'Em Eat Cake," *Washington Post*, April 7, 1979, p. A12.

57. "Carter Silences Officials of Crippled Atom Plant," *Chicago Tribune*, April 3, 1979, p. 6, sect. 1.

58. David Burnham, "President Establishing Commission to Study Nuclear Reactor Mishap," *New York Times*, April 6, 1979, p. 1.

59. Thomas O'Toole and Bill Richards, "A-Plant Violated U.S. Rules, NRC Is Told," *Washington Post*, April 5, 1979, p. 1.

60. Walter Pincus, "HEW Sees No Health Risk, Will Monitor Area," *Washington Post*, April 5, 1979, p. 1.

61. Harry Kelly and Robert Young, "Carter Orders Phasing Out of Domestic Oil Price Controls," *Chicago Tribune*, April 6, 1979, p. 1.

62. For examples of coverage of antinuclear groups and individuals see: A. O. Sulzberger Jr., "Nuclear Critics Plan Political Moves and Mass Protests," *New York Times*, April

7, 1979, p. A39; Stephan J. Lynton, "Antinuclear Protesters Call for Construction Ban," *Washington Post*, April 9, 1979, p. A12.

63. "Nader Leads Protest Against a Coast Plant," *New York Times*, April 8, 1979, p. A28.

64. A series of very long articles the *Washington Post*, published during lingering and post-crisis periods, lengthy chronologies and documentaries in *New York Times* and in-depth articles appearing in the weekend sections of all three publications were not included in the data. All of these very long articles contained, at least in part, previously published material.

65. Judith Miller, "Ouster of Energy Official Urged," *New York Times*, April 4, 1979, p. A16. David Burnham, "Atom Mishap Called product of Errors, *New York Times*, April 5, pp. 1, B15.

66. Peter Milius, "Crisis Has Ended at Nuclear Plant," *Washington Post*, April 10, 1979, p. 1.

67. Charles Mohr, "President Contends it is Impossible to 'Abandon' U.S. Nuclear Energy," *New York Times*, April 11, 1979, p. 1.

68. Terence Smith, "President Names Panel to Assess Nuclear Mishap," *New York Times*, April 12, 1979, p. 1.

69. Jack Nelson, "Carter Letter Urges Larger A-Program," *Washington Post*, May 4, 1979, p. A12.

70. Walter Pincus, "A-Emission at Pa. Plant Revised Up," *Washington Post*, May 4, 1979, p. 1.

71. Jo Thomas, "H.E.W. to Study Accident Effects in A-Plant Area," *New York Times*, May 30, 1979, p. 1.

72. Joanne Omang, "9 Babcock & Wilcox A-Power Plants to be Altered, NRC and Utilities Agree," *Washington Post*, April 28, 1979, p. A4.

73. "Nader Coalition Plans Nuclear Policy Protest," *Washington Post*, April 19, 1979, p. A9.

74. "Nader Blasts Atomic Power at 'Teach-in'," *Chicago Tribune*, May 6, 1979, p. 22, sect. 1.

75. "Gov. Brown, Differing With Carter, Bids U.S. Abandon Nuclear Energy," *New York Times*, April 26, 1979, p. A18.

76. Jon Margolis, "65,000 in Nuclear Protest," *Chicago Tribune*, May 7, 1979, p. 1; Paul W. Valentine and Karlyn Barker, "The Protesters," *Washington Post*, May 7, 1979, p. 1; Wendell Rawls Jr., "65,000 Demonstrate At Capitol To Halt Atomic Power Units," *New York Times*, May 7, 1979, p. 1.

77. Joanne Omang, "Kennedy Asks New Plant Moratorium," *Washington Post*, May 8, 1979, p. 1.

78. David Burnham, "Carter Tells Protesters Closing All Nuclear Plants is 'Out of the Question'," *New York Times*, May 8, 1979, p. A18; "Carter Defends A-Plants," *Chicago Tribune*, May 8, 1979, p. 1.

79. Eleanor Randolph, "U.S. 'Operated Almost Blind' in Nuclear Crisis," *Chicago Tribune*, April 13, 1979, p. 1.

80. T. R. Reid and Ward Sinclair, "Nuclear Plant Mishap Initially Confused NRC," *Washington Post*, April 13, 1979, pp. 1, A8. (Quote taken from p. A8.)

81. T. R. Reid and Bill Peterson, "NRC Considered Creating Accident it Understood," *Washington Post*, April 14, 1979, pp. 1, A6. (Quote taken from A6.)

82. Charles Mohr, "Nuclear Officials Feared a Disaster in First Days After Reactor Mishap," *New York Times*, April 13, 1979, p. 1, A11.

83. Edward Walsh, "Nothing Indicates Change in Carter View on Nuclear Power," *Washington Post,* May 25, 1979, p. A10.

84. Joanne Omang, "Uncomputerized Regulators Shun Nuclear Leaks and Drips, *Washington Post,* April 15, 1979, p. A10.

85. "Breeding Nuclear Danger," *New York Times,* May 17, 1979, p. A22.

86. "The Meaning of Three Mile Island," *New York Times,* April 12, 1 p. A22.

87. "The Kemeny Commission's Duty," *New York Times,* April 15, 1979, p. 16E.

88. "Digging Into Three Mile Island," *Washington Post,* May 12, 1979, p. A16; "The People Who Run Reactors," *Washington Post,* April 19, 1979, p. A26.

89. "Who Pays for a Nuclear Shutdown?" *Washington Post,* April 29, 1979, p. B6.

90. "Let's Not Overreact at Home." *Chicago Tribune,* April 10, 1979, p. 2, sect. 3.

91. "The Nuclear Panel's Mandate," *Chicago Tribune,* April 16, 1979, p. 2, sect. 3.

5. THE ATTEMPTED ASSASSINATION OF PRESIDENT REAGAN

1. Ed Magnuson, "Six Shots at a Nation's Heart," p. 25.

2. Lou Cannon, "The Shooting," *Washington Post,* March 31, 1981, p. 1.

3. Articles about the assassination attempt that appeared in *Newsweek* and *Time,* April 13, 1981 as well as reports published in the *New York Times, Washington Post,* and the *Chicago Tribune,* on March 31, 1981 were used for the description of the events surrounding the attempt to assassinate President Reagan.

4. Peter Goldman, "American Nightmare," *Newsweek,* April 13, 1981, p. 29.

5. Goldman, "The Budget: Bumps Ahead," *Newsweek,* March 30, 1981, p. 23.

6. Rowland Evans and Robert Novak, "The Honeymoon is Definitely Over," *Washington Post,* March 30, 1981, p. A19.

7. Kenneth W. Thompson, ed., *The White House Press on the Presidency,* pp. 35, 42.

8. *Ibid.,* p. 35.

9. Jody Powell, *The Other Side of the Story* p. 39.

10. Thompson, ed., pp. 35, 36.

11. David Stockman, *The Triumph of Politics: Why the Reagan Revolution Failed,* p. 12.

12. Steven R. Weisman, "The President and the Press," *New York Times,* Sunday Magazine, October 14, 1984, p. 71.

13. Thompson, ed., p. 37.

14. "Reagan Calls Budget Slash Only First Step," *Chicago Tribune,* March 21, 1981, p. 2, sect. 1.

15. Kirkland in Wonderland," *Chicago Tribune,* March 21, p. 8, sect. 1.

16. "A Right to Welfare?" *Chicago Tribune,* March 27, 1981, p. 2, sect. 1.

17. "Hitting the Ground Feuding," *Chicago Tribune,* March 26, 1981, p. 2, sect. 3.

18. "Rewriting the Tax Bill," *Washington Post,* March 22, 1981, p. D6.

19. "Requiem for CETA," *Washington Post,* March 29, 1981, p. B6.

20. "Deregulated Sausage," *Washington Post,* March 29, 1981, p. B6.

21. "Congress and the Reagan Cannonball," *New York Times,* March 22, 1981, p. 18E.

22. "Raking Leaves," *New York Times,* March 24, 1981, p. A18.

23. Lee Lescase and Lou Cannon, "Reagan to Keep Soviet Grain Embargo," *Washington Post,* March 29, 1981, p. A4; Lou Cannon, "Reagan's Disapproval Rating Laid to Promise Keeping," *Washington Post,* March 22, 1981, p. 1.

24. Spencer Rich, "Working Poor Seen Hit by Planned Welfare Cuts," *Washington*

Post, March 21, 1981, p. A4; Spencer Rich, "Reagan's Workfare Program Failed in California, Report Reveals," *Washington Post,* March 30, 1981, p. A4.

25. "U.S. to Crack Down on Misuse of Funds," *New York Times,* March 22, 1981, p. A31; Bernard Weinraub, "Reagan Cut Held to Affect 20% of Welfare Families," *New York Times,* March 24, 1981, pp. 1, B11.

26. Stephen Roberts, "House Democrats Mounting Drive to Reduce Impact of Budget Cuts," *New York Times,* March 22, 1981, p. 1.

27. Bernhard Weinraub, "Feminists Attack Reagan Administration Plan to Curb Aid for Abortions," *New York Times,* March 26, 1981, p. B13; Bernhard Weinraub, "Feminist Groups Attack Reagan Budget Cutbacks," *New York Times,* March 27, 1981, p. B8.

28. "Reagan Plans Assault on U.S. Fraud, Waste," *Chicago Tribune,* March 22, 1981, p. 3, sect. 1.

29. James Coates, "Reagan's 'Fraud War' Flops; Dems to Attack," *Chicago Tribune,* March 22, 1981, p. 14.

30. Howell Raines, "Reagan Wounded in Chest by Gunman," *New York Times,* March 31, 1981, p. 1' " 'Honey I forgot to duck . . .'," *Chicago Tribune,* March 31, 1981, p. 4.

31. David S. Broder, "Reagan Wounded by Assailant's Bullet," *Washington Post,* March 31, 1981, p. 1.

32. "Who's Minding the Store?" *New York Times,* April 1, 1981, p. A30.

33. Lee Lescaze, "Reagan, in Good Spirits, Making a Fast Recovery," *Washington Post,* April 1, 1981, p. 1.

34. Victor Cohn and Susan Okie, "Reagan Bouncing Back Like a Man in His 50s," *Washington Post,* April 1, 1981, p. A14; B. Drummond Ayres Jr., "Amid the Darkest Moments, a Leaven of Presidential Wit," *New York Times,* April 1, 1981 p. A18; "Bullet Ruined My New Suit: Reagan," *Chicago Tribune,* April 1, 1981, p. 3, sect. 1.

35. Barry Sussman, "Shooting Gives Reagan Boost in Popularity," *Washington Post,* April 2, 1981, p. 1.

36. "Again the Gunman Strikes," *Chicago Tribune,* March 31, 1981, p. 2, sect. 2.

37. "Together," *New York Times,* March 31, 1981, p. A18; "Slicing Through 'Soft' Science," *New York Times,* April 4, 1981, p. A22.

38. "Crisis and Reassurance," *Washington Post,* April 2, 1981 p. A22.

39. "The Other Kind of Spending," *Washington Post,* April 3, 1981, p. A14.

40. Adam Clymer, "Short-Term Gains Seen for G.O.P. by Politicians," *New York Times,* April 1, 1981, p. A24.

41. Howell Raines, "Meeting at Hospital," *New York Times,* April 1, 1981, p. 1.

42. "Reagan Hails Men Who Protect Him," *Chicago Tribune,* April 5, 1981, p. 8, sect. 1; Bill Peterson, "President is Lively, Alert; Fever Abates," *Washington Post,* April 5, 1981, p. 1.

43. " 'Strong' Reagan Message to Soviets," *Chicago Tribune,* April 6, 1981, p. 2, sect. 1.

44. Bill Peterson, "President is Lively, Alert; Fever Abates," *supra,* note 42. Lawrence K. Altman, "Reagan's Condition called 'Good'; He Sees Aides as Fever Goes Down," *New York Times,* April 5, 1981, p. 1.

45. Adam Clymer, "2 Leading Democrats Join Drive Against Reagan Economic Plan," *New York Times,* April 8, 1981, p. A18.

46. Warren Weaver Jr., "Aide Rejects Charges that Budget Portends a 'Disaster' for Elderly," *New York Times,* April 7, 1981, p. B9.

47. Arthur Siddon, "Thompson Backs Reagan Cuts, Ready to Ask for State Tax Hike," *Chicago Tribune,* April 8, 1981, p. 2, sect. 1.

48. Lou Cannon, "Reagan to Leave Hospital Today or Tomorrow," *Washington Post,* April 11, 1981, p. 1.

49. "Reagan Aims for TV Speech," *Chicago Tribune,* April 7, 1981, p. 6, sect. 1.

50. "Ragers and Fatalists," *New York Times,* April 5, 1981, p. 20E.

51. "Beware the New Park Rangers," *New York Times,* April 5, 1981, p. 20E; "Don't Punish the Economic Messenger," *New York Times,* April 7, 1981, p. A18; "Relief, but Not Leadership, for Detroit," *New York Times,* April 10, 1981, p. A30.

52. "Victims of Hasty Budget-Cutting," *Washington Post,* April 5, 1981, p. C6; "Help for the Auto Industry," *Washington Post,* April 9, 1981, p. A18; "Working Poor," *Washington Post,* April 10, 1981, p. A18.

53. "Discouraging Work," *Chicago Tribune,* April 8, 1981, p. 2, sect. 6. "Reagan Farm Program," *Chicago Tribune,* April 9, 1981, p. 2, sect. 3.

54. Steven R. Weisman, "President Returns to the White House; Says He Feels 'Great', " *New York Times,* April 12, 1981, p. 1.

55. Howell Raines, "Reagan Orders Staff to Repudiate Report of Compromise on Tax Cut," *New York Times,* April 14, 1981, p. 1.

56. Hedrick Smith, "Reagan Plans a Drive to Regain Momentum on Economic Package," *New York Times,* April 14, 1981, p. 1.

57. "Reagan Hopes to Woo 3 Foes of Budget Plan," *Chicago Tribune,* April 15, 1981, p. 8, sect. 1; "Reagan Enlists Ford to Lobby," *Chicago Tribune,* April 21, 1981, p. 8, sect. 1.

58. Lou Cannon, "Prospects Are Gloomy for Economic Plan, Reagan is Told," *Washington Post,* April 15, 1981, p. 1.

59. "Doctor Feared 'We might lose' Reagan," *Chicago Tribune,* April 15, 1981, p. 7, sect. 3.

60. Barry Sussman, "At Day 100 the People Like Reagan," *Washington Post,* April 25, 1981, p. 1.

61. Adam Clymer. "Kennedy Bids Democrats Fight Republican 'Reaction'," *New York Times,* April 13, 1981, p. B3.

62. "Congressmen Sue to Restore Jobs for VA," *Washington Post,* April 25, 1981, p. A6.

63. "Legal Services for the Poor," *Chicago Tribune,* April 13, 1981, p. 23, sect. 1.

64. "100 Days," *New York Times,* April 22, 1981, p. 22E.

65. "The Alternative Tax Cut," *Washington Post,* April 12, 1981, p. D6.

66. "Counting Up the Costs," *Washington Post,* April 17, 1981, p. A12.

6. THE GRENADA INVASION

1. The following material was used for the description of the invasion: Hugh O'Shaughnessy, *Grenada: An Eyewitness Account of the U.S. Invasion and the Carribean History that Provoked it;* Invasion reports in *Newsweek,* November 7, 1983; *Time,* November 7, 1983; *New York Times,* October 26, 1983; *Washington Post,* October 26, 1983; *Chicago Tribune,* October 26, 1983.

2. "Reagan Speech of October 25," *Congressional Quarterly Weekly Report,* October 29, 1983, pp. 2258–2259.

3. Ed Magnuson, "D-Day in Grenada," *Time,* November 7, 1983. p. 22.

4. Dr. George H. Gallup, *The Gallup Poll Public Opinion 1983,* pp. 170, 249.

5. "Reagan: Planning for '84," *Newsweek,* October 17, 1983, p. 25.

6. Ralph Kinney Bennett, "Grenada: Anatomy of a 'Go' Decision," p. 75.

7. "Letters," *Time,* Dec. 5, 1983, p. K2.

8. "President's Speech on Military Spending and a New Defense," *New York Times,* March 24, 1983, p. A20.

9. "Reagan Charge of Bases on Grenada Denied," *Chicago Tribune,* March 11, 1983 p. 14, sect. 1.

10. *Ibid.*

11. "Briefing," *New York Times,* March 26, 1983, p. A7.

12. "Hemisphere Diversions," *New York Times,* March 31, 1983 p. A22.

13. Patrick E. Tyler, "U.S. Tracks Cuban Aid to Grenada," *Washington Post,* February 27, 1983, p. 1.

14. "Leader of Grenada is Reported Killed by Troops," *New York Times,* October 20, 1983, p. 1; "Prime Minister of Grenada Dies in Military Coup," *Washington Post,* October 20, 1983, p. 1.

15. Edward Cody, "Grenada Puts Military on Alert, Warns of U.S. Threat to Invade," *Washington Post,* October 24, 1983, p. A4.

16. "The Horror in Grenada," *Washington Post,* October 22, 1983, p. A14.

17. Lou Cannon and David Hoffman, "Invasion Secrecy Creating a Furor," *Washington Post,* October 27, 1983, p. 1.

18. Phil Gailey, "U.S. Bars Coverage of Grenada Action; News Groups Protest," *New York Times,* October 27, 1983, p. 1.

19. Michael T. Kaufman, "Airports Seized, Drive on Capitol Faces Stiff Fire;" Hedrick Smith, "2 Americans Killed;" Barnaby J. Feder, "U.S. Was Warned By Mrs. Thatcher;" Frances X. Clines, "Days of Crisis for President: Golf, a Tragedy and Secrets;" Bernard Gwertzman, "An Invasion Prompted by Previous Debacles;" *New York Times,* October 26, 1983, p. 1.

20. Jim Joagland, "U.S. Invades Grenada, Fights Cubans;" Patrick E. Tyler and David Hoffman, "U.S. Says Aim is to Restore Order;" John Burgess and Michael Getler, "2 U.S. Fatalities are Reported;" Lou Cannon, "Strategic Airport, Hostage Fears Led to Move;" *Washington Post,* October 26, 1983, p. 1.

21. Raymond Coffey and Storer Rawley, "Why U.S. Acts," *Chicago Tribune,* October 26, 1983, p. 1; "12 Cubans Die," *Chicago Tribune,* October 26, 1983, p. 1.

22. B. Drummon Ayes Jr., "U.S. Says Grenada Invasion is Succeeding; 600 Cubans Seized After Heavy Resistance," *New York Times,* October 27, 1983, p. 1; David Hoffman and Fred Hiatt, "Weinberger Says U.S. May Stay for Weeks," *Washington Post,* October 27, 1983, p. 1; "1,000 More GIs Sent Into Grenada Battle," *Chicago Tribune,* October 27, 1983, p. 1.

23. "Ham's View: 'Gunfire Outside Our Campus'," *Washington Post,* October 26, 1983, p. A10.

24. George de Lama, "Isle Ringed With a Wall of Silence," *Chicago Tribune,* October 27, 1983, p. 4, sect. 1.

25. "Which Threat in Grenada?" *New York Times,* October 26, 1983, p. A26.

26. "Why Invade Grenada?" *Chicago Tribune,* October 26, 1983, p. 14, sect. 1.

27. "A Grave Act," *Washington Post,* October 26, 1983, p. A26.

28. "Grenada: The Morning After," *Washington Post,* October 27, 1983, p. A22.

29. *Ibid.*

30. Raymond Coffey and Storer Rawley, "Why U.S. Acts," *Chicago Tribune,* October 26, 1983, pp. 1, 10. (Quoted from p. 10.)

31. Steven V. Roberts, "Capitol Hill is Sharply Split Over the Wisdom of Invading Grenada," *New York Times,* October 26, 1983, p. A22.

32. Dan Balz and Thomas B. Edsall, "GOP Rallies Around Reagan; Democrats Divided on Grenada," *Washington Post,* October 26, 1983, p. A8.

33. "Responses Are Wide-Ranging," *New York Times,* October 27, 1983, p. A21.

34. Hedrick Smith, "Reagan Says Cuba Aimed to Take Grenada; Bastion Reported To Fall, Battle Goes On," *New York Times,* October 28, 1983, p. 1.

35. David S. Broder, "Speech Seen Buttressing Support," *Washington Post,* October 28, 1983, p. 1.

36. Robert D. McFadden, "From Rescued Students, Gratitude and Praise," *New York Times,* October 28, 1983, p. 1.

37. "Medical Students Recount Tale of Tense Escape From Grenada," *Washington Post,* October 28, 1983, p. A17.

38. "Cubans Were 'Out to Get Us,' Evacuated U.S. Students Say," *Washington Post,* October 28, 1983, p. A17.

39. Dori Meinert, "2 Say They Had No Fear but are Glad to be Here," *Chicago Tribune,* October 28, 1983, p. 6, sect. 1.

40. Michael Hirsley, " 'Rangers Were the Best'." October 28, 1983, pp. 10, Sect. 4.

41. Steven V. Roberts, "Move in Congress," *New York Times,* October 28, 1983, pp. 1, 12.

42. Roberts, "O'Neill Criticizes President; War Powers Act is Invoked," *New York Times,* October 29, 1983, p. 1.

43. "The 7 Democratic Candidates Weigh In," *Washington Post,* October 29, 1983, p. A12, "Mondale Assails Grenada Move and a Lack of Security in Beirut," *New York Times,* October 28, 1983, p. A12.

44. "Queen is 'Immensely Displeased'," *Chicago Tribune,* October 28, 1983, p. 1.

45. George de Lama, "Grenada Soldiers Shed Uniforms, Cheer Americans," *Chicago Tribune* November 1, 1983, p. 4, sect. 1; "Islanders 'Tickled Pink" at Invaders, a Wounded Marine Says," *New York Times,* October 31, 1983, p. A11.

46. "The Grenada High," *New York Times,* November 2, 1983, p. A30.

47. "Goliath in Grenada," *New York Times,* October 30, 1983, p. 18E.

48. "The Week That Was," *Washington Post,* October 30, 1983, p. C6.

49. "Who is in Charge?" *Washington Post,* November 1, 1983, p. A10.

50. "Balancing Will and Credibility," *Chicago Tribune,* October 1983, p. 2, sect. 5.

51. "Grenada—and Mount Suribachi," *New York Times,* October 28, 1983, p. A26.

52. "Censuring the Invasion," *Washington Post,* October 28, 1983, p. A22.

53. The Grenada News Ban," *Chicago Tribune,* October 28, 1983, p. 18, sect. 1.

54. Bernard Gwertzman, "Grenada Fighting is Ended, U.S. Says: Mop-Up Continues," *New York Times,* November 3, 1983, p. 1.

55. Frances X. Clines, "It Was a Rescue Mission, Reagan Says," *New York Times,* November 4, 1983, p. A16.

56. Frances X. Clines, "Medical Students Cheer Reagan at a White House Ceremony," *New York Times,* November 8, 1983, p. A10; David Hoffman, "Day of Grief," *Washington Post,* November 5, 1983, p. 1; Storer Rowley, "Reagan Greets Students, Raps 'Rescue' Critics," *Chicago Tribune,* October 8, 1983, p. 6, sect. 1.

57. Patrick E. Tyler and Walter Pincus, "Captured Documents to be Made Public," *Washington Post,* November 3, 1983, p. 1; "Grenada Arms Deals Claimed," *Chicago Tribune,* November 3, 1983, p. 20, sect. 1; Gwertzman, "Grenada Fighting is Ended, U.S. Says; Mop-Up Continues," *op. cit.*

58. Rick Atkinson, "Bush Views 'Awesome' Captured Arms Display," *Washington Post,* November 11, 1983, pp. 1; Judith Valente, "Grenada's Guns," *Washington Post,* November 13, 1983, p. B1.

59. Hedrick Smith, "Capitol Hill Outcry Softens as Public's Support Swells," *New York Times,* November 4, 1983, p. A18.

60. Hedrick Smith, "O'Neill Now Calls Grenada Invasion 'Justified' Action," *New York Times*, November 9, 1983, p. 1; T. R. Reid and Margaret Shapiro, "Hill Democrats Back Reagan on Grenada Action," *Washington Post*, November 9, 1983, p. 1. Dorothy Collin, "O'Neill Shifts on Grenada," *Chicago Tribune*, November 9, 1983, p. 1.

61. "Move for Impeachment is Begun by 7 in House," *New York Times*, November 11, 1983, p. 13; "Seven Democrats in House Seek Reagan's Impeachment," *Washington Post*, November 11, 1983, p. A26; "Scoon Slaps Strict Curbs on Grenada," *Chicago Tribune*, November 11, 1983, pp. 1, 2.

62. Hedrick Smith, "Members of House Differ on Invasion," *New York Times*, November 10, 1983, p. 11.

63. Robert Pear, "Washington Rally Draws Thousands," *New York Times*, November 13, 1983, p. A17; Bill Peterson, "Cranston Calls Reagan 'Trigger-Happy'," *Washington Post*, November 22, 1983, p. A4.

64. Bernhard Weinraub, "Reporter's Notebook: Darkness and Light on the Isle of Spice," *New York Times*, November 4, 1983, p. A18.

65. "U.S. Asked to Stay on Grenada," *Chicago Tribune*, November 6, 1983, p. 18, sect. 1.

66. "Most Grenadians Applaud U.S.," *Washington Post*, November 6, 1983, p. A19.

67. "Grenada: All Things Considered," *Washington Post*, November 9, 1983, p. A18.

68. "Grenada: Getting Out," *Washington Post*, November 15, 1983, p. A14.

69. "The Mouse That Grinned," *New York Times*, November 5, 1983, p. A26.

70. "Grenada, by O'Neill, by Orwell," *New York Times*, November 10, 1983, p. A26.

71. "Our Military Blunders," *Chicago Tribune*, November 19, 1983, p. 10, sect. 1.

72. "Castro vs. (Some) Censorship," *New York Times*, November 22, 1983, p. A30.

7. CONCLUSIONS

1. Richard Brody, "International Crises: A Rallying Point for the President?" p. 42.

2. Daniel C. Hallin, *The "Uncensored War,"* p. 213.

3. See chapters 2 through 7 for press–president relationship during Kennedy, Johnson, Carter, and Reagan presidencies.

4. Tom Wicker, "In the Nation," *New York Times*, March 5, 1985, p. A27.

5. These charges against the press are described in the introduction.

BIBLIOGRAPHY

"A Path for Reasonable Men." *Newsweek,* April 19, 1965, pp. 25–26.
"An American Tragedy 1967—Detroit." *Newsweek,* August 7, 1967, pp. 18–26.
Bagdikian, Ben H. *The Effete Conspiracy.* New York: Harper & Row, 1972.
—— *The Media Monopoly.* Boston: Beacon Press, 1983.
Balz, Dan and Thomas E. Edsall. "GOP Rallies Around Reagan; Democrats Divided on Grenada." *Washington Post,* October 26, 1983.
Bennett, Ralph Kinney, "Grenada: Anatomy of a "Go" Decision." *Reader's Digest,* February 1984, pp. 72–77.
Bogart, Leo. "The Public's Use and Perception of Newspapers." *Public Opinion Quarterly* (Winter 1984), pp. 716–717.
Braestrup, Peter. *Big Story.* New Haven: Yale University Press, 1983.
"Brief Interlude." *Newsweek,* July 17, 1967, pp. 22–23.
Brody, Richard. "International Crises: A Rallying Point for the President?" *Public Opinion,* Dec./Jan. 1984, pp. 42.
Brody, Richard A. and Benjamin I. Page. "The Impact of Events on Presidential Popularity: The Johnson and Nixon Administrations." In Aaron Wildavsky, (ed.). *Perspectives on the Presidency.* Boston: Little, Brown and Company, 1975, pp. 136–148.
Carter, Jimmy. *Keeping Faith.* New York: Bantam Books, 1982.
"Carter: Black and Blue." *Time,* March 5, 1979, pp. 10–13.
Cater, Douglass. *The Fourth Branch of Government.* Boston: Houghton Mifflin, 1959.
Cirino, Robert. *Don't Blame the People.* New York: Vintage Books, 1971.
Coffey, Raymond and Storer Rawley. "Why the U.S. Acts," *Chicago Tribune,* October 26, 1983.
Cohen, Bernhard C. *The Press and Foreign Policy.* Princeton, N.J.: Princeton University Press, 1963.
Cronin, Thomas E. *The State of the Presidency.* Boston: Little, Brown and Company, 1975.
Detzer, David. *The Brink.* New York: Thomas Y. Crowell, 1979.
Donovan, Hedley. *Roosevelt to Reagan.* New York: Harper & Row, 1987.
Efron, Edith. *The News Twisters.* Los Angeles: Nash, 1971.
Entman, Robert. "The Imperial Media." In Arnold J. Meltsner, ed., *Politics and the Oval Office.* San Francisco: Institute for Contemporary Studies, 1981.
Epstein, Edward Jay. *News From Nowhere.* New York: Vintage Books, 1974.
Executive Office of the President Energy and Policy Planning. *The National Energy Plan.* Cambridge, Mass.: Ballinger, 1977.
Gans, Herbert J. *Deciding What's News.* New York: Vintage Books, 1980.
Gallup, George H. *The Gallup Poll Public Opinion 1935–1971.* New York: Random House, 1972.
—— *The Gallup Poll Public Opinion 1983.* Wilmington, Del.: Scholarly Resources, 1984.

Gitlin, Todd. *The Whole World is Watching*. Berkeley: University of California Press, 1980.

Goldman, Peter. "American Nightmare." *Newsweek*, April 13, 1981, p. 29.

—— "The Budget: Bumps Ahead." *Newsweek*, March 30, 1981, p. 23–24.

Graber, Doris. *Mass Media and American Politics*. Washington, D.C.: Congressional Quarterly Press, 1980.

Gromyko, Anatolii Andreievich. *Through Russian Eyes: President Kennedy's 1036 Days*. Washington, D.C.: International Library, 1973.

Grossman, Michael Baruch and Martha Joynt Kumar. *Portraying The President*. Baltimore: Johns Hopkins University Press, 1981.

Grunwald, Henry. "Trying to Censor Reality." *Time*, Nov. 7, 1983, p. 102.

Halberstam, David. *The Best and the Brightest*. New York: Random House, 1972.

—— *The Powers That Be*. New York: Dell, 1979.

Hallin, Daniel C. *The "Uncensored War": The Media and Vietnam*. New York: Oxford University Press, 1986.

Hamilton, Charles V. "America in Search of Itself." *Political Science Quarterly* (Fall 1982): pp. 487–493.

Hess, Stephen. *The Washington Reporters*. Washington, D.C.: Brookings Institute, 1981.

Hofstadter, Richard, and Michael Wallace. *American Violence*. New York: Knopf, 1968.

"Hundred-Day Mark." *Newsweek*, April 19, 1965, p. 26.

Huntington, Samuel P. *American Politics: The Promise of Disharmony*. Cambridge: Belknap Press of Harvard University Press, 1981.

Iyengar, Shanto, Mark D. Peters, and Donald Kinder, "Experimental Demonstrations of the "Not-so-minimal' Consequences of Television News Programs." *American Political Science Review* (Dec. 1982): pp. 848–858.

Jordan, Hamilton. *Crisis*. New York: Putnam, 1982.

Kennedy, Robert F. *Thirteen Days*. New York: New American Library, 1969.

Kern, Montague, Patricia Levering and Ralph Levering. *The Kennedy Crises*. Chapel Hill: University of North Carolina Press, 1983.

Kernell, Samuel. *Going Public*. Washington, D.C.: Congressional Quarterly Press, 1986.

Klapper, Joseph T. *The Effects of Mass Communication*. Glencoe, Ill.: Free Press, 1960.

Lang, Gladys Engel and Kurt Lang. *The Battle for Public Opinion*. New York: Columbia University Press, 1983.

Lang, Kurt and Gladys Engel Lang. *Politics and Television*. Chicago: Quadrangle, 1968.

Lazarsfeld, Paul, Bernard Berelson and Hazel Gaudet. *The People's Choice*. New York: Columbia University Press, 1944.

Linsky, Martin. *Impact*. New York: Norton, 1986.

Lippmann, Walter. *Public Opinion*. New York: Free Press, 1949.

Magnuson, Ed. "D-Day in Grenada." *Time*. Nov. 7, 1983, pp. 22–28.

—— "Six Shots at a Nation's Heart." *Time*, April 13, 1981, pp. 24–38.

Miller, Merle. *Lyndon: An Oral Biography*. New York: Putnam, 1980.

Mohr, Charles. "The Press: How to Use It or Lose It." *The New York Times*, June 28, 1984, p. 24.

Moynihan, Daniel P. "The Presidency and the Press." In Aaron Wildavsky, ed., *Perspectives on the Presidency*. Boston: Little, Brown, 1975.

Mueller, John E. *War, Presidents, and Public Opinion*. New York: Wiley, 1973.

Neustadt, Richard E. *Presidential Power*. New York: Wiley, 1976.

"Next: Challenges at Home." *Time*, April 2, 1979, pp. 12–13.

Nimmo, Dan, and James E. Combs. *Nightly Horrors*. Knoxville: University of Tennessee Press, 1985.

O'Shaughnessy, Hugh. *Grenada: An Eyewitness Account of the U.S. Invasion and the Caribbean History That Provoked It.* New York: Dodd, Mead, 1984.

Page, Benjamin I. and Robert Y. Shapiro. "Effects of Public Opinion on Policy." *American Political Science Review* (March 1983), pp. 175–190.

—— "The Mass Media and Changes in Americans' Policy Preferences: A Preliminary Analysis." Paper Delivered at the 1983 annual meeting of the Midwest Political Science Associations, Chicago, April 20–23.

Page, Shapiro and Glenn R. Dempsey. "The Mass Media Do Affect Policy Preferences." Paper delivered at the annual meeting of the American Associations for Public Opinion Research, McAfee, N.J., May 16–19, 1985.

—— "What Moves Public Opinion?" *American Political Science Review* (March 1987), pp. 23–43.

Pious, Richard M. *The American Presidency.* New York: Basic, 1979.

Polsby, Nelson W. *Congress and the Presidency.* Englewood Cliffs, N.J.: Prentice Hall, 1964.

Powell, Jody. *The Other Side of the Story.* New York: William Morrow, 1984.

"Power—and the Ticking of the Clock." *Newsweek,* May 10, 1965, pp. 35–39.

Rainie, Harrison. "Media 'always against us,' Shultz says of Grenada ban." New York *Daily News,* Dec. 16, 1983, p. 25.

Reedy, George E. "The President and the Press." In Kenneth W. Thompson, cd, *Three Press Secretaries on the Presidency and the Press.* Lanham, Md.: University Press of America, 1983.

Salinger, Pierre. *With Kennedy.* Garden City, N.Y.: Doubleday, 1966.

Sandman, Peter M., and Mary Paden. "At Three Mile Island." In Doris Graber, ed., *Media Power in Politics.* Washington, D.C.: Congressional Quarterly Press, 1984.

Schlesinger, Arthur M., Jr. *A Thousand Days.* Boston: Houghton Mifflin Company, 1965.

——*The Imperial Presidency.* Boston: Houghton Mifflin, 1973.

Schudson, Michael. *Discovering the News.* New York: Basic, 1978.

Shaw, Donald, and Maxwell E. McCombs. *The Emergence of Political Issues: The Agenda-Setting Function of the Press.* St. Paul: West Publishing, 1977.

Sidey, Hugh. *John F. Kennedy, President.* New York: Atheneum, 1963.

Sigal, Leon V. *Reporters and Officials.* Lexington, Mass.: D.C. Heath, 1973.

Small, William. *To Kill a Messenger.* New York: Hastings House, 1970.

"Small-Stick Diplomacy." *Newsweek,* March 5, 1979, pp. 37–39.

Sorensen, Theodore C. *Kennedy.* New York: Harper & Row, 1965.

Stockman, David. *The Triumph of Politics: Why the Reagan Revolution Failed.* New York: Harper & Row, 1986.

Stoler, Peter. *The War Against the Press.* New York: Dodd, Mead, 1986.

Tebbel, John, and Sarah Miles Watts. *The Press and the Presidency.* New York: Oxford University Press, 1985.

"The GOP: It's Spring." *Newsweek,* April 17, 1967, pp. 31–32.

Thompson, Kenneth W., ed. *Ten Presidents and the Press.* Washington, D.C.: University Press of America, 1983.

—— *The White House Press on the Presidency.* Lanham, Md: University Press of America, 1983.

—— *Three Press Secretaries on the Presidency and the Press.* Lanham, Md: University Press of America, 1983.

U.S. Riot Commission Report. New York: Bantam Books, 1968.

Viguerie, Richard A. *The New Right: We're Ready To Lead.* Falls Church, Va: Viguerie, 1981.

Weissman, Steven R. "The President and the Press." *The New York Times Magazine,*
    Oct. 14, 1984, pp. 34–83.
White, Theodore H. *The Making of the President 1972.* New York: Bantam Books, 1973.
Wicker, Tom. "In the Nation." *The New York Times,* March 5, 1985, pp. A27.
—— *On Press.* New York: Viking Press, 1978.
Will, George F. "The Price of Power." *Newsweek,* Nov. 7, 1983, pp. 142.
"Wing and a Prayer." *Newsweek,* May 22, 1967, p. 26.

News articles, news analyses, and editorials published in *The New York Times, The Washington Post,* and the *Chicago Tribune* which were relevant to the subject matter of this study were read, examined, and coded for the following periods:
Cuban Missile Crisis: Aug. 22, 1962 through Jan. 31, 1963.
Dominican Republic Invasion: Jan. 1 through May 22, 1965.
Detroit Riots: July 1, through August 31, 1967.
Three Mile Island Accident: Jan. 1, through May 31, 1979.
Assass. Attempt Reagan: March 21, through April 26, 1981.
Grenada Invasion: Jan. 1, through Nov. 25, 1983.

INDEX